AUSTRALIA
THE QUIET CONTINENT

AUSTRALIA

The Quiet Continent

BY

DOUGLAS PIKE

*Professor of History,
Australian National University;
formerly Professor of History in the
University of Tasmania*

SECOND EDITION

CAMBRIDGE
AT THE UNIVERSITY PRESS
1970

Published by the Syndics of the Cambridge University Press
Bentley House, 200 Euston Road, London N.W.1
American Branch: 32 East 57th Street, New York, N.Y.10022

© Cambridge University Press 1962
This edition © Cambridge University Press 1970

Standard Book Numbers:
521 07745 1 clothbound
521 09604 9 paperback

First published 1962
Reprinted 1966
Second edition 1970

Printed in Great Britain
at the University Printing House, Cambridge
(Brooke Crutchley, University Printer)

CONTENTS

	List of Illustrations	*page* ix
1	A Remote Continent	1
2	A Lonely Land	25
3	Survival: 1788–1820	44
4	Separation: 1820–40	65
5	Expansion: 1840–60	83
6	Transition: 1860–80	105
7	Readjustment: 1880–1900	127
8	Federation: 1900–20	146
9	Disillusion: 1920–40	172
10	Nation: 1940–68	193
11	Destiny	223
	Index	234

LIST OF ILLUSTRATIONS

PLATES

I (a) The *Pamir*, the last of the grain ships
   (b) The Ross-Smith brothers arrive at Darwin,
       1919   *facing p.* 20

II (a) Donkey team on a South Australian station
    (b) Wool waggons at Port Augusta, 1879   *facing p.* 21

III (a) Camels carrying sleepers for the East–West
         railway, 1914
     (b) Mail car on the Birdsville track, 1934

IV (a) Mt Connor, Central Australia, a flat-topped
        mass of quartzite, 800 feet high and two miles
        long
    (b) The station gate

V (a) The Dorrigo tablelands in the north of New
       South Wales
   (b) One of the few clearings in the Warrumbungle
       Range, Guneemooroo

VI (a) Hobart, Tasmania, 1855
    (b) Hobart, Tasmania, 1967   *between pp.* 52 *and* 53

VII (a) King William Street, Adelaide, 1885
     (b) King William Street, Adelaide, 1968

VIII (a) Queen Street, Brisbane, 1883
      (b) Brisbane today

IX (a) Merino ram, 1882
    (b) Merino ram, 1910
    (c) Merino ram, 1958

X   (a) Panning gold

(b) A Bush inn, Willunga   *between pp.* 84 *and* 85

XI   (a) The first stump-jumping plough, 1876

(b) Murray steamer and barge unloading stores, about 1900

XII   (a) Railway engine and carriages, 1873

(b) The 'Overland' express between Melbourne and Adelaide, 1960

XIII   (a) Sheep shearing, 1870

(b) Sheep shearing, 1959

XIV   (a) Farm land in southern New South Wales

(b) A typical scene near a station homestead

between pp. 116 *and* 117

XV   (a) South Australians about to depart for 'New Australia' in Paraguay, 1893

(b) The Federal Convention, Adelaide, 1897

XVI   (a) Imperial Bushmen's Corps about to depart for South Africa, 1900

(b) First Australian Light Horse Brigade in Palestine, January 1918

XVII   Copper mining in Queensland: the Mount Morgan mine, 1959

XVIII   Sydney from the air   *between pp.* 148 *and* 149

XIX   (a) Perth from the air

(b) Melbourne from the River Yarra

XX   Four famous Australians

(a) Alfred Deakin

(b) Rt Hon. John Forrest

(c) Sir Charles Kingsford-Smith

(d) Sir Donald Bradman

XXI   (*a*) W. M. Hughes appealing for military recruits in Sydney, 1939

      (*b*) The Customs House, Darwin, after a Japanese air raid, 1942

XXII   Green Snipers' Pimple, Finisterre Range, New Guinea   *between pp.* 180 *and* 181

XXIII   A modern 'Mullenizer'—a five-ton steel ball dragged by two heavy tractors—clearing Soldier Settlement plots in the Heytesbury Forest, Victoria
                                           facing p. 212

XXIV   (*a*) A condemned terrace, Adelaide

       (*b*) One of the houses that replaced it   *facing p.* 213

MAPS

1   Australia 15,000 years ago   *page* 2

2   The sea exploration of Australia   9

3   The land exploration of Australia   33

4   Australia by 1863   102

5   The Gallipoli campaign, 1915   163

6   The war in the Middle-East, 1915–18   165

7   Battlefields in northern France, 1916–18   167

8   The North African campaign, 1940–2   195

9   The war in the Pacific, 1941–5   198–9

10   The New Guinea campaign, 1942–4   201

11   Australia, 1863–1968   213

DIAGRAMS

1   Shipping to Australia from the old world   17

2   Distribution of dwelling-houses by states, 1871–1901   135

3   Population of capital cities in proportion to total in each state, 1881–1968   153

4   Growth of factory industries, 1928/9–1967/8   211

ACKNOWLEDGEMENTS

The publishers express their thanks, for permission to use copyright illustrations, to the following:

A. D. Edwardes Esq. (Plates I(a), II(b)); South Australian Archives (Plates I(b), II(a), III(a) and (b), X(a) and (b), XI(b), XII(a), XIII(a), XV(a) and (b), XVI(a)); Australian National Travel Association (Plate IV(b)); Australian News and Information Bureau (Plates V(a) and (b), VI(b), XIV(a), XIX(a) and (b), XX(a), (b), (c) and (d)); Tasmanian Museum and Art Gallery (Plate VI(a)), South Australian Government Tourist Bureau (Plates VII(a); XIII(b)); Advertiser Newspapers Limited (Plate VII(b)); Brisbane City Council (Plate VIII(a)); Queensland Government Tourist Bureau (Plate VIII(b)); G. G. Hawkes Esq. (Plate IX(a), (b) and (c)); *Journal of the Royal Agricultural Society of South Australia* (Plate XI(a)); Victorian Government Tourist Development Authority (Plate XII(b)); *The Courier Mail* (Plate XIV(b)); Australian War Memorial, Canberra (Plates XVI(b), XXI(b), XXII); Mount Morgan Limited (Plate XVII); New South Wales Department of Tourism (Plate XVIII); Associated Newspapers Limited, Sydney (Plate XXI(a)); International Harvester Company (Plate XXIII); South Australian Housing Trust (Plate XXIV(a) and (b)).

NOTE TO THE SECOND EDITION

For this edition Professor Pike has corrected errors in the text and revised and added new material to the chapter on developments since 1958. He surveys important political events in Southeast Asia since the mid 1950s, in particular, Australia's involvement in the defence of Malaysia and in Vietnam. Professor Pike tells the story of the success of the excavations for minerals and technological advance in the 1960s and of the remarkable urban and industrial growth and expansion of Australian agricultural production in the last decade. Five plates have been replaced with new photographs and the diagrams have been brought up to date. There is also a new index.

CHAPTER I

A REMOTE CONTINENT

Most Australian history is about landsmen. Most of their novels, films and art depict the lonely outback, and the wide open spaces are supposed to have made an air-minded nation. Nine out of ten Australians, however, live on the coastal fringe, mostly in crowded cities. Their continent separates two large oceans, and twelve thousand miles of sand, cliff and swamp define their earthy boundaries. Their beaches and bronzed life-savers are popular, but they have no sea-faring tradition. The ships that carry their oversea cargoes and eager travellers are mostly built in old-world ports and manned by old-world crews. Adventurous boys do not run away to sea; they go bush instead. The great ocean wastes set few Australians dreaming, yet the sea that isolates them from the rest of the world has helped to shape their history.

Twice as far from England as South Africa and with no near neighbour such as Canada has, Australia is geographically an extension of South-east Asia. In bygone ages when sea levels were low, Australia's northern shore was separated from the Asian mainland only by narrow straits that hindered the passage of animals, but not of migrating tribes. East of the deep Timor Trench, the present Arafura Sea and Torres Strait were dry, and early arrivals may have reached Tasmania by land. Some fifteen thousand years ago rising sea levels stopped migration and isolated Australia. While the old world progressed, the sea guarded the mystery of the southern continent and held its native people in stone-age bondage. When the sea at last gave up its secret, the first comers from Europe were not impressed by the uninviting northern front that Australia turned towards the old world. When colonization began in 1788 at Sydney, much of the continent's coast was still unknown. Later exploration by sea proved that

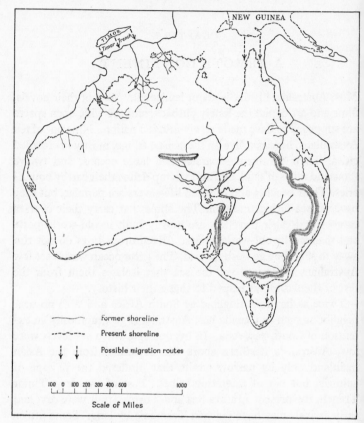

Map 1. Australia 15,000 years ago.

Australia's backdoor was to be its most used entrance. Land exploration lagged behind while small and isolated settlements on these southern shores were planted from the sea. Some of these settlements—Hobart (1803), Launceston (1804), Brisbane (1824), Perth (1829), Melbourne (1835), Adelaide (1836) and Darwin in the north (1865)—became the seaside capitals and major ports of separate colonies. Their progress depended on sea links with Britain. They looked to the mother country for men, money and manufactures, but the long voyage to Australia was unprofitable and unpopular until the colonies produced return cargoes of raw materials. The wool, gold and grain wanted by England scattered Australia's population and delayed the growth of urban industry. Sea communications thus became entangled with development.

The years of pioneering struggle were unduly lengthened by weak links with the outside world, but they also helped Australia to make its own traditions. With little aid from England's industrial revolution, early settlers had to grapple barehanded with a wilderness, or perish. If isolation slowed their progress, the great sea barrier quickened their initiative. If distance kept them grimly practical, their own achievements gave them pride in their new land. If they depended on British markets they found a new freedom in their isolation: they were secure while Britannia ruled the waves. Thus sheltered and remote, the Australian communities took shape as peaceful outposts of British civilization. Although Asia was near, one of their favourite anthems proclaimed

> Australia's sons let us rejoice,
> For we are young and free,
> We've golden soil and wealth for toil,
> Our home is girt by sea.
> Our land abounds in nature's gifts
> Of beauty rich and rare.
> In history's page let every stage
> Advance Australia fair.
>
> Should foreign foe e'er sight our coast,
> Or dare a foot to land,
> We'll rouse to arms like sires of yore
> To guard our native strand.
> Britannia then shall surely know,
> Beyond wide ocean's roll,
> Her sons in fair Australia's land
> Still keep a British soul.

3

Australia's belated discovery and exploration were the most obvious effects of its isolation by sea. For good or ill, Asians were not interested in settling the southern continent. What they knew of Australia before Europeans came is uncertain; its gradual discovery was more closely linked with Europe's maritime history. The Portuguese came first, drawn by spices to the East Indies and other oriental lands where industrious inhabitants promised trade and conquests for Christianity. The island world well known to Chinese, Arabs and Malays was discovered anew, and fresh knowledge was added by Spaniards sailing across the Pacific Ocean to contest Portugal's hold on the Moluccas.

These were brave voyages. Ships were soon worm-eaten in tropic waters, and until copper sheathing solved this problem, crews had cause to be discontented. Although every landfall meant water and fresh food, their leaders ventured into southern oceans with unfamiliar stars to guide them. The Southern Cross gave less accurate direction than the Pole Star in the north; they pressed on with only crude instruments to point the way. Of latitude they were reasonably sure, but longitude was roughly guessed at by dead reckoning. Although these bold navigators were not looking for a southern continent, they proved where it could not be by finding more sea than land.

Their old maps showed a *terra australis* sprawling from Africa to America and reaching north to Ceylon. Asian pilots and traders had another legend, an island peopled with black savages and abounding in gold. With these confused notions, southern exploration went on for three hundred years, each landfall being mistaken for a continent and then proving to be an island. Dom Jorge de Meneses thought he had found *terra australis* for Portugal when he sheltered off New Guinea's northern shore in 1526. Eighty years later Pedro Fernandez de Quiros made the same mistake when he claimed Austrialia de Espiritu Santos in the New Hebrides for Spain. His pilot Luis Vaez de Torres sailed on to prove that the New Hebrides were islands. Further on he found

4

the strait that proved New Guinea was an island too. This discovery remained a secret, filed in the archives of Spain, whose
monarch now ruled Portugal and had no ambition to expand his
possessions in far eastern waters.

Control of the spice trade passed to the Dutch whose United
East India Company soon had factories at key places in the Indies.
From one of these the *Duyfken* was sent to see what New Guinea
offered by way of trade and gold. This pinnace under Wilhelm
Jansz sailed along the island's southern shore and crossed to the
west coast of the peninsula now called Cape York. Here in unsuccessful search for water and food some of the crew were killed
by natives. Jansz was back at Batavia with an unhappy report in
June 1606, a few months before Torres found the strait that bears
his name.

This first recorded discovery of the mainland had little importance, but the next landings showed how greatly Dutch seamen
advanced the art of navigation. The old route to the Indies from
the Cape of Good Hope hugged the African coast and did not turn
east until it reached the equator. Sailors found this passage slow
and unhealthy, unless they caught the seasonal monsoons. The
Dutch with more seaworthy ships soon discovered a quicker way.
By sailing east from the Cape for 4000 miles before turning north,
they cut the passage from Holland to Batavia from eighteen months
to six. When in 1611 Commodore Brouwer first braved this
southern ocean route and found the westerly winds that blew
regularly in the roaring forties, he provided the key that unlocked
the south land.

Within five years Dirk Hartog in the *Eendracht* found the island
now named after him. Others followed to add their fragments to
knowledge of a coast that seemed to stretch from Cape Leeuwin to
North-west Cape. In 1622 two boats reached Batavia with sailors
wrecked on this western shore in the English *Trial*. Already the
Dutch were asking questions. Was this coast worth possession?
Could it provide refreshment for ships between Batavia and South

Africa? Was it the legendary southern continent or the Asians' fabled island?

Ships sent to investigate came back with gloomy answers. South of the shore found by the *Duyfken*, an expedition lost its way in reefs and shallows. The leader reported: 'We have not seen one fruit-bearing tree, nor anything men can make use of.' One ship parted from the others and sailed west to give its name to Arnhem Land, where the natives were 'poor and abject wretches' with manners that shocked even mutinous sailors. On the southern side of the continent, the *Gulden Seepaart*, headed for Batavia, made landfall near Cape Leeuwin and turned east to chart the coast for 1000 miles. The unbroken monotony of the Australian Bight killed their enthusiasm and drove them back with a cheerless report of an empty arid shore.

In 1636 Anthony Van Diemen became Governor General at Batavia. His ambition to extend the boundaries of empire combined with the skilled planning of Abel Tasman to make a notable contribution to exploration. The *Heemskerck* and the *Zeehan* left Batavia in August 1642 under Tasman's command to explore 'the remaining unknown part of the terrestrial globe'. From Mauritius the expedition swept south-east to find and name Van Diemen's Land, and cross the Tasman Sea to New Zealand, which Tasman thought a southern continent. The ships then turned north to Fiji and returned to Batavia. Tasman was sent next year with orders to find land and trade instead of ocean waste. This time he traced part of the northern coast of what was now called New Holland, but brought back no news of gold and silver mines. The disappointed masters of the Dutch East India Company turned to more profitable business. Their interest in 'voyages of curiosity' was gone.

The next European visitor to New Holland's shore was the Englishman William Dampier. In January 1688 this roving sailor found and named Cygnet Bay after his ship. A three months' stay revealed no more of country and natives than the Dutch already knew, but Dampier's journal, published on return to London, brought him before the First Lord of the Admiralty who sent him back to New Holland. With a troublesome crew in the *Roebuck*, Dampier left England in 1699. By way of Brazil and the Cape of Good Hope, he came to Dirk Hartog's Island. Beyond it he found Shark Bay, and explored six hundred miles of north-western coast before shortage of water drove him to Timor. The *Roebuck* 'founder'd thro' perfect Age' before he reached home and Dampier turned again to privateering. Although his discoveries were not important, his writings brought the romance of southern seas to the notice of his countrymen. Like Robinson Crusoe and Lemuel Gulliver, Dampier showed what Englishmen might do on the fringes of the empires held by Holland and Spain. As these powers waned in the eighteenth century, France and England became the leading competitors for trade, colonies and naval power. In 1763 they were temporarily released from the absorbing business of war by the Peace of Paris. The voyages of discovery that followed were often for the sake of science, but Plassey and the Heights of Abraham were not forgotten. The French and English ships were small and often patched, but they were better equipped for exploration. The modern method for determining longitude had been discovered, quadrants and sextants were coming into use, and the dread of scurvy had been lessened by limejuice.

The most notable French explorer was the Chevalier de Bougainville, who had fought under Montcalm against the English in Canada. In 1768 he crossed the south Pacific and discovered the Great Barrier Reef before he turned north for Batavia by way of northern New Guinea. Was this first sign of an eastern shore another group of islands, or did it join the known coast of New Holland to make a single continent? Mapmakers were busy with theories. Alexander Dalrymple, hydrographer to the English East India Company, appealed to geography to prove that New Holland must stretch far to the south-east; land masses in northern and southern hemispheres must be equal to give equilibrium to the earth's motion. Foreigners might divert them-selves with small islands; let British ships look for the continent and add its vast resources to the Empire. Dalrymple wanted to be sent on this mission, but when opportunity came he was passed over and James Cook was chosen.

This labourer's son from Marton in Yorkshire had served his apprenticeship in the coal ships of Whitby and won his first command during the Seven Years War. Peace found him survey-ing the difficult waters of Newfoundland with a skill that earned him attention from the Royal Society. At forty he was promoted to first lieutenant to lead an expedition to the south seas where the transit of Venus was to be observed on 3 June 1769. His ship, the Whitby-built *Endeavour Bark* of 368 tons, was four years old and victualled for eighteen months. Among her complement of ninety-four the most prominent was Sir Joseph Banks, a wealthy botanist with great family influence.

The *Endeavour* sailed from England in August 1768 with orders to discover the southern continent once the astronomical work was done. By way of Cape Horn, Tahiti was reached next April. An observatory was built, the island charted, the ship overhauled and its stores replenished. In August Cook sailed for New Zealand where he took formal possession and disproved Tasman's claim that it was a continent. Then he turned to Van Diemen's Land, but a gale drove him off course and his first landfall was Point Hicks. For three weeks he struggled north seeking a harbour. On 29 April 1770 he found shelter in Stingray Bay. Shore parties found water and fuel, but the natives were unfriendly and provided no food. Although the country was sandy and poor, Banks and his natural-ists collected such varied plant specimens that the name of the anchorage was changed to Botany Bay. As they sailed north charting the coast other fruitless landings were made, but no harbour was found where the ship's fouled bottom could be scraped. Inside the Barrier Reef were dangerous shoals, outside

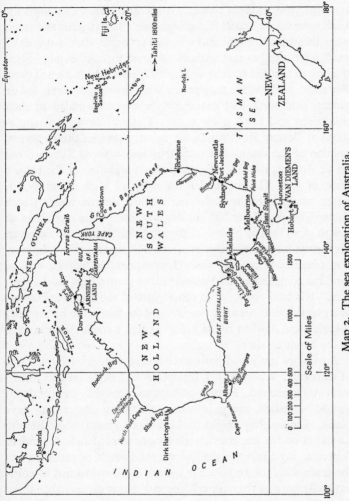

Map 2. The sea exploration of Australia.

were tremendous seas. The shore was nowhere inviting until an accident brought them closer to it. Near modern Cooktown the *Endeavour* struck a coral reef at high tide. Ballast, guns and stores were thrown overboard and she was refloated after a full day's work with windlass and anchors. A great piece of coral plugged the hole in her hull and she was hurriedly beached in a small river. For three weeks while the damage was repaired, the crew fed on greens, fish, turtle and kangaroo; the botanists added to their collections and Cook made charts. The natives were as shy as those at Botany Bay, but fertile country revised the explorers' opinion of the coast. Not until they rediscovered Torres Strait on 21 August, did Cook formally take possession of the eastern coast of New Holland under the name of New South Wales. Seven weeks later the *Endeavour* reached Batavia where Dutch shipwrights found her hull cut down by coral to no more than an eighth of an inch in places. Although Cook had no chronometer, his surveys were remarkably accurate. His report to the Admiralty was remarkably modest too. 'I presume this Voyage will be found as compleat as any before made to the St. Seas on the same acct.' His later work lay in other parts of the Pacific. For two years he sailed in Antarctic waters, and for four more he explored Siberian and Alaskan coasts before he met a tragic death in 1779 at the hands of Hawaiian natives.

Australia's last found parts were first settled, reversing the line of discovery. Where earlier Europeans had explored and turned away unimpressed, British enthusiasts thought the continent should be settled, and gave reasons that were clearer than their plans. Botany Bay might make a home for United Empire Loyalists or for the convicts no longer wanted in independent America. Settlement might forestall the French, or provide ports for trade with the Indies. Sir George Young dreamed of cultivating flax to give the navy cordage and canvas cheaper than those from Russia. The factor that won the day was isolation. Botany Bay was 12,500 miles from London and 6000 miles from America's nearest coast. Convicts unable to protest were to be sent to New South Wales, so Lord Sydney said, because of 'the remoteness of its situation, from whence it is hardly possible for persons to return without permission'. In this distant gaol they might work out their own salvation by supplying stores for the fleet in India.

This plan won grudging consent from the East India Company, which held the monopoly of British trade in all regions lying between the Cape of Good Hope and Magellan Straits. So long as its rich China trade was not threatened, the Company had no cares what happened at Botany Bay, but Governors were often reminded of its rights. When the first fleet with its eleven ships arrived in 1788, Captain Arthur Phillip was forbidden to allow the building of private craft that might encroach on the Company's trade. Early ships chartered by the government to carry convicts and stores had to seek the Company's permission to proceed to China for return cargoes, for the new land yielded no exports for many years.

Until 1810 New South Wales was mostly an Admiralty concern, and sea captains guided its destinies. Coastal surveys, naval stores and strategy held high priority. A week after Phillip landed, a French expedition under Comte de La Pérouse reached Botany Bay and others followed. Flax plants refused to thrive, but dis-coveries made in search of runaway convicts gave promise of ships' timber and masts, while newly found harbours made the coast seem more hospitable. Some of these were discovered by the surgeon George Bass in his tiny eight-foot boat *Tom Thumb*. In 1798 he was sent with eight men to explore the southern coast in a whaleboat. A journey of six hundred miles in boisterous seas brought them to Westernport where waves and tide convinced Bass that he had found a strait separating Van Diemen's Land from the mainland. With his friend Matthew Flinders he later proved his guess was right, by sailing around Van Diemen's Land.

Back in England the charts of Bass encouraged Sir Joseph Banks to propose that coastal exploration be completed. King George

Sound had been discovered by Captain George Vancouver on his way to North America's west coast in 1791, and Lieutenant James Grant had named Cape Northumberland in 1800. Fifteen hundred miles of uncharted southern coast thus remained for Flinders's expedition in the *Investigator*. The leader was an excellent choice, precise in his use of instruments and skilled in scientific observation. From Cape Leeuwin he worked east charting and recording in close detail. In Spencer Gulf he hoped to find a strait dividing New Holland from New South Wales, but narrowing shores soon brought disillusion. His work was nearly done when, in April 1802, he met a French ship. Flinders promptly cleared decks for action, but its commander, Nicolas Baudin, flew a flag of truce, for shells and butterflies were his chief quest. After friendly talks, the ships parted.

Next year Flinders circumnavigated the continent, bringing the leaking *Investigator* back to Sydney with great difficulty. He then sailed for England in a small locally built schooner. In December 1803 he put into the enemy port of Mauritius where a French governor held him prisoner for six years. Meanwhile Baudin's maps of the continent were published with French names for its southern features. These were soon changed when Flinders was freed. Although the Admiralty preferred the names of New Holland and New South Wales, Flinders's title of Australia for the whole continent came into use after his *Voyages* were published in 1814.

With maritime exploration completed, the sea provided Australia's first exports that brought the antipodes a little closer to the outside world. While Phillip carved out a settlement on the shore of Port Jackson, a British whaler first entered the East Pacific Ocean. Its voyage was very successful, although Spanish restrictions reduced the value of Chilean ports as victualling bases. When reports reached England that the Tasman Sea abounded with sperm whales, Port Jackson gained attraction. In 1791 five transports delivered their convicts and sailed straightway for whales. Bad weather spoilt the catch and the captains decided that they had chosen the wrong season. For ten years Governors lamented that fishing had not been fairly tried, but no British whalers came until war with Spain drove them from the coast of Chile. By 1803 fishing grounds were established from New Zealand to Australia, with bases at Port Jackson, Norfolk Island and Hobart. As well as sperm whales in the open sea, there were black whales, seals and sea elephants to be caught in coastal bays.

At first British whalers were hampered by the India Company's monopoly. After many appeals, licences were granted to fish in the Tasman Sea, but blubber, skins and seal oil were not to be sent to China, and if brought into England without permission, were likely to be seized as 'exports from a prohibited area'. One cargo in 1805 was actually confiscated, causing severe loss to the Sydney merchants who shipped it. Such discouragement played into the hands of American sailors. Port Jackson's settlement was four years old when men from Nantucket came with their first cargoes. Their whalers pressed hard on the heels of George Bass and Matthew Flinders. Each year their sealers came in greater numbers bringing news and welcome stores to Port Jackson, but perplexing Governors by their independence. They helped convicts to escape, captured native women, and slaughtered seals regardless of age or sex. Worse still, they were more successful than British whalers and ran off with their best harpooners. What could the Governors do? Again and again they appealed to London for advice. The Colonial Office had none to offer until the Company's monopoly of trade in New South Wales came to an end in 1813. Then Parliament placed a heavy duty on whale oil sent from Australia in foreign bottoms, and forbade local owners to trade with the mother country in ships of less than 350 tons. American whalers were not hurt and British merchants not helped by these two impositions. Colonial complaints soon had them modified, but they had some lasting effects on Australia's sea communications with the old world.

With whaling and shipbuilding handicapped, moneyed men in Sydney found that it paid better to invest in sheep and land. Sydney colonists did little fishing until the heavy duties on oil were removed in 1828. Their ventures then made rich profits, even though seals and sea elephants were becoming scarce. In 1833 whale products accounted for half the exports from New South Wales. Sydney merchants soon had forty ships and twelve hundred men in deep sea fishing, as well as many bay stations on the coast and in New Zealand. Hobart's fishing trade was better and lasted longer. In 1841 Van Diemen's Land had thirty-five licensed stations manned by more than a thousand men. More ships and men hunted the deep-sea sperm whale, while mainland stations from Twofold Bay to Swan River were visited each year. When bay whaling declined, sailors from Hobart roved far south and north in search of new grounds. Until indiscriminate killing crippled sperm fishing, Hobart held its reputation as a whaling base.

Colonial shipbuilding had a less spectacular rise and fall. A few small craft were built at Sydney from sheer necessity before the Company's monopoly ended. After that their size increased; small brigs were in demand for trade between the settlements that strung along the coast. By 1848 each colony had shipyards of some kind. The largest were in Hobart and Sydney. Shipping companies were formed, some using locally built ships, others bringing steamers or their engines from Scotland. North from Sydney was Newcastle with its coalfields and the rich Hunter River valley. Beyond was Clarence River with its cedar, and a host of Pacific Islands with sandalwood and trepang much prized in China. The coastal trade flourished, but oversea trade had to be carried in British bottoms. While the Navigation Acts remained in force, all the colonists could do was to gather cargoes at the major ports and wait for ships.

Sydney with its fine harbour and older settlement was favoured as a terminal port by ships from Britain, but Hobart early became popular as the first port of call. Its heyday gradually passed after Melbourne and Adelaide were founded. Perth was too far north to be visited often by ships on the roaring forties route; it did not flourish until the Suez Canal was regularly used by Sydney-bound steamships.

The long Australian run got only the dregs of British shipping while quicker profits were to be had elsewhere. Convict transports chartered by the government were almost the only exceptions, yet even the condition of these ships was scandalous and brought many official inquiries. In time transports became less lethal, but they were never designed for comfort, except for first-class passengers. Private ships were irregular, small and often ill-found. In the tropics, heat warped the deck planks and sprang the caulking of their seams, leaving cracks for water to pour through in heavy southern seas. To make their voyages pay, ships had to wait for months while cargoes were assembled, thereby losing their crews and sometimes their skippers to better jobs ashore. To offset such delays high prices were charged for passengers and freight until sheep-owners produced enough wool for regular back-loading.

In the 'thirties governments began to give free passages to migrants. More ships were attracted, but few were A 1 at Lloyd's or even copper-sheathed. Government regulations were often evaded to make the horrors of the five months' journey nearly as bad for emigrants as for convicts. Cooped into overcrowded, ill-ventilated holds, steerage passengers had to make their own arrangements for sleeping, eating and privacy. In bad weather they were kept below for weeks at a time in loathsome damp and darkness. At journey's end they gladly left the sea behind for ever.

Such steerage passages cost £35 but fell to less than £20 when wool offered return cargoes. No better ships came; but wool was light and bulky, and because it could not be packed deep in wet holds, it needed heavy ballast. This gave the whalers an opportunity. Their barrels of oil and bone made a profitable ballast that was not spoilt in wet holds. Tubs of tallow and bags of copper ore fulfilled the same purpose when whaling declined in the 'forties. Little other payable ballast could be used until ships improved. The few heavy cargoes of grain and flour sent to England were mostly ruined by salt water. Insurance could only be had at 3s. 6d. a bushel; when this was added to freight and duty charges, colonial farmers were practically cut off from oversea markets. Unable to export their surplus, wheatgrowers were left with unused acres and bitter thoughts. Corn law repeal brought them no relief; but English agents, persuaded to explain their problems to Parliamentary committees on shipping, helped to win repeal of the Navigation Acts in 1849. Immediately agriculture increased. Americans and other foreigners came to compete for cargoes, and British owners soon had new ships on the Australian run. They were larger and cheaper as freighters, and more important, they kept cargoes dry. Before the year 1850 ended, insurance on wheat and flour was down to 1d. a bushel.

After 1851 the gold rush brought more ships and more immigrants. The swollen population needed all the local grain, and although agriculture expanded rapidly, no flour was available for England until the 'sixties. Gold also brought private investors and speculators. Their incoming cargoes and government expenditure on railways and migration transformed the Australian run. From squalor and stagnation it rose to great importance in the eyes of British ship-owners. Ballast was no longer a dominating influence. The Blackwell firms of Green and Money Wigram diverted their ships from the Indian trade and built new 1000-ton frigates that could reach Sydney in eighty days. Lund's Blue Anchor Line, and the Black Ball and White Star Lines of Liverpool, placed orders with American shipyards for large passenger-carrying clippers to compete for the emigrant trade. Anderson's Orient Line ran to South Australia, while Walker of London sent his smart barques to Hobart and Brisbane. Against such companies, local ship-owners were no match although they managed to

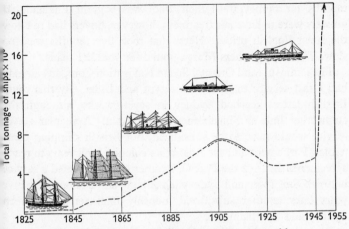

Fig. 1. Shipping to Australia from the old world.

hold the coastal trade. It grew more profitable as settlement extended, and more steamers and auxiliary ships were used. When iron supplanted wood, most colonial shipyards closed. One of the few remaining docks at Sydney was owned by Thomas Sutcliffe Mort, a far-sighted pioneer who served his adopted country well.

Mort came from Lancashire in 1838 to work for the Hunter River Navigation Company. When it failed he became a Sydney auctioneer, and promoted railways, mining, farming, shipbuilding, sheep-raising and working-men's profit-sharing schemes. New ventures of any kind excited him and his enthusiasm was infectious. His name lives on in the great land, stock and wool firm of Goldsbrough, Mort and Company. The man is almost forgotten, yet few have striven so zealously outside politics to strengthen the links between England and Australia. Many of his projects were ahead of his time but later became famous Australian institutions His wool sales begun in 1843 were a notable example. They aimed to save small growers from waiting months for money until their wool was sold in England. If growers were to have fair treatment, however, buyers had to know the latest English prices. News that took five months was too slow. With many others Mort agitated for speedier mails.

The Peninsula and Oriental Steam Navigation Company already had a fast service to China *via* Egypt and India. By this route English letters reached Sydney in seven weeks, although the connecting link at Singapore was uncertain. A regular steam service would have to be subsidized, but British shipping companies, Parliament and the Australian colonies took years to reach agreement. In 1852 the P. & O. steamer *Chusan* opened a service between Singapore and Sydney *via* Albany and Melbourne. Five years later another subsidized monthly mail started between Sydney and Southampton.

Completion of the Suez Canal in 1870 brought the colonies closer to England by a few hundred miles, although these were offset by costly canal dues. For ten years only P. & O. ships used the Suez route for the Australian run, while subsidized steam packets between Sydney and San Francisco, terminus of America's new transcontinental railway, brought mails with equal speed from Europe. The American link was broken by 1880 when Suez won favour with the passenger trade. Freighters continued to sail round the Cape but the day of clippers was over. Although they survived until the twentieth century, few new sailing ships were built. Old lines were taken over by steam companies whose ships rapidly increased in size and more slowly reduced the time of voyage. By 1890 it was down to forty days, and German and French lines had joined the regular run. Isolation was reduced, but British ship-owners still kept the lion's share of trade.

This monopoly had long disturbed many colonists. Britain provided not only oversea shipping but most of Australia's immigrants and manufactures. Each colony was also deeply in debt to London banks, yet apart from precious metals, only wool and wheat seemed to be wanted in Britain. Was Australia doomed to be forever a rural backwater, its whole economy subject to fluctuating oversea markets?

On their large estates sheep-owners bred only merino flocks and aimed only at increasing wool clips. Little thought was spared for pasture improvement or fat lambs for meat consumers. Throughout vast areas native plants were killed by over-stocking, and trees that seemed to hinder the growth of grass were recklessly killed by ring-barking. Soil erosion followed, to be quickened by the rabbit pest and the sharp hooves of sheep hemmed in by fences. The land's stored riches were plundered each year to increase the supply of wool for Britain's hungry mills. The meat trade was an unprofitable side-line for most graziers until refrigeration was introduced. Valuable pioneering work was done in Victoria by James Harrison who made his journalism pay for his ice-making experiments. In Sydney, Mort carried out other tests but did not live to see the first successful shipment of beef and mutton sent to London on the refrigerated *Strathleven* in 1879. The export of frozen meat gradually increased, more refrigerated ships came and Australia gained another valuable source of income. More important, the perfection of cold storage gave new life to dairymen and fruitgrowers; the rising oversea demand for perishable foods made closer settlement possible for smallholders without much money.

The problems of wheatgrowers were less easily solved. Like the graziers, they plundered new land to increase their exports. Like the graziers, they often complained when the weight and quality of their shipments were disputed by unscrupulous buyers in England. Graziers got over the difficulty by using local sales, which by 1880 disposed of one-third of Australia's clip, but farmers appealed to their governments. In each colony samples were taken to make a standard called f.a.q. (fair average quality). Before dispatch, wheat cargoes were measured by this standard and sold by it in England. Although wheatgrowers also invented ingenious machinery, little science was applied to farming until the 'eighties when new strains of wheat were bred to overcome disease and resist drought. Later superphosphate was introduced; although it doubled the yield, protein value was often lost. Thus Australian flour, famed for its whiteness, gradually became less suitable for bread-making unless other varieties of higher quality were added. This could be done in England where grain from many countries was received, but it made Australian flour hard to sell on other markets.

Dependence on Britain also troubled townsmen. Apart from things like bricks, beer and bread, they could not compete with British manufactures. Some colonies struggled to foster urban industry, but their markets were small and scattered. Although railways were spreading, the capital cities were more closely linked with Britain than with each other. When federation of the colonies became pressing, most of the delegates to the 1890 convention had to travel to Sydney by sea. It seemed appropriate that the first Commonwealth constitution was drafted on a ship, even if rumour claims that one of its makers was seasick.

Some colonists were also alarmed by problems of defence; others, made complacent by isolation, relied on protection by the British navy. In times of peace, privates were hard to recruit for the volunteer militia and were often outnumbered by their officers; men responded readily only when the mother country was at war. The first to serve the Empire was a contingent from New South Wales sent to the Sudan campaign in 1885. From sea attack, New South Wales could always boast special protection, for the Royal Navy had a small station at Sydney. Other colonies felt less secure. The presence of four Russian warships in the Philippines during the Crimean War prompted Victoria to buy an armed sloop for local defence and twelve years later two other men-of-war were added. In 1883 when Papua was annexed, Queensland commissioned three small gunboats, and South Australia the cruiser *Protector*. These independent 'navies' did not deter the colonies from accepting a share in the cost of a new British

PLATE I

(a) The *Pamir*, the last of the grain ships

(b) The Ross-Smith brothers arrive at Darwin, 1919

PLATE II

(*a*) Donkey team on a South Australian station

(*b*) Wool waggons at Port Augusta, 1879

squadron which was not to be moved without their consent from Australian waters.

At federation in 1901, the *Protector* and naval brigades from Victoria and New South Wales were serving with the Royal Navy in China's Boxer War, and Australian contingents were with the imperial forces in South Africa. Five years later, however, Germany's growing naval strength caused Britain to withdraw some of her squadron from Sydney, and the Federal Government began to plan a Royal Australian Navy. The Commonwealth had already taken over the colonies' old gunboats, but now new ships were bought and manned as far as possible with Australian crews. Sydney's Cockatoo Island dockyard was also taken over for building destroyers and auxiliary ships. By 1914 the squadron was complete and ready for its part in the first World War.

Meanwhile federation had revived other dreams of independence. The remote Commonwealth was to become a paradise for working-men, a laboratory of social reform. But four million people could not fill a continent nearly as large as Europe, or raise standards of living simply by turning their backs on the world. To develop unused resources, population and investments were needed and Britain alone would supply them. Agents in London invited families to escape the cramped squalor of 'awful old England', and promised glowing opportunities to all comers. For four years until 1914 British migrants poured into Australia. Non-British countries began to demand Australian produce and sent more ships for cargoes. Some new industries and markets were opened, without much weakening of the ties with Britain.

Oversea trade came to an abrupt stop with the Kaiser's war. Shipping was disrupted and British markets and supplies were cut off. Scarcity of imported iron and steel forced Australia to develop heavy industries. Furnaces blown in during the war remained to supply the needs of peace. Increasing demand for cars and trucks reopened sea routes to America, while Japanese shipping activity in Australian waters helped to bring Asia closer. During the war a Labor government began to form an Australian Commonwealth Line. Its first ships were bought in England and others locally built. With prizes of war and the powerful 'Bay' steamers, the Commonwealth Line had a fleet of fifty-three soon after peace was declared. The best of them competed strongly with old-established companies on the Australian run, but the Line was given a bad name as a 'socialist enterprise'. With the onset of world depression in 1930 most of the Commonwealth ships were laid up in Sydney Harbour, and later the so-called 'barnacle fleet' was sold at great loss to a combine of its English rivals.

During the 1920's Australian industry developed slowly behind the shelter of a rising tariff wall. New markets for wool and meat brought changes in the old pastoral pattern. Britain still demanded merino wool, but other buyers now competed for the clips from flocks which also supplied fat lambs for export. Although Australians were careless salesmen, markets were found to take the wheat, dairy produce and dried fruits unwanted by England. In return, foreign exports were accepted. Britain's share of Australia's trade shrank and immigrants came from southern Europe to supplement the flow of Britons. Some newspapers even sent reporters abroad to gather oversea news. But old habits died hard. Although American cars were popular and Japanese goods cheap, 'buy British' was a powerful slogan. Britain was still 'home' to many in Australia. They travelled abroad with British passports, Britain spoke for Australia on international councils, Britain lent the money for local development and a British banker came to advise Australian governments when depression began in 1930.

As markets collapsed and international payments became difficult, Australia joined Britain and other Dominions in a trade agreement. Britain again became the biggest supplier, but when British markets could not take all their produce, Australians were forced to reduce their imports and manufacture more of their own goods. New industries were not easily created. New skills had to be learnt, new sources of power developed, new factories and houses built and new water supplies provided. The tooling-up process was costly and lack of money made it slow.

While Australia groped its way towards industrial independence in these uncertain years, Australian airmen were challenging its isolation. In March 1919 the Commonwealth Government offered a prize of £10,000 for the first flight from England to Australia. It was won next December by Captain Ross Smith and his brother; with two engineers they made the trip in twenty-eight days. Their adventures and mishaps were more than matched by the ingenious Ray Parer whose seven months' flight in a £70 plane brought him to Australia too late to win the prize. Bert Hinkler, another competitor, gave up at Rome, but nine years later he took off alone with a small pack of food and a thermos to reach Darwin in fifteen days. The same year Charles Kingsford Smith went with C. T. P. Ulm to the United States to organize a trans-Pacific flight. Between Hawaii and Fiji was a long non-stop stage that called for a plane specially strengthened to carry extra fuel. Preparation of the *Southern Cross* attracted attention. Two Americans were added to its crew as navigator and engineer. Their radio told the world of a hazardous flight. Blinded by storm and rain, they made the long hop from Honolulu to Suva in thirty-four hours, then battled on to land in Brisbane, deaf but exultant. In 1934, as a feature in Victoria's centenary celebrations £10,000 was given as a prize for an air race from England. Hinkler's record to Darwin had already been lowered by Kingsford Smith to seven days. The air race ending in Melbourne was won by the Englishmen C. W. A. Scott and T. Campbell Black in a few minutes less than three days.

As the distance from England was narrowed, few Australians saw that Asia was also closer, until world war made it plain. Help went to Britain as before, but when Japanese forces threatened, American aid was welcomed. Wartime arrangements gave Australia its first own diplomatic representatives and more independence in international councils. Peace brought responsibility for British Commonwealth affairs in Japan and a Nationality Act that proclaimed Australian citizenship. Fabulous prices for wool and food provided funds for more industrial independence, while immigrants from Europe swelled the consumers' ranks that now attracted the factories as well as the goods of oversea firms. Radio, jet planes and fast ships banished isolation, but the sea remained—a comforting barrier between Australia and the outside world.

CHAPTER 2

A LONELY LAND

Australia with three million square miles of land is nearly as large as the United States of America and fifty times bigger than England. It is the Cinderella of continents: the youngest in settlement by Europeans, the most isolated by geography, the most reluctant to yield natural resources, the smallest in population. It stretches from ten degrees south of the equator half-way to the Antarctic Pole, while forty degrees of longitude separate clock time in Sydney and Perth by two hours. Size alone can be misleading; apart from the temperate 600,000 square miles that border the eastern and southern coasts, more than three-quarters of the continent is fated to be desolate and empty unless some miracle of science makes it habitable. Distance and isolation within Australia are the counterparts of its remoteness from the rest of the world.

Australia is noted for its sunshine, although it also has a variety of climates from monsoonal tropic summers to bleak, snow-bound winters. Unlike other continents, its highest mountain reaches only 7328 feet and its longest river has no proper mouth. Beyond the hilly coastal fringe there are no forests, and as the plains sweep inland even the tough acacia refuses to grow. The sparsely peopled grazing lands give way at last to desert with no known possibility of settlement.

The wide open spaces have lured men to great hardship and heroism. The boasted possibilities of the land have made a myth akin to the American 'Go west young man'; but no myth can make the desert blossom like a rose, for Australia is a land of feast or famine. Its crowded cities as well as lonely sheep stations know how floods alternate with water scarcity. The southern coast has regular winter rains and the north a reliable summer 'wet', but in between rainfall fluctuates widely. Records show Australia as the driest continent, though averages have little meaning. On parts of Queensland's coast annual falls vary from 10 to 70 inches, and in the dry interior the inches are sometimes years apart. But irregular droughts alone do not make deserts. The lakes shown on maps of Australia are not always dry pans of encrusted salt. On rare occasions floodwaters fill them and rain often inundates their parched surroundings, but high temperatures and winds cause quick evaporation. Where soil moisture dries too rapidly for plants to grow, there is desert. On its margins nature has produced weird drought-resistant shrubs with salty leaves and insulated roots. Their grudging growth will sometimes carry one sheep to fifty acres when the scant feed is carefully nursed by resourceful stockmen who reckon on one good year out of seven. Where rainfall is higher, the better growth of grass and trees helps to check evaporation. Since all imported crops need a growing period of at least five months, soil moisture is too unreliable for farming in more than two million of Australia's square miles. Farms are concentrated on the coastal fringe where their foodstuffs combine with flowing rivers and other resources to make a few large cities possible. These capital cities were founded to exploit the hinterland on which they mostly lived. The empty miles between them effectively separated their communities whose jealous rivalries delayed the emergence of an Australian nation.

More by luck than good management the first settlement was made where nature was least unkind; even then the pioneers from England were forced to struggle for their very existence. When Captain Arthur Phillip arrived with the first fleet, he soon found Botany Bay unsafe for anchorage and made his settlement a few miles north on the southern shore of Port Jackson, the best natural harbour in the world. Here he founded Sydney on 26 January 1788. Fresh water, fish, game and timber were there in abundance, although the soil and seasons failed to yield the European crops expected of them. Where stone-age Aboriginals thrived, convicts and their guards nearly perished. As the two years' supply of food from England was depleted, rations of salt pork and weevilly rice were reduced below the level of sustenance. The occasional kangaroo brought in by shooting parties was reserved for the sick. Clothes and boots could not be replaced, spades and axes were too inferior for use, and the work of clearing and building soon came to a standstill. The marquees and tents of the officers gave less shelter than the wattle and daub huts of the convicts. Livestock strayed in search of greener pastures, and rainstorms washed the seed from primitive gardens. His people nearly naked and starving, Phillip sent for relief to Norfolk Island where he had started a settlement, but the ship was lost. After thirty months' privation, the second fleet straggled into Port Jackson with half its human freight dead or dying. Its store ship *Guardian* had come to grief on an iceberg. The starving time went on until more food arrived from India and Batavia, and new fields for growing grain were found near Parramatta.

By 1800 a few settlers were learning to adapt themselves to their new country, but they did not love it. Most officers viewed their surroundings through English eyes and set the tasks with little imagination. Convicts hacked away at heavy timber and grubbed out tangled roots to make clearings on the pattern of English farms. Logs were painfully sawn into planks that warped and cracked before the cuts were finished. With fine sandstone close at hand, the officers chose to make bricks from indifferent clay, and waited tediously for imported lime and slates to finish their houses with high-pitched roofs patterned in England to throw off snow that never fell in Sydney. Except for their verandas, Sydney's narrow-windowed villas set down amid gardens of imported plants might have been on the outskirts of Brighton or Cheltenham. Their rosewood furniture, like their books and newspapers, came from England; but homesickness only made the country a less congenial nursery for transplanting English life and ideas. To them the bush was hostile, hard and cruel; everything that grew in it was tough and spiky. The harsh sun poured through the dull drooping leaves of gum trees to splinter on dry ground below. No local plant could be coaxed to make food; no indigenous animal gave milk for human use; no native tree yielded edible fruit. Nor could any Aboriginal natives be trusted, for they never behaved as English officers thought they should. Their timidity usually kept them beyond the white man's range; when curiosity did prevail it was suspected as treachery. As sketched by Governor King, one native family became no more than scantily clothed, dark Europeans.

The penal settlement was also ruled on English patterns. Although the community was very small, sharp distinctions were drawn between bond and free. The officers formed an élite with privileges denied to smaller fry, but enterprise and resource could not be wholly monopolized. Most of the convicts were apathetic and shiftless, but a few aimed at improving their lot. Phillip tried to encourage them with small grants of land, a move towards converting the antipodean gaol into a colony of peasant proprietors. When twenty-five acres proved insufficient for an experienced farmer to feed his own family, the land grants to emancipated convicts had to be increased in size. Officers also shared in the hand-out, but their grants were much larger. As Sydney grew and the number of emancipists increased, well-situated land rose in value. Speculators began to ask for even bigger grants at river junctions and other places of likely future importance. Because these grants were seldom put to immediate use, *bona fide* settlers were forced further afield. Isolated farmers with little money soon learned new lessons in bushcraft. Sheets of bark roofed their huts, and slabs split from straight grained trees made their walls and furniture. They wasted less time in clearing; long after the first ploughs arrived they used only hoes to 'tickle' the ground between the stumps, yet it gave them 'laughing' crops of Indian corn. On the fertile upper reaches of the Hawkesbury River they suffered from floods and fire, but learned to be cautious and persevering. Necessity also increased their ingenuity. They learned quicker than well-to-do officers with convict labour to use draught oxen and to fashion crude vehicles from forked trees with sawn logs for wheels. In these rude conditions their sons were born to grow into sturdy independence, skilled in the ways of the bush and less tied than their parents to a few acres of farm land.

By 1810 Sydney had ample food, although grain was still imported in poor seasons. Country to north and south had been explored for a hundred miles. Rich coal seams had been opened south of Botany Bay and north at Newcastle on the Hunter River, but little new farming land was found. The settlement seemed to be hemmed in by the Blue Mountains which rose sharply from the plain forty miles west of Sydney. Within the enclosed area fertile land with water was becoming scarce. Officers, emancipists and a small trickle of settlers from England pressed for more and larger grants. This was not merely greed. Keen observers prophesied a brighter future for sheep than for wheat, and they were right. Australia proved to be one of the cleanest countries in the world for animal health. The scourges of the old world have all come and been conquered, chiefly by isolation. Some, like the dreaded foot and mouth disease, have found no native animals to spread them. Others like rabies have been fought by quarantine. Even common complaints like sheep scab have been stamped out by careful segregation and treatment. These unromantic triumphs have left stock-owners free to improve their breeds and increase their numbers.

One prominent early sheep-owner was John Macarthur, who started farming at Parramatta. Restless and imaginative, he looked for other sources of wealth. By mating an Irish ram with coarse Bengal ewes he bred lambs that grew a mingled fleece of wool and hair. Spanish merinos from South Africa grew even better fleeces, and Macarthur began to dream of a wool industry that would bring New South Wales prosperity and population. This dream took him to England where he won high praise for his wool and a promise of large land grants. His purchase of seven merino rams and three ewes from the Royal Stud, Kew, was even more important.

Macarthur's quarrels with the government exiled him from New South Wales for years, but his wife and other enthusiasts carried on the breeding experiments. By 1812 he could write from London that 'wool of our most improved kind will sell for a guinea a fleece'.

Next year a severe drought ruined the crops, dried up the creeks and brought heavy losses among the flocks and herds. Clearly new pastures were needed if New South Wales was to prosper. Gregory Blaxland, herding hungry cattle in a Blue Mountain valley, became sure that the 4000-foot range could be crossed by following the tops of the ridges. Like many others he had already followed up the deepest gorges only to find unscalable cliffs. With Governor Macquarie's blessing, Blaxland started his journey in May 1813. His companions were William Charles Wentworth, a young colonist, William Lawson, a progressive settler, and four convict servants. For fourteen days they struggled through dense scrub and rugged country to reach the mountains' western side, where they saw plains wide enough 'to support the stock of the colony for the next thirty years'. The three explorers were each rewarded with 1000 acres of land. Convict labour was used to build a road over their route. In January 1815 Governor Macquarie and his lady travelled over it on horseback to lay out the new town of Bathurst, 120 miles west of Sydney. A military guard was posted to prevent convicts and other unlicensed intruders from using the road, for Macquarie wanted no expansion. Left alone, he would have turned his back on the vast interior, and concentrated settlement close to Sydney; but the successful exploration had broken down the gaol walls. No longer was New South Wales merely a penal settlement. Its possibilities for wool were beginning to attract money from England and the attention of the British Government. Before new settlers could be persuaded to immigrate, however, three other problems had to be solved.

The first was strategic. After Waterloo, French ships returned to the coast they had left alone since the peace of 1802. Their shell-gathering and scientific charting were suspected in Sydney and

London, and steps were taken to forestall any settlement by the French. Baudin's expedition to Van Diemen's Land in 1802 was as innocent as the names of his ships—*Géographe* and *Naturaliste*, yet it led to formal British possession of the island and its occupation next year by Lieutenant Bowen. He was soon joined by Lieut.-Colonel David Collins, lately released from his unwelcome task of forming a convict settlement at Port Phillip. Bowen's site at Risdon Cove also failed to suit Collins, so the convicts and their guards were moved across the Derwent River to Hobart, and a second settlement was made at Launceston. Then the thousand free settlers on Norfolk Island were removed to the Upper Derwent where they began at last to thrive with the aid of sheep from Macarthur's flock. Remote Macquarie Harbour on the west coast was chosen to replace Norfolk Island as a convict station for the worst criminals. The visit of the French explorer Freycinet in 1819 caused no alarm in Sydney, but seven years later D'Urville's expedition led to a settlement at Westernport that soon failed, and another at King George Sound under Major Lockyer who assumed Britain's claim to the whole of Australia. At Port Essington another short-lived settlement aimed to safeguard the northern coast. Each of these stations was manned by convicts, and thereby helped to dispose of the second problem, the segregation of prisoners.

Although peace in Europe brought increased transportation to New South Wales, ways were found to separate the bond from the free. Each year Van Diemen's Land got an increasing proportion of exiled prisoners, while barracks confined the convicts in Sydney, and many others were sent to work out their salvation in the country. A penal station was already planted at Newcastle; now another was made at Port Macquarie, and Norfolk Island was re-occupied. In 1822 the Surveyor-General, John Oxley, seeking further northern sites, came to Moreton Bay where a shipwrecked sailor living with the Aboriginals showed him the Brisbane River. Two years later a small party of convicts was landed to begin the settlement of the future State of Queensland.

With strategy and convicts disposed of, there remained the third problem, new pastures for rapidly increasing flocks and herds. The key to good grazing was water, so for ten years explorers busied themselves with the western rivers. Oxley traced the Lachlan and the Macquarie till he lost them in shallow swamps and reedbeds. On his heels came Allan Cunningham, government botanist, to find the Liverpool Plains, the Darling Downs and more west-flowing streams. In the south Charles Throsby reached the Murrumbidgee River before stockmen and explorers found its higher reaches on the Monaro tableland. Following them came the adventurous colonial-born Hamilton Hume, to form a cattle station near Lake George. In 1824 he was asked by Governor Brisbane to explore the unknown country towards Spencer Gulf, but chose instead to head south for Bass Strait. With him went William Hovell, a sea captain turned settler. They found the Hume River (now known as the Upper Murray) and several of its southern tributaries. In the tortuous foothills of the Australian Alps the two men quarrelled, and pushed on in dignified silence to reach Corio Bay before shortage of provisions turned them homeward. Each new discovery opened up vast areas of well-watered grazing land and stockmen steadily moved into them; but the mystery of the western rivers remained. Did they join to flow into the ocean in some bay missed by the coastal explorers, or was there an inland sea? The man who unveiled the mystery was Charles Sturt.

Born in Bengal, Sturt was educated at Harrow, fought in Spain and Canada, and served in France and Ireland. Sent to Sydney with his regiment, he sought further adventures. In 1828 his first exploration brought him more hardship than excitement. In spite of severe drought, he managed to reach the Darling River. The water was salt and his party nearly perished; even the emus and wild dogs were gasping with thirst. Next summer Sturt set out to trace the Murrumbidgee. Its deeply chiselled course made land travel slow and difficult, so he decided to divide his party. The whaleboat in his equipment was fitted together and a skiff was

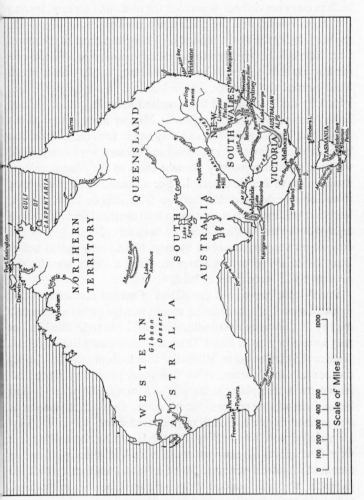

Map 3. The land exploration of Australia.

Scale of Miles

0 100 200 300 400 500   1000

33

built to carry provisions. Sturt took the boats and six men, leaving the others behind with the cattle and horses to form a depot. On the second day the skiff smashed on a snag and most of the stores were ruined. The whaleboat whirled downstream at a fearful rate for a week before it swept into a broad and noble stream which Sturt named the Murray. Three hundred miles further it was joined by the Darling and five hundred miles beyond it entered Lake Alexandrina. The treacherous Murray mouth stopped the party from reaching the sea, and they had to turn back. Sturt was blind and sick, provisions were short and the men were weary. Eight weeks of upstream journey brought them to the Murrumbidgee depot, only to find it deserted. For seventeen more days they rowed on so exhausted that the men fell asleep on their oars. At last Sturt made a camp and sent two men overland for help. Relief arrived as the last scraps of food had been served out. By slow and easy stages the party reached Sydney, but months passed before Sturt could see to write his report. After a longer wait he was rewarded with 5000 acres of land.

Sturt's epic voyage was the climax of several explorations that revealed a river system draining an area nearly as large as Canada's mighty St Lawrence river basin. Gaps still had to be filled in, but they were only gaps as Major Thomas Livingstone Mitchell found. Jealous of Sturt's success, Mitchell set out to show that the Darling did not join the Murray. After that guess proved wrong, he explored the fertile plains south of the Murray, and when he lost himself blamed the errors in Sturt's maps. On reaching the sea he was amazed to find a small European settlement at Portland Bay. Its main purpose was whaling, but the Henty brothers who ran it were forerunners of many settlers to leave Van Diemen's Land in search of mainland pastures. Some crossed Bass Strait with their sheep in 1835 and founded Melbourne and Geelong; others tried to buy the entire southern coast from Portland to Port Lincoln, but were forestalled by plans in England to found a new colony in South Australia. This was started in 1836 with a whaling station on

34

Kangaroo Island; surveys and land sales at Adelaide soon followed. Free from all convict stain, the colony with its 80-acre sections was meant to be an agricultural paradise, yet before a sod was turned, sheep were brought from Hobart for meat and wool growing. Stockmen from New South Wales were not far behind. Large numbers of cattle and sheep were overlanded to Port Phillip and South Australia.

Further west, the Swan River settlement was also planned in England as a convict-free colony. After a promising start in 1829 it languished in isolation beyond the reach of eastern flocks. One overlander, Edward John Eyre, did try to discover a stock route from Adelaide, but to the west and north he found no flowing streams beyond Gulf St Vincent. In February 1841 he set out for King George Sound, pressing courageously into unknown water-less country with one faithful black boy. By digging in sand below the cliffs and by collecting dew with a sponge, they found barely enough moisture to keep them alive until in extreme distress they sighted a French whaler. The friendly captain cared for them and gave provisions that brought them to the end of their trying ordeal in five months. Eyre's exhausting trip revealed no new grazing country but it set new standards of endurance for future explorers.

In 1841 the eastern mainland ceased to be a receptacle for con-victs, and British migrants were flowing into the widely scattered Australian settlements. The colonies of Van Diemen's Land, South Australia and Western Australia were separated by distance and by government from New South Wales, and revelled in their indepen-dence. Within each colony the policy of concentrated settlement was replaced by New South Wales' pattern of dispersion. Five million sheep now spread inland from Sydney over a grassland belt 800 miles long by 300 wide. Imported grain set ambitious men free from dull routines of farming and many sheep-owners reckoned land in square miles instead of acres. Unauthorized occupation earned them the title of squatters; their isolated runs bordering the rivers and creeks gave them control of all nearby unwatered land, and drove newcomers farther afield. Over long empty miles stockmen and shearers tramped or rode in search of jobs, while bullock waggons lumbered annually to the coast with wool to return with a year's supply of stores. Their tracks cut across unfenced plains, to find at shaded river crossings some primitive inn, nucleus of a future township.

While grass and water called to greater loneliness farther out, sheep-owners had little sympathy for the Aboriginal natives. As the so-called waste lands were occupied, whole tribes were dispossessed of their traditional hunting grounds. Governors' policies were humane, but primitive food-gatherers were no match for the white invader. The native had to change his ways or fight for his sacred lands. Whether he chose dependence or clash, the end was death, lingering or sudden. Sheep and the rough characters that looked after them were usually the victims and the cause of misunderstanding between old and new Australians, but the natives suffered most. Near Perth half the males of one tribe were killed in the 'battle' of Pinjarra in 1834. In Van Diemen's Land settlers combined to end a 'black war' by driving the natives into Tasman Peninsula; when force failed, coaxing succeeded and tribal remnants were taken to Flinders Island to die out in uncongenial surroundings. In South Australia natives were sometimes given poisoned flour or shot on sight by voluntary police and vengeful stockmen. Early squatters near Port Phillip boasted the murder of forty natives in one district and two whole tribes in another. In New South Wales seven shepherds killed and burned the bodies of more than twenty men, women and children in the notorious Myall Creek massacre of 1838; and yet the execution of the offending stockmen was widely disapproved. The killings, however numerous, accounted for fewer Aboriginal deaths than did the white man's diet and diseases. Estimated at 300,000 in 1788, native numbers shrank by two-thirds before governments seriously gave them protection.

Dispersion of settlement went on more speedily as squatters learned to use lighter equipment. Huts and hurdles for yarding sheep each night became less important once the native threat was removed and poison baits thinned out the dingo. Until the famous Kelpie sheepdog became popular in the 'seventies, the collie was a useful substitute with small flocks. By 1840 a stockman could carry all his gear on a light hunting saddle. He needed no firearms or ropes; a short plaited whip was effective enough. Heavy cast-iron kettles and cooking pots were left in camp; he used instead the empty cans that were becoming popular as food containers. Black tea, boiled mutton and loaves of 'damper' cooked in hot coals became a standard diet. Imported sheets of galvanized iron were beginning to be used to catch the rain from homesteads and shed roofs, while heavy square ships' tanks gave better water storage than wooden barrels. The iron sheets were not to be had in corrugated ugliness for another twenty years; meanwhile progressive owners used the flat sheets for troughs to water stock at their wells, although old hands preferred the trunks of hollow trees. Other innovators were beginning to build walls of earth to dam gullies and shallow creeks, thus allowing their sheep to reach grass miles away from the rivers. But progress in water conservation was slow while new pastures beckoned.

The limits of grass and water were first reached in South Australia where Charles Sturt again turned to exploration. In 1844 he left Adelaide for country west of the Darling, hopeful of finding a way round the horseshoe of salt lakes that seemed to stop the colony's northern expansion. For six months Sturt's party was marooned at Depot Glen, the only permanent water in a parched waste. When rain fell Sturt pushed north towards the centre of the continent, but found only desert. The party got back to the Darling by carting water in bullock skins for use on long dry stages. Sturt's report was gloomy but it had one important effect. By encouraging South Australians to return to their original plan of agricultural settlement, the colony was saved from domination by big pastoralists.

In New South Wales the explorers also turned north. Ludwig Leichhardt, a venturesome German, led the way with a successful overland expedition to Port Essington in 1844. New rivers and fine cattle pastures made him ambitious to cross the continent from east to west. On his first venture in 1846 he lost his livestock and provisions, and was back among the sheep stations in six months. Next year he started again but completely disappeared; except for a few trees marked 'L', no authentic trace of his party was ever found. Meanwhile the unbelieving Major Mitchell was again concocting theories. This time he hoped to find a river by which squatters' produce could be carried to the northern coast and sold in the Dutch East Indies. He set off with waggons and a boat to find the river at its source. The boat was destined to be used only as a trough for watering cattle. Mitchell travelled north from station to station till he reached the last on the Warrego River. Across the Great Dividing Range he found a fine stream flowing in the right direction. Exultantly he gave it the Queen's name, believing it to be the source of the River Victoria which entered the sea at Cambridge Gulf. His second-in-command, Edmund Kennedy, found later that Mitchell's river turned south to join the Barcoo and Cooper's Creek. The mystery of their irregular flow towards Lake Eyre was solved by Augustus Charles Gregory while searching for Leichhardt. Gregory with two brothers had already explored the Murchison and Gascoyne rivers in Western Australia. Further journeys took him north to trace the Victoria River from its mouth, and other streams flowing into the Gulf of Carpentaria, before the new colony of Queensland made him its first Surveyor-General in 1859.

That year also brought intercolonial rivalry for the glory of first crossing the continent from south to north. In Victoria £6000 was raised by public subscription and doubled by the government for an elaborate scientific expedition. It was placed in charge of Robert O'Hara Burke, a showy police inspector with little experience as a leader. He quarrelled with his officers and left them at the Darling to follow with the heavy equipment, while he hurried on with William John Wills and six other men. At Cooper's Creek a depot was formed, but Burke was too impatient to wait for the arrival of the slow-moving party. In December 1860 he set off for the northern coast. With three men he reached the mangrove swamps of the Flinders estuary in February. Without seeing the ocean they hurried back to Cooper's Creek. One man died before they got there to find the depot deserted. Its guards had Burke's orders to wait for three months; they stayed five weeks longer, and had gone only ten miles from the camp when the three starving men reached it. Enough stores were buried by a marked tree to take Burke to the Darling, but the impetuous leader now decided to head for the nearest station in South Australia. The mistake was fatal. Burke and Wills soon died from exhaustion. King survived only by making himself useful to a native tribe. A search party from Melbourne found him in September 'wasted to a shadow, and hardly to be distinguished as a civilized being except by the remnants of clothes on him'. Other search parties from Brisbane saw more of the northern country than Burke did on his hasty trip, and their reports brought cattlemen into the tropical Gulf country. From Adelaide, John McKinlay also joined the search. After hearing that King had been found, he pushed on to the Gulf; like Burke and Wills he crossed the continent but failed to reach the actual sea. That honour was reserved for John McDouall Stuart.

Stuart carried a giant's energy in his nine-stone frame. As a professional surveyor he spent years on the frontier of settlement marking out new runs and selling information about land and minerals to Adelaide speculators. By 1859 stockmen had found a passage through the horseshoe of salt lakes and Stuart pressed through the gap to discover the Macdonnell Range and new creeks and pastures on the western side of Lake Eyre. He soon had another goal. South Australia's government offered £2000 to the first person to cross the continent, for there were whispers that the

London to Java telegraph was to be extended to Australia, and a mainland terminus was wanted. Cambridge Gulf appeared to Stuart as the best place to land the cable from Java, so for two years he tried to reach the Victoria River. Until the government gave him an escort for protection from the natives, his expeditions were absurdly light, and the waterholes he found, sometimes fifty miles apart, all forced him east of his course. He drove his men and horses to the limits of endurance in his determination to go north-west, but every attempt was baffled. His last journey brought him by way of the Mary River to bathe his hands and face in the Indian Ocean in July 1862. Stuart won the government reward and South Australia won the Northern Territory in spite of Queensland's opposition. Ten years later a transcontinental telegraph line linked Adelaide to Darwin's cable terminus.

The telegraph line soon became a jumping-off place for western exploration. Ernest Giles went out from it to discover Lake Amadeus and the ranges skirting the fearsome Gibson Desert. He also tried to reach Perth, but without success until camels were used. With their aid Giles and his party got to the western coast and back, sometimes travelling over 300 miles without water. Meanwhile the colonial-born John Forrest looked for Leichhardt, travelled overland to Adelaide around the Bight, and beat the South Australians in crossing from the western coast to the overland telegraph line. His mantle then fell on his brother Alexander who found and traced some of Western Australia's northern rivers.

By 1880 major exploration was complete. Cattle spread from east to west across the northern tropics. Although the Timor buffaloes brought to Port Essington in 1824 increased rapidly, English Shorthorn and Durham breeds were afflicted by redwater and cattle tick. Long distance from markets was a more permanent problem. Even when meat works were opened at Wyndham, Darwin, Cairns and other ports, cattle had to walk hundreds of miles to reach them. A few railways stretched long tentacles into the interior and some districts benefited, but costs were too high for outback railways that could only count on livestock for freights. In Western Australia special ships now take cattle to Perth and Singapore, while some inland stations airlift their carcases. Elsewhere large road trucks and trailers are used to move stock without losing their condition. Cattle are at their best soon after the summer 'wet' and must be marketed then, for the country is not fit for crops that could fatten them regularly through the year. Northern cattle-growing is thus ill suited for venturesome men with small means. Some runs are larger than Wales, and all are isolated, although pedal wireless, aeroplanes, cars and the Flying Doctor service make some old-timers grumble about 'living in the suburbs'. They need not fear disturbance from the south; they live beyond the jealous eye of governments, in remote regions that are easily forgotten.

Sheep-owners have the same sturdy independence but less opportunity to use it, for their country merges with farmland, and governments have always clipped their runs to provide farms for the landless. More sheep now water at dams and wells than at running streams. The last great dispersion of flocks came with the discovery of artesian basins which cover one-third of the continent. The first artesian water tapped in 1879 in north-west New South Wales was quickly followed by other finds. (Queensland alone now has nearly five thousand artesian and sub-artesian bores, ranging in depth from ten feet to seven thousand and yielding a daily flow of 300 million gallons.) Although artesian water was often too full of mineral salts for irrigation, miles of ploughed drains and huge earth storage tanks took it to distant grass that sheep could not otherwise reach. Enormous new pastures were thus opened, with governments providing bores along new stock routes. Travellers could now rely on regular water supplies, but although the dread of thirst was lessened, the flow from bores also decreased as much water ran to waste. This added bitterness to the intercolonial quarrels already rife over the use of River Murray for navigation and irrigation. Other vexations increased ill-feeling. South

Australia monopolized trade with the Darling, Broken Hill and south-west Queensland, while Victorian railways ruined South Australia's River Murray commerce by carrying the wool and produce of southern New South Wales to Melbourne. Victoria was also blamed for introducing the wild rabbit which by 1880 was a serious pest ravaging all farm and grazing land in spite of costly fences along colonial boundaries. Meanwhile imported weeds, burrs, warts and thistles were spreading their noxious growth to distress farmers and woolgrowers. Worse still, unions of shearers, miners and waterside workers were combining their raucous voices in demands that seemed to threaten the moneyed interests in each colony. As the colonies were already jealous rivals for oversea immigrants, trade and investment, these earthy quarrels helped to bring about Australia's federation as a political device for conquering some of the problems of distance and separation. Drought and depression, however, were problems that not even federation could solve.

The peak of pastoral expansion was passed by 1890; pastures had been too ruthlessly exploited. Inland Australia was already in depression; the desert fringe was eaten out and its red soil blown to the four winds; rivers were filling with silt, land was becoming exhausted and wool prices were falling. Country-bred families were turning to the cities before the great drought of 1902 reduced sheep numbers by half. With superphosphate and good seasons farm land soon recovered, but woolgrowers were slow to mend their ways. The hazards of their occupation were gradually reduced by better breeding and more careful use of pastures. With the coming of motor transport, the dominance of wool and other primary produce was challenged by growing urban industries, but some of the importance of distance remained. The Australian states clung jealously to their separate rights, and the old distinctions between town and country, and between graziers and farmers, survived the drift to the cities.

Although major exploration had been completed and bright city lights drew more people than the wide open spaces, a few townsmen still yearned for unknown lands. A new chapter was added to the annals of exploration by the gallant parties that braved the Antarctic continent. In these intrepid journeys the name of Mawson deserves to be linked with Amundsen for skill and with Scott and Shackleton for courage. English-born and Sydney educated, Douglas Mawson first saw the Antarctic with Shackleton's expedition in 1909. From headquarters on Ross Island the party pioneered the route that Scott was soon to use on his disastrous return from the South Pole. With Professor Edgeworth David of Sydney, Mawson shared the first ascent of Mt Erebus, and also the finding of the southern magnetic pole. Two years later Mawson led the first purely Australian expedition to the Antarctic. On one long sledge journey his two companions died and most of the food was lost. Mawson's lone struggle back to camp was an epic of human endurance, a stirring tale even when told in simple detail in his own *Home of the Blizzard*. Back in Australia he gave long years to the study of geology, but Antarctica still called and he led two more expeditions in 1929 and 1931. After the second World War he advised the Commonwealth Government on the research parties that established scientific stations on Macquarie and Heard Islands. The base on the Australian section of the Antarctic mainland was named after him—a worthy tribute to one of many who triumphed over distance and isolation.

CHAPTER 3

SURVIVAL: 1788–1820

New South Wales had a bad start. Its beginnings as a remote gaol gave it a bad name that was not improved by the misdeeds of its gaolers. It did not emerge as a land of hope and second opportunity until formal recognition as a Crown colony in 1823 brought a more regular flow of private money and free migrants. Their coming gave a greater emphasis to the differences between bond and free, and to a longer-lived question that had already arisen. Was expansion to be controlled by the colony or by the mother country?

To many convicts, as to free migrants who followed them, New South Wales was a land of no return where they might nevertheless find freedom, independence and security. To others, New South Wales meant temporary exile from whence shrewd dealing would soon return them to wealthy ease in England. In unsettled minds speculation vied with security. From the beginning, seasons of feast and famine invited all men to gamble, although some also relied on hard work. Yet neither luck nor hard work had value unless backed by capital. Convicts and guards had little cash or credit, and the colony's chief income came from British grants for the penal establishment. These funds, as well as land and labour, were at the disposal of Governors, whose good favour was the key to success. This patronage created jealous rivalry, and continued long after development brought private investment by absentee owners. Their ties with the British Government won them rich pickings and the distrust of those without influence. Investors and their agents wanted quick development and first claims to government help. As expansionists they were faced by colonists whose resentment of a privileged élite and of remote control warranted the title of isolationists. In time the isolationists' demand for self-

44

government was granted, but expansion still depended on British money, migrants and markets. The struggle went on in changing forms, but the pattern took shape in the opening years.

New South Wales was meant to be a penal settlement, but it soon became a peculiar mixture of gaol and colony. The convicts were too few and too oppressed for the birth-stain to last. The Australian nation was not to be built on social misfits and outcasts; yet the gaol was important as the first grim scaffolding.

One reason for founding New South Wales was to relieve the pressure on Britain's crowded prisons. The number of offences punishable by transportation had steadily grown since 1597 when it was first introduced. Most convicts were sent to British colonies in North America. Nearly a thousand were being transported each year when the War of Independence closed these dumping grounds. As a temporary measure the Hulks Act was passed in 1776 and convicts were sent to disused ships moored in the River Thames. They were soon insanitary and overcrowded. The heavy prison death-rate had already attracted the attention of reformers who demanded a better penitentiary system. Edmund Burke told Parliament that British gaols held at least 100,000 prisoners sentenced to transportation. Although a more careful count by John Howard revealed only 5000, the number was rising and the addition of more hulks at Portsmouth was only a temporary solution. The government decided that transportation must start again and looked for a suitable place. Africa's west coast, Gibraltar, the West Indies and the Falkland Islands were suggested, but Botany Bay was chosen. In May 1787 the first fleet was on its way.

In the next eighty years Australian colonies received some 160,000 convicts. They came in an irregular flow to varied destinations. Only 11,200 arrived before 1810; after Waterloo the number increased each year to reach a record of 5600 in 1835. By 1840 when New South Wales ceased to take convicts, it had received 52 per cent of the total; Van Diemen's Land got 42 per

45

cent by 1852, and 6 per cent went to Western Australia between 1850 and 1870. The age groups fluctuated widely from 12 to 80, although most convicts were not too old to fit themselves to new ways. Their criminal records varied from petty theft to atrocious offences. On the transports, young and old, lifers and those with shorter sentences were herded together to share their vices and boast their criminal prowess. Most persistent criminals were later isolated in remote penal stations, and the rest of the bond were soon outnumbered by the free. When transportation ended the colonies had a population ten times larger than the total number of convicts transported. In this growth free immigration was far more important than the natural increase from convict stock. At first the ratio of male to female convicts was three to one, and later rose to seven to one; Western Australia got no female prisoners at all. After transportation ceased in eastern Australia this unbalance of the sexes was corrected by a heavy intake of free migrant women, especially single girls from famine-distressed Ireland. Even then the number of colonial-born did not catch up and pass the number of those born outside Australia until the 1870s.

Legend has won a sympathy not wholly deserved for convicts supposedly transported for no more than poaching rabbits, stealing silk handkerchiefs and sharing in political disturbances. Such trivial offences were common among the early arrivals, for Britain's penal code was harsh and uncertain, and enclosures drove evicted peasants into petty theft to avoid starvation. The laws of England, with more than 160 capital offences, were said to be written in blood, and the gallows were overworked. As wholesale executions were impossible, large numbers of criminals, not always the least vicious, were respited after seeing the judges solemnly don their black caps. This led to much injustice and made the law and its punishments seem ridiculous. Before New South Wales was founded, some magistrates were already turning to transportation as a merciful alternative to hanging, while juries were known to return verdicts of guilt for thefts valued at a few pence less than the 40s. of stolen goods that by law merited death. Criminal law reformers had little success while revolution and war lasted in France. When Bonaparte fell most of the convicts sent to New South Wales had been sentenced to no more than seven years' transportation. Fifteen years of peace brought slow changes in the law, and with it came better police and crime detection. Glaring injustice was removed, but severity remained as the standard check on law-breakers. Few thought of fitting punishment to the crime, although some hoped that transportation would reform bad characters.

By and large the convicts were a worthless lot, and justified the complaint that Britain was hiding its shame in the antipodes. There were of course some notable exceptions. The best known were the five Scottish 'martyrs', scandalously tried and sentenced for sedition in 1793; six Dorchester labourers transported for administering illegal oaths at Tolpuddle in 1834; seventy-two seditious Chartists; about 250 Canadian rebels of 1838; and some 350 United Irishmen from the rebellion of 1798. These political prisoners were too few to be representative of the mass. Most were emancipated early, although many of the Irish, in company with their countrymen, staged a rebellion in 1804 that brought quick retribution; some rebels were shot, some hanged, some flogged and many others sent to fearsome exile on Norfolk Island or to Newcastle coal mines specially opened for their reception.

Professional malpractice and the gentleman's crime of forgery accounted for a few more special cases that were soon granted pardons in the colony. One erring lawyer was set free to allow his creditors to sue him for debt. Others were given tolerable work as government clerks in Sydney, although repeated misbehaviour earned some of them a bad name and hard manual labour.

More than one-third of the convicts came from Ireland where enclosures and political unrest were followed by overpopulation and famine to make poverty more acute than in England. The proportion of agricultural workers among the transported Irish was

47

always higher than those from England even in times of rural distress. Field labourers suitable to pioneer a new land were far outnumbered by town workers sentenced for theft. Some may have been country-bred, and unemployment may have driven them into crime; but the remaining records of their criminal careers suggest that distressed casual law-breakers were fewer than depraved professional thieves. Moral standards were low, and even the law seemed to favour employers. The first fleet had one incurable rogue who was flogged for making counterfeit coins from pewter spoons and military buckles, yet the four-pound weights supplied by the shipping contractor for the second fleet were ounces underweight and brought him no punishment.

Colonial Governors from Captain Phillip onward lamented the habit of indolence and vice that made convicts dread hard work. English reformers took up the tale to prove that transportation was most efficient in adding further corruption and infamy to a class already saturated in crime. Although exile in the antipodes was at first a terrifying sentence and some early convicts begged instead to be hanged at home, familiarity soon bred contempt as glowing reports of New South Wales trickled back to England. A few boasted of crimes deliberately committed to earn a free passage to New South Wales. One young woman avowedly intent on joining her convict husband was gaoled three times for shoplifting before she was transported; in Van Diemen's Land her continued thefts won her a permanent place in the house of correction.

Severe sentences and frightful transports were brutalizing enough, but the secondary punishments meted out as discipline to unruly convicts were far worse. Treadmills, chain gangs, solitary confinement and heavy irons were trivial compared with floggings that sometimes exceeded five hundred lashes. Such punishments were seldom just, for they could be awarded on the slender evidence of employers alone. When law reform did reach New South Wales fifty lashes became the maximum, but by that time penal stations had been built and troublesome convicts were disciplined within their walls. Life in these stations was savage and degrading. A prisoner sent to Norfolk Island was said to lose the heart of a man and get that of a beast instead. Women convicts were usually punished in government factories where they picked and spun wool. Conditions at the Parramatta factory were so disgusting that new arrivals were segregated from old inmates. But these secondary punishments were reserved for convicts who committed crime while still under sentence of transportation, and many escaped them altogether.

As a penal sentence transportation was very flexible. Government supplied rations and clothes, but convicts in Sydney found their own lodgings until regular barracks were opened. Some built crude huts, others boarded in return for work and many more were assigned as servants to freemen. As the Crown owned the services of all convicts under sentence, the government was supposed to take first choice when transports arrived, and to make regulations under which its rejects were allotted to private employers. A master had to house his assigned servants and pay a wage for work done outside regular hours. Flogging or return to the government could only be ordered by two magistrates; a servant could also complain if regulations were broken, but he had no way of leaving a harsh master.

With power in employers' hands, assignment made transportation grossly unjust as a form of punishment, for more depended on how a convict could work than on his criminal record. Competition for masons, blacksmiths, carpenters and capable domestic servants was always keen, and skilled labourers could count on reasonable treatment, but assignment was a lottery for the unskilled. Although everyone had to work, servants in homes and shops usually found life less unpleasant than those in gangs. Small settlers, particularly ex-convicts, often treated their one or two labourers as members of the family; though this meant endless toil there were other compensations. Some big employers were humane, and some hoped good conditions would produce good work, but other masters and overseers relied on cruelty and contempt. Convicts could only retaliate by thieving, burning, breaking tools and losing livestock, but always at risk of the lash.

The alternative to assignment was government service in a wide variety of work and conditions. A few convicts went into offices or to other skilled work; most toiled in gangs cutting timber, quarrying stone, clearing land, making bricks and building hospitals, churches, barracks and wharves. As settlement spread government farms were opened in many places and more attention was given to building roads and bridges. For these heavy tasks the government selected the strongest newcomers and added its own troublesome convicts and those unwanted or unmanageable as assigned servants. The most incorrigible were sent to coal mines and penal stations, but the rest were placed in chain gangs under the care of military guards and overseers. These men were mostly promoted convicts whose cruel authority enabled them to settle old scores and make the chain gangs notorious. In heavy irons the prisoners worked ten hours a day with primitive tools; their food was coarse and monotonous, their clothing was poor, and at night they were locked in huts too crowded to lie down. Chain gangs offered no incentive for good behaviour although a good report from a bribed overseer might win promotion or pardon. The government always needed constables, guards, warders and overseers. 'Set a thief to catch a thief' brought results, if not just ones, and many convicts stayed in these positions of trust after their sentences expired.

Most convicts had served at least a year in British gaols and transports before they arrived. Absolute pardons were given to those with completed sentences. Governors also had power to grant conditional pardons to worthy men with unfinished sentences, on terms that prevented them from leaving the colony and made them accept New South Wales as a permanent home. These pardoned men and their families were called emancipists, and with the freemen they soon outnumbered those in servitude. Some were granted land, but very few made successful settlers.

A small handful of ex-convicts became very wealthy. One was Simeon Lord who served his sentence for stealing cloth and had a fortune from trade, ships and land within ten years. Another prosperous trader was Mary Reibey, transported at thirteen for borrowing a neighbour's pony. These were rare exceptions; most convicts when freed joined the ranks of town and country labourers to compete hopelessly with assigned servants. A later form of conditional pardon was the ticket of leave for which a convict could apply after serving part of his sentence. If good conduct could be proved and maintained, the ticket allowed a convict to work where he wished within a specified district. This solved some difficulties of assignment, kept down the numbers in government service and reduced public expense. But the local government was faced with rising costs as settlers demanded more police protection. This brought increased taxes which added to other tangled problems that were producing bitter strife.

These quarrels started with the first fleet which brought not only convicts and seamen, but officials, marines and officers with their wives and children as well. Wise and ingenious, Captain Phillip was the right Governor for a new settlement, though his stay was too short and too few of his assistants shared his humane views. The three companies of Royal Marine Light Infantry sent to defend New South Wales were uncooperative. They refused to police the convicts and made mischief by consorting with the women and encouraging crime, yet they resented Phillip's authority that included them in short rations and put convict overseers in charge of work parties. When their officers were asked to join the Advocate-General in trying criminal offenders, they complained that such tasks were outside their military duties. Their greatest grievance was that Phillip had no power, as he had with emancipated convicts, to make grants of crown land to soldiers. Before this power was given, the discontented marines were being replaced by a regiment specially recruited for garrison duties. The first of this New South Wales Corps arrived in 1791.

It remained for twenty years, a motley collection with a strength of about 500, sometimes maintained by the addition of picked convicts. Its officers came and went, for light duties left ample time for squabbles and duels, but in spite of their fuss over rights and the honour of the regiment, most of them were attracted by the promise of land grants. With their families and those of government officials they made a peculiar body of first free settlers in a peculiar colony.

The early Governors were called autocrats because of their extraordinary powers. The British Government decided how many convicts were sent and the Secretary of State in London issued frequent instructions, but distance and slow mails left the Governors in almost complete control of the colony's expansion. Although the gaol was their chief concern and their regulations favoured land settlement for the permanent reform of the pardoned, they also commanded the use of convict servants and the rate of government spending. Thus the disposal of land, labour and capital depended on each Governor's individual discretion, within the pattern of administration made by Captain Phillip.

At first private investment was slight. During the Napoleonic Wars coin was scarce in England and little could be spared for New South Wales even if it had been thought necessary. Governor Phillip was given no treasury and no petty cash. The salaries of government officials and garrison officers were paid into accounts in England. Although seamen, convicts and guards did bring some money, their coins were few and varied. Most good cash was soon spent in buying goods from ships. Left without money for local currency, Sydney had to devise a substitute. Some payments were made by barter, and wages were usually paid in kind. Rum was the most popular part of them, although meat and flour were used more commonly. Like tea, tobacco and sugar, spirits of any kind were supposed to be an incentive to extra work and a relief from dullness. As an article of barter, a bottle might swap for ten pounds of flour or four ounces of tobacco, but it changed hands

PLATE III

(*a*) Camels carrying sleepers for the East–West railway, 1914

(*b*) Mail car on the Birdsville track, 1934

PLATE IV

(a) Mt Connor, Central Australia, a flat-topped mass
of quartzite, 800 feet high and two miles long

(b) The station gate

PLATE V

(*a*) The Dorrigo tablelands in the north of New South Wales

(*b*) One of the few clearings in the
Warrumbungle Range, Guneemooroo

PLATE VI

(*a*) Hobart, Tasmania, 1855

(*b*) Hobart, Tasmania, 1967

very few times. Thirst was too insatiable for rum to be the sole substitute for money, and wages were rarely paid in spirits alone or in the sugar and grain that produced illicit grog.

The chief substitutes for cash were promissory notes with which men, from Governor to convict, settled their debts. Written on any scrap of paper, these notes were easily torn or forged. They were made out for any value from a few pence upwards, and sometimes specified payment in kind. Some had ink that soon faded and others circulated for a long time before they were redeemed. Those drawn by prominent men were accepted at face value, but varying discounts were charged for less reputable notes with less hope of redemption. However useful for local business, this muddled currency could not be used to pay for the imports on which the colony depended. With no private investments or exports to balance trade, the mother country was left to foot the bill. Most supplies came from England in convict transports, but food and livestock from other places were bought with the Governor's drafts or bills that had to be presented at the British Treasury in London for payment in gold. Although this delay made traders charge a small discount for handling them, Treasury Bills were reliable and convenient especially for payment of big sums. Drawn 'for Government services in New South Wales' by authority of the Governor, they gave him almost complete control over the colony's imports. The only limits to his spending were his own prudence and the tolerance of the British Treasury.

Under early Governors, the government was chief storekeeper as well as chief investor. Its commissariat issued provisions and clothes to convicts and garrison, sold other stores for promissory notes and handled the Treasury Bills that paid for incoming goods. When land was granted, the government store victualled the settlers, provided their seed, tools and stock, and bought their grain and meat at generous prices. Payment was sometimes made in store receipts that soon were prized as though they were bank-notes; more often produce was bartered for goods imported by the store. By this buying and selling the government was the most important trader in the colony.

The worst of Sydney's starving time was over when ill-health brought Phillip's resignation in 1792. In five years New South Wales had cost the British Government more than £500,000. At £130 for each transported convict, this was too much for Westminster critics, who thought the place should be abandoned. But half the money had been spent on transports and supply ships; the rest went in food, stores, livestock and administrative costs. Although the expense was high, it had provided links with the outside world and brought the beginnings of trade. The penal settlement was well planted and it propped up the private enterprise of free settlers. This nurture by a careful Governor, however, was not enough for budding expansionists. They were glad to see Phillip go, for his departure brought to power the commanding officer of the New South Wales Corps.

Three years of military interregnum played havoc with Phillip's dreams. He had granted 3440 acres of land to 72 settlers, two-thirds of them ex-convicts. They farmed one-third of the 1700 acres under crop in 1792, yet according to the Deputy-Governor they were a useless lot. Some found their land infertile because they relied more on hope than on manure. Others did no work at all and had their land seized for debt or bartered it for rum. Such idleness justified new instructions from London that land granted to former convicts was not to be sold unless properly worked for five years. A more welcome instruction authorized grants to officers as a speculation that could be sold when they left. These rules brought great confusion. Carelessly kept records showed few grants larger than 120 acres, but details of size were often omitted. Although some land still went to emancipists and even to prisoners under sentence, officers in garrison and government were better placed to press for choice sites, and thus got for themselves, their henchmen and their debtors the lion's share of the 15,000 acres granted during the interregnum. Phillip's orderly plans were bandoned as irregular town sections gave Sydney narrow winding treets, and country grants invaded the good land at Parramatta where he hoped to concentrate penal settlement. However sensible he development of a new colony on neat patterns, geography was against it. Haphazard expansion did lay the foundation of big estates and hurry the colony towards self-support. By 1795 private settlers with 2500 cultivated acres were growing seven times more wheat than the government farms, and the year's work of clearing promised to double the crop.

Most of this progress was made possible by the assignment of convict labour. Orders from London allowed each officer two convict servants victualled by the government store for two years; rations for other labourers must be supplied at his own cost. During the interregnum this rule was ignored. As many as ten male convicts and three females supported by the government were assigned to some officers, while servants were given to other settlers according to their status. Instead of civil magistrates, military officers assumed the power to order secondary punishments for unruly servants, and other devices were used to procure more cheap, docile labour. The working time in government service was reduced to four hours in the morning, leaving convicts free for private employ until late afternoon. To make sure that they worked at low wages, two separate ration scales were introduced for masters and men, in place of the equal allowances Phillip had given to bond and free. From Parramatta prison farms, many convicts were sent to Sydney to build new barracks for the Corps. This reduced the government harvest and made the public store more dependent on food supplies grown by private settlers whose servants, in turn, received their rations from it.

The vicious circle was completed by the officers' control of trade. At first they bought the cargoes of visiting merchants and chartered ships to bring the 'many necessaries' that Sydney lacked. Although they combined, purchase was not easy, for an officer's private bill against his salary in England was not always accepted. When the

Corps's paymaster agreed to issue bills payable on presentation to regimental agents in London, military officers gained better access to foreign trade. After Phillip left, the Treasury Bills drawn by their obliging Commandant gave the officers' combination a complete monopoly of imported goods and of the government store. One shipmaster refused to sell his cargo unless his large stock of rum was taken as well. The whole cargo was bought, in spite of a rule that spirits were not to be used for trade. Within a month barter in rum was bringing the combination enormous profits. More cargoes followed and illicit stills became common as settlers found that wheat brought more when brewed into liquor than when sold to the government store. Traffic in drink got out of hand, but remained very profitable in kind, if not in money. By its aid military traders cheaply acquired the land, livestock and produce of their debtors, and allowed no grain or meat except their own to reach the government store, or any of its imported goods to go out except at their advantage. Famine in 1794 increased their power and the degradation of their luckless victims. No one in Sydney dared to oppose them.

Authorities in London heard little of these official misdeeds. They learned instead of the increasing depravity of convicts and the hopelessness of their reform. Reports showed Sydney deluged in sin, with drunkenness, murder and robbery as common crimes. But nothing was done, for the colony's cost to the British Government fell by half after Phillip left; a bigger decrease in the number of incoming convicts seemed to escape notice. The interregnum ran its course with expansionists enriching themselves at the expense of government and would-be settlers.

Governor John Hunter came in 1795 to find complete reform impossible without the use of force; the colony was too dependent on the trading officers. Civil government, however, had to be restored. Hunter was old and upright. He reinstated civil magistrates and brought some order into the granting of land; but his attempts to break the officers' monopoly of rum and trade were resented by the élite who complained to their powerful friends in England. Orders to stop spending and stop interfering with private traders soon forced Hunter to compromise. The hours of convicts in government service were lengthened, but assignment increased because more servants were now given to employers who offered to support them privately. Although more food was grown, more convicts arrived to eat it; as public officers were still the biggest customers at the government stores, their monopoly of trade increased in value.

Each year more sentences expired to create new problems. Bond and free became harder to distinguish; convict clerks added more confusion by taking bribes to alter the records, and many undeserved certificates of freedom were issued. Some ex-convicts left on visiting ships, some went to India as army recruits, and some were reconvicted and sent to Norfolk Island. Many who stayed were corrupted by rum and debt. A few went into trade and the most favoured were allowed to import goods, but not liquor. This rum restriction strengthened instead of breaking the officers' monopoly, for Hunter also prohibited illicit stills and had public houses licensed. In vain, Hunter reported every small sign of reform to London; after five years he was dismissed for spending and interfering too much.

When Philip Gidley King became Governor in 1800 emancipist settlers fared a little better. King was a business-like ruler with a passion for order. Careless administration distressed him as much as ramshackle buildings. His convicts soon had Sydney looking like a flourishing town, but the Colonial Office dashed his hopes of government reform. For details within his control, such as assignment and trade, he issued endless streams of regulations. Most were ignored because they could not be enforced. King blamed the military officers, but government officials and magistrates were among the worst offenders. Some had joined the trading ring and others were big land-holders. The Reverend Samuel Marsden, prison chaplain and superintendent of labour, had more acres and assigned servants than anyone else. As a magistrate he was dreaded by convicts, yet rum helped to build his church and missionary ships did his trading. His sermons denounced lawbreakers, but he took no notice of regulations.

King was determined to break the officers' power, but they had got rid of one 'naval tyrant' and were unwilling to tolerate another. The clash came quickly. Men in government pay were forbidden to trade, and ships with rum cargoes were ordered out of port. The government storekeeper was told to give preference to growers instead of resellers and King himself attended to see that this was done. Led by Captain John Macarthur the officers retaliated by refusing to attend a loyal celebration at Government House. When the Corps's commanding officer objected, Macarthur challenged him to a duel and wounded him seriously. King promptly sent the offender to England for trial and thus won four years' freedom from a very disruptive influence. With other officers he had less luck. While these quarrels raged, Irish convicts rebelled and the garrison had to be used to restore order. Unable to manage without the officers, King encouraged emancipist traders to compete with military dealers. Merchant speculators like Robert Campbell from Calcutta were welcomed with land and favours although they brought shiploads of spirits. Thousands of copper coins were sent from England to take the place of promissory notes, and payment of wages in rum was prohibited; a maximum rate of interest was fixed for loans and the government store was allowed to give goods on credit to needy settlers. These changes increased the profit in rum, widened the trading combination, and united the free, nicknamed exclusives, against the emancipists.

Because half the granted land was held by a score of military officers and government officials, King increased the number of conditional pardons and gave emancipists sheep and cattle with their land grants. In seven years he doubled the area of granted land. Some went to big settlers like John Blaxland who came with letters of credit, got free passages and freight, 8000 acres and 80 convict servants supported by the government store. Much granted land still went to the officers through debt and thirst. When gout brought King's departure in 1806, the government had 1200 sheep, and 600 small settlers had 20,000 between them. Although officers had 62,000 sheep they grew less grain than the small farmers of whom five out of six were emancipists.

Trouble between exclusives and emancipists was brought to a head by the fourth Governor, Captain William Bligh. Already famous for the *Bounty* mutiny and great resolution as a sailor, he believed in harsh discipline, and was nothing like the olive branch that Sydney needed. He tried to help struggling farmers and to enforce King's regulations with a rough-tongued zeal that was soon felt in every corner of the colony. To settlers flooded by the Hawkesbury River he was a friend in need, but others thought him interfering. His punishments of erring convicts were severe and he had no mercy for freemen who ignored his prohibition of barter in rum. By taking advice from a few unscrupulous emancipists with scores of their own to settle, he became more unpopular. Exclusives opposed him bitterly and it was rumoured that even the Aboriginals wanted to get rid of him. His worst enemy, however, was the haughty and aggressive John Macarthur.

The two men first quarrelled over land; Bligh tried to prevent Macarthur from enlarging his already generous holdings and from picking his own site for his land grants. As Macarthur had resigned his commission in the Corps but not his leading place in the trading combination, he demanded the officers' support against Bligh and his scheming councillors. The opening skirmishes were petty. Soldiers made fun of Bligh's daughter in church, and bullied freemen who sought his favour. In turn the Governor had a fence pulled down on Macarthur's town lease, refused to allow his import of stills, and fined him heavily because a convict stowed away on one of his ships. For not paying this fine Macarthur was brought to court, where he objected to trial before a judge who was an avowed enemy and in his debt. The military officers who made up the court supported Macarthur's protest and asked Bligh to appoint another presiding judge. Bligh answered by putting Macarthur into the common gaol. Furious officers soon released him. The barracks' guns were trained on Bligh's residence. Using one as a desk, Macarthur wrote a short petition calling on the Corps Commandant, Colonel George Johnston, to depose the Governor before more damage was done to property, liberty and life. The paper was signed by a few excited supporters, and the Corps, led by its band and followed by cheering crowds, marched to Government House. Bligh, busily destroying papers in a back room, was not found for some time; legend had him hiding under a bed. He was put under arrest and Johnston took control.

The second military interregnum began in January 1808 and lasted for two years. Bligh's henchmen were dismissed and lost their land. Civil government was suspended and officers enriched themselves and their supporters with land grants, convict labour and government livestock. Only their import trading was limited, because the Commandant, doubtful of his powers, hesitated to sign bills on the British Treasury.

In London Bligh's overthrow was condemned as mutiny, but the rebels in Sydney kept him under guard for twelve months before he was allowed to leave. He went no further than Van Diemen's Land, until the arrival of a new Governor, Colonel Lachlan Macquarie, brought him back briefly to Sydney. Bligh did not reach England until October 1810, long after Johnston, Macarthur and the other witnesses. In June 1811 Johnston was tried by court-martial, found guilty and cashiered, but allowed to return to Sydney where he had much property. Macarthur was less fortunate; he remained in exile for seven years. To the further discomfort of the rebels, Macquarie brought his own regiment to replace the New South Wales Corps. Most of its officers sold their land and stock but a few remained. Their power was gone, yet with other exclusives they carried on the fight against tyrant Governors. Friction continued although Macquarie made many changes.

Lachlan Macquarie was a dignified Scot with little humour to temper his vanity. The role of reformer suited him well, for he was resolute and sincere even when he blamed others for spoiling his plans. With great energy he toured each district of the growing settlement to see for himself how his charges lived. This early inspection convinced him that New South Wales had a fine future; if abuses were checked it could be a model reformatory and, in good time, a free and self-supporting colony. The dream was not new but Macquarie tried for twelve years to fulfil it. One part of his plan was to segregate those under servitude. He assigned fewer servants and instead built barracks, opened government farms and employed more convicts on public works. Chain gangs clanking their fetters made Sydney look like a penal station, and did not encourage exclusives to help emancipists to forget their past as Macquarie insisted they should. Tongues wagged unkindly when he invited successful emancipists to his home. It was bad enough to give a ticket of leave to Francis Howard Greenway, transported for fourteen years for concealing his bankruptcy, and make him government architect. But the choice of William Redfern, convicted for siding with mutineers at the Nore, as Macquarie's family doctor shocked the exclusives; the junior officers hastily left when the Governor brought him to their mess. Emancipists appointed as magistrates were also ostracized. The Reverend Samuel Marsden's refusal to sit on the bench with one of them led to many squabbles. More serious disputes came when Macquarie wanted permission for ex-convict attorneys to plead in court. The new Judge, Ellis Bent, firmly refused; his hot-headed brother and assistant became so offensive over the request that he was removed from office.

Sympathy for reformed emancipists made Macquarie intolerant of lawless freemen. One group led by a doubtful character was arrested for trespass in the grounds of Government House. The

Governor sent the women to prison and had the men flogged. This punishment of freemen without proper trial brought an exclusives' protest that did not enhance the Governor's reputation in London. Freemen had other complaints. Macquarie kept his regiment out of trade, and out of mischief by keeping the colony in order. The settlement was divided into police districts, and for the first time regulations were enforced. Macquarie boasted of the improvement in manners and morals, and of a decrease in crime and drunkenness. Orphanages and schools were opened, and marriage was encouraged by granting tickets of leave to convict couples who could support themselves. The trade in spirits was better controlled. Public houses were fewer and prices more moderate, but Macquarie used more rum payments than any other Governor. The contractors who built Sydney Hospital were given among other things a monopoly to import spirits for more than three years.

Macquarie's aim was to curtail the Treasury Bills that revealed his heavy spending to authorities in London. He gradually reduced the price of meat and grain bought by the government store, so that it needed fewer imported goods for barter. This helped the private stores and justified the removal of many settlers and servants from support by the government. It also encouraged speculation in the private promissory notes that circulated as currency and changed their value each day. To give the colony a fixed currency Macquarie wanted to start a bank, but London refused. He was sent instead 40,000 Spanish dollars from India in 1812. Each was turned into a ring coin by cutting from its centre a 'dump'. This made the 'holey' dollars difficult to export, but when they did not circulate freely in Sydney, Macquarie decided to abolish irregular currency by establishing the Bank of New South Wales. Its charter of 1817 displeased the Colonial Office, and the Bank had to be reorganized ten years later. At first its banknotes were outnumbered by government bills and store receipts, but they helped to drive out less reputable paper currency.

In spite of his care, Macquarie's Treasury Bills increased as more prisoners arrived. By 1817 New South Wales had cost some £4 million. Critics in London argued that thirty years of settlement should have produced some better export than Treasury Bills. In Sydney big land-owners agreed; in addition they blamed the distant government that enabled autocratic Governors to discourage expansion and private investment. As Colonel Johnston wrote: 'If it is the intention of Ministers merely to keep the country to answer the purpose of an immense gaol for the reception of the vilest of the vile, the sooner they declare it the better, in order that the respectable industrious part of the community may have an opportunity afforded them of disposing of what they possess here, and of seeking a country in which they may find some other security for it than the mere will and caprice of a Governor or Secretary of State.'

Such criticism persuaded the Colonial Office to make a thorough inquiry. The task went to a judge from Trinidad, John Thomas Bigge, who spent two years on it. He was soon at loggerheads with Macquarie over the employment of convicts on unproductive public works and over the treatment of emancipists. Bigge found emancipists filling the public offices, dominating trade and holding nine-tenths of the 250,000 acres granted in concentrated settlement. Emancipists also had nine-tenths of the land under cultivation and more than half the livestock. Clearly their settlement was well established and full of promise, but when they claimed the civil rights to which free British subjects were entitled, Bigge was not impressed. He found the exclusive landowners more convincing. According to John Macarthur democratic feeling had already taken too deep a root and threatened Great Britain with the loss of her dependency; isolationist aims were only to be defeated by granting large estates and convict labour to an élite of 'ancient families' whose wealth and property could produce a colonial aristocracy. Macarthur also claimed that the salvation of New South Wales was not in fancied freedom but in fine wool; it alone would bring

63

private investment, reduce government costs, supply raw material for British factories and bind mother country more firmly to colony. Bigge's report was written under the exclusives' spell. Macquarie was recalled. Assignment increased. Exploration and settlement spread to make Bigge appear as a prophet. British investors, from peers to commoners and including Bigge himself, turned to New South Wales for speculation. To isolationists, however, Bigge's 'nauseous trash' was merely a transcript of what expansionists had done for thirty years and were to go on doing for thirty more.

CHAPTER 4

SEPARATION: 1820–40

The ten years after Macquarie were a sober prelude to the rapid movements of the next decade. Population, swollen by immigration, multiplied five times to reach 190,000 by 1840. Wool exports multiplied forty-five times to reach 27,000 bales. Sheep spread over thousands of square miles in the east, while possession of New Holland gave Britain the whole continent and the beginnings of a new western colony. What New South Wales lost in territory others gained; Van Diemen's Land was given independence and room was made for South Australia. Changes in administration brought British banks, companies and private investors to compete with local speculators for prizes in land and wool. With rising prosperity anyone could better himself. In all the hustle of expansion only the Colonial Office seemed to hinder progress. This common grudge slowly dissolved the bad feeling between exclusives and emancipists, but also created new divisions. The first cautious transfer of control from London to the antipodes gave political influence to wealthy landowners whose greed for power united less privileged colonists in demanding the civil rights of free Englishmen. Delay sharpened appetites for political independence, even though the colonies depended on British investment for new opportunies to expand.

In 1820 New South Wales was at law no more than a prison. Convicts and the freemen who outnumbered them were ruled by a Governor whose authority rested only on a commission from the Crown and instructions from the Colonial Office. For years the legality of regulations, land grants and conditional pardons had been doubted because they lacked the consent of Parliament; of all the Governors' questioned orders only customs duties had its direct sanction. The plight of freemen provoked no interest at

Westminster until 1823 when a Judicature Act made New South Wales into a Crown colony. Even then Parliament took no chances with emancipists. A new charter of justice created a Supreme Court where military juries were to be used in all criminal trials; in civil cases an ordinary jury was permitted only if both parties asked for it. A new constitution created a Legislative Council to advise the Governor, but without power to check his autocracy. He alone could introduce the colonial laws that now took the place of regulations, and his special votes gave him power to pass them. As a step towards self-government, the Council was disappointing. Most members were senior government officials, and the non-official Councillors were chosen for their wealth, not because they represented the colonists. With exclusive juries and Councillors, emancipist hopes fell, until a champion came to their rescue.

Colonial-born and fearless, William Charles Wentworth had already made a name as an explorer, barrister and writer. His lifelong passions were leadership and constitutional law. Later he became a bitter enemy of democracy, but in 1824 his friends and clients were emancipists. As an ardent patriot he believed that the designs of self-seeking exclusives could only be defeated if full citizen rights were gained for every freeman in New South Wales. When petitions to the Crown brought no reform, he published the *Australian*, with help from two radical journalists. In fiery editorials they flayed the government for misrule. When other newspapers joined the attack, the Governor tried to silence the press. The battle raged for three years without truce. The Legislative Council remained an exclusive preserve, but in slow stages emancipists were given a share in trial by jury, and military juries were abandoned. Another important victory was won in 1840 when the mother country struck New South Wales off the list of places to which convicts could be sent.

The Judicature Act was accompanied by other changes that hastened expansion. One was currency reform. Its object was uniform coinage based on sterling, but foreign money had to be driven out first. In 1822 Sydney received large shipments of dollars. Valued by their silver content, they became official currency for three years. Their arrival coincided with a boom of prosperity that attracted new banks and moneylenders, whose loans to speculators rapidly pushed up the price of land and sheep. The boom also attracted foreign cargoes. Soon the dollars were flowing out and with them went other foreign coins. Sydney was left with another shortage of cash. This crisis coincided unhappily with a drought to cause great distress. Prices collapsed and many speculators were ruined. Banks and merchants were left with promissory notes for £200,000 that could not be paid until British coin was brought in. By 1830 the currency problem was solved and confidence was restored, but the crisis left many bitter feelings.

A second reform dealt with land. When Macquarie left, surveyors were still struggling to make order out of the chaos of early grants. Too much land had been given away carelessly; of 650,000 granted acres only one in twenty was cleared or cultivated. Authorities in London slowly began to see some value in colonial land. Their first step was to ensure that it was given to men with enough money to work it. New rules allowed land to be granted to a settler only if he had at least £500 in money, livestock or equipment. He was also given one assigned servant for every hundred acres, but the land was not to be sold for five years. The maximum grant of four square miles—and more could be bought for 5s. an acre—showed the change in government policy. Where small farms had once been encouraged, large estates were now favoured. The rules were much abused and trickery was common. The same £500 transferred from one applicant to another often secured a number of grants. *Bona fide* settlers were not easily distinguished from speculators, and influence with officials still won choice sites. Certainly the five million acres granted in eastern Australia during the 'twenties were not matched by an equivalent investment of capital. Most grants went to British investors. Colonel Potter Macqueen, M.P., for example, was given 10,000 acres of freehold with another 10,000 held in reserve. The Australian Agricultural Company gained a million acres at a nominal price; Bigge and Macarthur were among its shareholders in a list that bristled with the names of bankers, shipowners and eminent politicians. Another company was given half a million acres in Van Diemen's Land. Few of these investors aimed to leave England, but many sent their poor relations and dependants as agents and labourers. They came in greater numbers after the Colonial Office allowed the cost of passages to be included in the capital required for land grants. In this way the free migration that by 1825 had brought only 5000 in three decades was more than equalled in the next five years.

The changes in law, currency and land policy were evidence of Britain's growing interest in the colony, but while isolationists welcomed the new opportunities, they resented the increase of distant control. They had faced the pioneering hazards through long years of neglect by the mother country; why should new-comers and absentees now profit from their work? These feelings were strong in New South Wales, but Van Diemen's Land had a double grievance. Remote control from London was bad enough; relayed through Sydney it was intolerable.

The settlements planted at Hobart and Launceston by Governor King had grown very slowly. They dimly reflected Sydney's progress, but avoided serious friction between exclusives and emancipists, and had no extreme abuses of military rule. The inevitable starving time was followed by trouble with runaway convicts and bushrangers. One notorious gang was led by Michael Howe. Transported for highway robbery, he escaped to become the terror of lonely settlers for eight years. Colonel Thomas Davey, the island's second Lieutenant Governor, was no match for him. Appointed through influence of a powerful patron, 'mad Tom' Davey was more eager to enjoy high living than to keep order. Although he did at last proclaim martial law, his Sydney superior declared it illegal. When Davey was replaced by William Sorell, the island gained a reliable ruler. Within a year 'Black' Howe was tracked down. Other bushrangers remained at large in wild country, but the main settlements were safe. They also became productive under Sorell's guidance. By assigning servants he persuaded settlers to grow grain for export to Sydney. He imported merino sheep, offered prizes for the finest wool and guaranteed a minimum price for all clips. Before he left in 1824 Van Diemen's Land had nearly as many sheep as the mainland and was attracting more free migrants with money and farming experience. What might have been pleasant rivalry between isolated neighbours was turned into bitter resentment by the island's legal dependence on New South Wales. Sorell struggled hard for local powers. By winning permission to issue Treasury Bills he set Hobart's trade free from Sydney's control. The opening of local courts brought immediate trial to criminals and saved civil litigants from costly journeys to Sydney. Land grants and other official business, however, had to be approved by the Governor of New South Wales until the Judicature Act gave Van Diemen's Land its long-sought separation.

The island's new constitution came into operation in 1825 under Colonel George Arthur. A Legislative Council was formed, but he seldom took its advice. For twelve years he ruled as a despot, altering laws that stood in his way, dismissing officials who would not work with him and defying instructions from London that did not please him. His plans were unpopular yet he followed them tirelessly. Convicts were his special care. To make transportation a dreaded punishment, Arthur treated determined prisoners with extreme severity. From notorious Macquarie Harbour incorrigibles were moved to stricter supervision at Port Arthur where the narrow neck of Tasman Peninsula made escape difficult. The less hardened in crime were given opportunity to reform as assigned servants. Free settlers who co-operated with the Governor's plans were given labour and land. To encourage law-abiding behaviour he increased the number of police. With a reinforced military garrison he waged a successful war on bushrangers, run-aways, and sheep-stealers. A tougher problem was the long-standing hostility between settlers and Aboriginals. When his orders did not stop ill-treatment of natives or their reprisals, Arthur decided to segregate the troublesome tribes. To drive them into Tasman Peninsula, three thousand soldiers, settlers and servants formed the famous line of 1830 that captured only a man and a boy at a cost of £30,000 and seven weeks' effort. When force failed, conciliation was tried. George Robinson, a pious Hobart contractor, was given the dangerous task of winning the natives' confidence. His four-year mission brought in 200 Aboriginals, the decimated remnant of thirty years' contact with whites.

Arthur's activities displeased the Colonial Office, but complaints from England disturbed him no more than the local clamour for civil rights. Rigid as rock he worked on to make the colony safe for reformed convicts. Schools and churches were multiplied. Roads and bridges improved travel. Arthur went everywhere fighting crime and immorality. His hand fell heavily on high and low without favour. His enemies were legion but the island prospered. Its wheatgrowers profited from convict labour and Sydney's recurring droughts. By 1830 private banks in Hobart and Launceston were offering British investors the highest legal rate of interest in the Empire. Six years under Arthur had brought a million acres of land grants, trebled the flocks and doubled the population of free migrants and convicts. Although the best parts of the island were filling fast, the empty southern mainland was close at hand to encourage expansion; but before flockmasters were ready to claim this new territory, investors from Britain opened a new colony in the west.

Western Australia was founded by Captain James Stirling in 1829. On an earlier mission to Australia he explored the Swan River and returned to England to press for its immediate settlement. Unless Britain acted quickly, he warned, the unclaimed half-continent would be taken by French or Americans. The

Colonial Office hesitated; Swan River was too isolated to defend and new settlements were costly. Stirling persisted; if a man-of-war were provided, he undertook to find migrants and settle the colony himself. When this plan was rejected he asked for a charter for an association that, in exchange for land grants, would take out settlers and govern the colony free of cost to the mother country. Stirling's glowing reports of Swan River soon brought other offers from speculators. One group led by Thomas Peel and Potter Macqueen proposed to send 10,000 settlers within four years, in return for four million acres of land. Reluctantly the Colonial Office gave way. Stirling was given charge of the new colony, with one man-of-war and one transport to carry his garrison, settlers and stores. Colonists were promised 200 acres for each labourer they took out, and 40 acres for each £3 they brought in livestock and equipment. These conditions displeased Peel's group, but although it dissolved, half a million acres were reserved for Peel himself if he landed his tenants and livestock within twelve months. After Stirling left, Parliament cautiously authorized the new colony by an Act that required renewal in five years. With much less caution, speculators painted rosy pictures of Swan River where families might easily gain quick fortunes and large estates, free from any convict taint. Before Stirling's first reports reached England, thirteen ships were on their way with 1500 migrants all eager for wealth, but mostly ill-suited for the hardship of pioneering.

Captain Fremantle arrived at Swan River to take formal possession of New Holland in May 1829. Stirling came a month later in the transport *Parmelia*. It ran aground in Cockburn Sound. In great confusion passengers, stores and livestock were landed on Garden Island. While other ships arrived to swell the crude settlement on its barren shore, Stirling went up Swan River in search of a town site. By August Perth had been surveyed and its blocks were available for selection, but already settlers were complaining that the sandy soil was unfit to cultivate. Their land hunger added to Stirling's survey problem, for he had to reserve large areas for

Peel and other favoured individuals before smaller settlers were served. While they waited confusion increased. Some had brought wooden cottages and farm tools, others had carriages and pianos, but food and money were scarce. The first sheep and flour sent from Hobart fetched high prices. Little cash was left for later cargoes, some of which suffered severe losses in transit. Their disappointed owners departed to prophesy disaster for the new colony. Thomas Peel arrived with his retinue in a veritable Noah's ark, too late to claim his reserve. Although he selected other sandy acres south of Cockburn Sound, most of his dependants broke their agreements and deserted. Sickness, starvation and straying stock left Peel with little more than bitter memories.

Despite these depressing reverses Stirling nursed the settlement gently and firmly. Exploration revealed scattered areas of well-watered land along the south coast and over the Darling Ranges. They were soon surveyed and settled, but large holdings increased the problems of distance. Not even Stirling's resolution could hold the disillusioned labourers and adventurers whose chief object now was to quit the colony. Even respectable settlers lost heart and left. The arrival of 1000 people in 1830 scarcely sufficed to keep the population steady at 1500. Perplexed by his people's plight, Stirling went to England in 1832 to plead for help. At the Colonial Office he asked for money, migrants, livestock, soldiers and clergy; where private individuals had invested £200,000 and taken all the risks, the Mother Country had spent only £40,000 and gained an asset of one million square miles of territory. The Colonial Office replied that settlers went out knowing no government aid would follow; let them therefore use their own enterprise. They could, however, have a Legislative Council, and what revenue it raised in taxes would be matched by a grant from the British Government.

These meagre concessions were not well received in Perth, but Stirling returned in 1834 to infuse new determination into the settlement. He led the fight against natives at the 'battle' of

Pinjarra, which shocked the Colonial Office but ended the talk of abandoning outlying districts. Where lesser men were discouraged, Stirling fought on. Within five years the colony had flour-mills, breweries, newspapers, a whaling base, a shipyard, an agricultural show and an annual Governor's ball. When Stirling resigned in 1839 some one and a half million acres had been granted. The sheep from the old world and Hobart had multiplied; wool was being exported and enough crops were being grown to feed the population whose numbers had crept past 2000. Although Western Australia was proud of Stirling's tenacious record, it had ceased to attract the British ships, money and migrants that made expansion possible. The lonely colony lagged behind its ambitious neighbours, yet the struggling settlers did not lose faith in their adopted home. They spoke wryly of their 'sand, sorrow and sore eyes', and in their isolation grew bitter against the indifference of Westminster and the eastern colonies.

Some of Western Australia's unpopularity in England was due to Edward Gibbon Wakefield, who began his reform of colonization while Stirling was planting the new colony. To Wakefield colonization was more than sending Britain's people to empty spaces in the colonies; British civilization must also be transplanted if colonies were to be held to the mother country by affection and respect. He approved the Swan River plan to encourage immigration of labourers by grants of land to employers, but he deplored the large holdings that dispersed settlement, wasted labour and brought needless hardship. Dispersion and cheap land, he argued, drove lonely settlers into brutish habits and made emigration a curse instead of a blessing. He offered to cure these evils with a simple prescription: land must be sold at a price sufficient to concentrate settlement, combine the varied skills of labourers and preserve the decencies of British civilization. In these conditions, the revenue from land sales could be used for the emigration of suitable young couples to the mutual benefit of colony and mother country.

73

Wakefield's systematic colonization was not a clear-cut plan, nor was it applied anywhere to his satisfaction. His *Letter from Sydney* (1829) gained him a few supporters and his *England and America* (1833) brought many more, but Wakefield would never translate his key words—sufficient price—into a sordid number of shillings. Whenever his disciples did so, he quarrelled with them and went off to find a new group willing to listen to his 'art' of colonization. From keen young Cambridge graduates he turned in succession to bankers, radical politicians and aristocratic speculators. In this process the noble dream of transplanted civilization suffered and the theory became known as a system of land sales and emigration.

While Wakefield thought chiefly of his theory, his disciples were eager to prove it in a new experimental colony. Australia's empty southern shore beckoned in 1830, and a settlement at Gulf St Vincent was planned, to be managed completely by Wakefieldians. Many changes had to be made before the Colonial Office agreed that its control of the new colony in South Australia could be shared by a Board of Commissioners responsible for land, emigration and government funds. In 1834 Parliament gave its approval on condition that £35,000 of land was sold before settlement began. Next year Commissioners were appointed. Although the new territory was unexplored, English buyers were offered one town acre and eighty country acres for £81 that would also provide them with emigrant labourers. Wakefield protested that this price was insufficient, and disowned the project, but the required amount of land was sold and in 1836 the pioneers left England.

The first arrivals made a whaling station on Kangaroo Island. They were followed by surveyors under Colonel William Light. Mainland exploration had scarcely begun before more ships arrived. On 28 December 1836 Governor John Hindmarsh landed to establish his government. With him came the Resident Commissioner J. H. Fisher. By next March the site of Adelaide was chosen and surveyed, and its acre blocks were allotted to buyers. Although brilliantly planned, the town was six miles from its port and

74

no provision had been made for transport. With stores to carry and houses to build, workmen were in great demand. Light's labourers were soon enticed away by high wages and the country survey came almost to a standstill. As immigrant families poured in provisions had to be imported from Hobart and Sydney; in paying for them Adelaide ran short of money. This vicious circle brought angry quarrels between Governor and Resident Commissioner. The bluff sailor Hindmarsh was bewildered by the colony's divided rule. He was responsible to the Colonial Office and he alone could draw on the government funds raised by the Commissioners. On the other hand, Fisher alone could draw on the Commissioners' land revenue. Which was to pay for speeding the survey and importing stores? Hindmarsh was craftily persuaded to draw bills for amounts beyond his authority, but he was defied by Fisher when he wanted to buy land for himself outside the concentrated area that Light was surveying near Adelaide. Soon Hindmarsh was dismissing officers and Fisher was reinstating them. When his orders were countermanded, Fisher worked through his friends to call public meetings and to start a newspaper in opposition to the one that supported the Governor. Stormy reports to London brought strong protests from English land-buyers who feared that friction might spoil their investment. Before long Hindmarsh and Fisher were both dismissed and Colonel George Gawler was given the dual role of Governor and Resident Commissioner.

Before Gawler arrived in October 1838, the concentrated country survey around Adelaide was finished but Light had resigned. Although some country sections were allotted, many preliminary buyers demanded better land further afield. To give them the promised first choice, Gawler was instructed to survey some 8000 square miles. This put an end to the theory of concentration and multiplied costs of government. By the end of 1839 land sales at 20s. an acre amounted to £300,000, but only one-third of this revenue was spent on the immigration of young couples; the balance was frittered away in London on publicity and less worthy purposes. The population rose to 15,000 by 1840 as settlers came from Britain, Germany and neighbouring colonies to share South Australia's boasted prosperity.

Most newcomers found that the prosperity had been exaggerated. A few pastoralists were doing well with sheep and cattle from Van Diemen's Land and New South Wales, and merchants were thriving in Adelaide, but there were unhealthy symptoms as well. The whaling station on Kangaroo Island had proved unprofitable and the delayed country survey prevented farmers from growing crops; Adelaide was still crowded with immigrants and still dependent on imported food. Much land was changing hands; some acres brought up to £2000, and speculators were subdividing near-by country sections. Money was scarce and most payments were made in land orders, promissory notes and private bills on English investors. Meanwhile luckless labourers went jobless until Gawler provided public works. This benevolence added to Gawler's mounting costs as immigrants came in greater numbers. When land sales slackened in 1840 Adelaide leaders began to criticize the servile spirit of dependence that Gawler seemed to foster. They preferred the free enterprise that had produced what they liked to call a record feat of colonization. In spite of valuable aid from Sydney and Hobart, they disdained their convict neighbours and boasted distinction as a home for free families. They claimed that South Australia was an English province just like Devonshire. Had not this freedom won them the first Municipal Corporation in the colonial Empire? South Australia, however, was separated from its neighbours by more than pride. Sydney in disrespect called it a humbug colony: Adelaide's speculation, urban growth and misused land fund had failed to prove the virtue of Wakefield's systematic colonization, yet its English patrons were trying to force high land prices and concentrated settlement on New South Wales.

The first attempt had come in 1831 when the Colonial Office decreed that Crown land in eastern Australia was to be sold by auction at a minimum price of 5s. an acre. This order, known as the Ripon Regulations, put an end to the free granting of land. In the next eight years nearly two million acres were sold, on occasions for 40s., but more often for the minimum price. Part of this revenue was used for emigration. The appointment of a London Committee brought a sudden drop in the cost of passages, but very few suitable migrants. Skilled labourers were outnumbered by paupers and orphan girls. In Sydney the system soon earned a bad name. Land-owners wanted young single men for up-country work. Some disappointed employers sent for Indian and Chinese coolies; others commissioned their own agents in London to provide their needed labour. When this private migration was exploited by ship-owners, the government had to intervene. Before long New South Wales had two systems. In London an official agent controlled emigration under the land fund scheme, and in Sydney the government offered bounties for the labour brought out by private employers. By these means eastern Australia gained some 70,000 immigrants during the 'thirties.

The Ripon Regulations were unpopular with pastoralists who thought 5s. too high, and with systematic colonizers who thought it too low. In 1838 the Wakefieldians triumphed and the minimum price was raised to 12s., but sheep-owners had their own answer to the mischievous half-truths of theorists. Settlement had already been restricted to the counties surveyed near Sydney. By 1836 the best land inside this area was granted or sold cheaply to large graziers. Little was left for newcomers or for the growing flocks of smaller owners who found trespass on Crown land easier than purchase. Each year new stations outside the surveyed counties were formed without the knowledge of government. This rapid spread played havoc with Wakefield's combination of skills, for each sheep-owner became a jack of all trades. British civilization was left behind as scattered males relapsed into primitive crudity. The unauthorized dispersion of squatters made nonsense of Wakefield's tidy dreams, yet systematic colonizers in London insisted that concentration be enforced. In Sydney the Governors were perplexed; the squatters' wool enriched the colony and their so-called lawlessness did not trouble the government. Surely theory was at fault if it contradicted practice. The subject dominated the dispatches between Sydney and London for years until the theorists agreed that wool-growing was the exception that proved their rule. A wise Governor, Sir Richard Bourke, had already found a temporary solution; in 1836 his Legislative Council passed an Act which brought dispersion within the law. For an annual £10 licence a squatter could occupy as much Crown land as he pleased, but he was given no title to land or to any improvements he might make. Shepherds still fought over grass and water as they had done since the days of Abraham.

This Act affected the sheep-owners from Van Diemen's Land who settled the southern mainland. The first comer was Edward Henty. His father, a Sussex farmer, had sent three sons to Swan River, but they were soon discouraged and rejoined the family which was now in Van Diemen's Land. As suitable cheap land was scarce on the island, Edward was sent to explore the mainland. He found a good site and applied for permission to occupy it. Without waiting for a reply, he took a shipload of labourers, livestock and equipment and in November 1834 landed at Portland Bay. Henty's brothers joined him before they learned of London's disapproval. They stayed to expand the settlement, but ten years later when Portland was officially opened as a town they received very little reward for their pioneering effort.

The settlers at Port Phillip Bay fared better. The first on the scene was John Batman. For capturing bushrangers and pacifying natives this jolly, colonial-born giant had been granted land by Governor Arthur, but his stock did not thrive and he wanted better pastures. When leave to settle the mainland was refused, he and his friends, including a government surveyor and Governor Arthur's nephew, decided to deal directly with the Aboriginal owners of the empty territory. In May 1835 Batman crossed

Bass Strait and found some natives who he claimed were 'chiefs'. From them he 'purchased' on behalf of his Port Phillip Association some 600,000 acres north of the River Yarra for a few blankets, knives and trinkets. In July land south of the river was claimed by a rival party organized by John Pascoe Fawkner, owner of a Launceston inn and newspaper.

These expeditions had unofficial blessing from Governor Arthur who hoped for control of the new settlement from Hobart. In Sydney Governor Bourke thought otherwise. In August he issued a proclamation that Batman's treaty with the natives was void, but although Bourke warned against unlicensed trespass at Port Phillip, he knew it could not be stopped. He appealed to the Colonial Office to turn this new dispersion to good account by selling land and opening new towns as centres of civilization and government. While his dispatch was on its way to London, enterprising settlers were crossing Bass Strait with large numbers of sheep. The land claimed by Batman was occupied months before protest from the Port Phillip Association brought a reluctant compensation of £7000 from the government in Sydney. By June 1836 some 30,000 sheep had arrived and 200 people were camped in huts and tents near Fawkner's new dramshop by the River Yarra. A visiting police inspector reported that the invaders had elected an arbitrator to settle disputes among themselves and with the aborigines.

By September Bourke had London's approval to authorize the settlement of Port Phillip as a district of New South Wales. Captain William Lonsdale was sent from Sydney to take charge. With him came customs officers, surveyors, convict servants and a military guard. Next March Governor Bourke himself arrived to proclaim the site of Melbourne and name its streets. With the auction of its first blocks in June 1837 the village began to grow. A year later when the first licences were issued to squatters, the Port Phillip District had more than 300,000 sheep. Most came from Van Diemen's Land, and the resolute Scots who brought

79

them were spreading steadily westward from Geelong to found the fortunes that later won them and their descendants a leading place in Melbourne affairs. Overlanders from New South Wales settled the northern plains. Some took the route used by the Sydney squatter, C. H. Ebden, when he crossed the River Murray with his flocks in 1835; a few latecomers followed the explorer Angus Macmillan over rugged mountain tracks into Gippsland.

Overland migration gathered momentum as word spread that the new pastures had reliable rainfall and easy access to ports. So many Sydney buyers came to dominate the land auctions at Melbourne and Geelong that the government decided to hold the next sales in Sydney. Busy southern settlers were thus left to the mercy of agents whose eager bidding pushed up the price of grazing land to more than 40s. an acre. The Scots, backed by colonial banks in Van Diemen's Land, were not ready buyers at first; they had their squatting licences and could move to good land further out. Their caution soon vanished as the surveys progressed and British banks opened branches in Melbourne. By 1840 land speculation had become a mania. Although sheep numbers rose to 800,000, good ewes could not be had for less than 30s. Grazing land rose to £9 an acre at government auctions, with prompt private resale for £50. From £37,000 in 1838 sales of Crown land in the Port Phillip District increased to £219,000 in 1840.

While squatters gambled for big stakes, Melbourne had its own inflation. Although little assistance was given to British migrants, Port Phillip's population reached 10,000 in 1840. Half the new arrivals swarmed into Melbourne to make a staggering demand for houses and land. As British money also poured in, the town was soon crowded with merchants, dealers, agents and auctioneers. Where wool worth £125,000 was exported, nearly £500,000 of goods were imported. Everyone overtraded, and moneylenders did a roaring business at high rates of interest. Land was the chief attraction; half-acre town blocks bought for £42 in 1837 were now resold privately for £9,450, while suburban land, subdivided into pocket handkerchief lots, yielded immediate profits of £400 an acre. The opening years were like a gay picnic, but not all the spending was reckless. Observers who deplored the showy champagne lunches and the absence of families did not recognize the ambition of young men who had unlimited confidence in Melbourne's future and their own success. As their determined independence made them hard to govern, especially when government originated in distant Sydney, Governor Bourke soon saw that the Port Phillip District needed a local superintendent. Charles Joseph La Trobe was chosen for the job and reached Melbourne in October 1839.

La Trobe was inexperienced in government, but wide travel fitted him to direct the growth of a new city. He began by clearing tree stumps from the streets and went on to drainage. Soon he was planning a public hospital, benevolent asylum, public library, university, water supply and botanical gardens. He could not fulfil any of these plans without permission from Sydney, and young Melbourne became impatient with his placid obedience to frustrating instructions. When he tried to explain the limits of local authority, three rival newspapers struggling for public favour scorned him and the Governor he represented. Bitter editorials gave reasons why La Trobe should not submit tamely to Sydney's selfish policies. Port Phillip was suffering injustice and heavy loss as a neglected extension of New South Wales. The District paid its own way and owed nothing to Sydney for its settlement. By 1840 nearly £400,000 of government revenue had gone to New South Wales where it was spent on public works while Melbourne went short of immigrant labour and much needed improvements. Convicts were another sore point. Port Phillip was free and had its own reasons for supporting the pleas to abolish transportation to New South Wales. Squatters had brought assigned servants, but no penal station marred the new settlement. Why should its freemen be dependent on a convict colony? As demands for separation gathered strength, the Colonial Office was blamed as much as the government in Sydney for retarding Melbourne's progress. Long before independent rule was won, Melbourne and Sydney were widely separated by regional pride and resentment.

In a frenzied scramble for land Australia was thus divided into isolated settlements, each jealous of its own small distinctions. Each loudly proclaimed its virtues in desperate rivalry for money and migrants. Yet the settlements had much in common. Their people and rulers were British. Transplanted British civilization struggled against less worthy growths in their new and different soils. Their churches and schools competed feebly with more earthy needs. With every man for himself, more respect was given to good luck than to good manners. Their common goal was independence measured in hard facts and figures. It seemed near in the booming days of 1840 when isolation was by choice. Isolation enforced by depression was soon to teach that dependence also had some virtue. The lessons were not forgotten. Although local loyalties prevailed, the paternal embrace of empire was a comfort.

CHAPTER 5

EXPANSION: 1840–60

The mid-century years were marked by unexpected events that brought the outside world much closer yet greatly strengthened separation within Australia. Every outer breach in the barriers of distance was matched by new internal walls of division. Depression was followed by new-found wealth and political independence to give new purpose to regionalism instead of producing a nation. The continent of 1860 had more jealously guarded disunity than ever before.

The rosy prospects of 1840 vanished in a financial slump. British investors were disappointed as every Australian mail brought news of speculation. Instead of productive rural industry, their agents boasted of boom prices for town land and asked for more money to keep prices soaring. In alarm, British investors ordered their agents to economize and began to ask for their money back. This check to inflation was felt first in South Australia where town speculation had been particularly reckless and even the food of settlers had been imported. Systematic colonizers saw their plans go awry. Land, labour and capital were thrown out of balance as investors stopped buying land, and immigrants continued to arrive in increasing numbers. To relieve their desperate needs Governor Gawler drew heavily on the South Australian Commissioners in London. He did not know that the Commissioners' funds had evaporated before his bills began to arrive from Adelaide, and the Commissioners did not know they were coming. No attempt was made to raise a loan in London until newspapers had the story and then, of course, it was too late.

News of the government's bankruptcy reached Adelaide in 1841. Bankers who had lent money wanted it back. Their debtors were forced to sell property, even the trinkets and treasures of their wives and daughters, and there were many insolvencies. Benevolent Governor Gawler was replaced by George Grey, a youthful military captain whose twenty-nine years had been packed with adventure. As resolutely as he had explored the inhospitable coast of Western Australia, he set out to make South Australia pay its way. The Colonial Office wanted to remove the population altogether; Grey drove it instead into the country by stopping all public works in Adelaide. Hundreds of town houses were emptied; shops were boarded up; cockney clerks and skilled tradesmen became shepherds and farm labourers. Each day the Governor became more unpopular as government debts remained unpaid, but he would not change his plans. Immigration was suspended for five years. Imports which amounted to £56 per head in 1838, shrank to £6 in 1843. The port was as deserted as the town; until it had worthwhile exports, Adelaide was too far from trade routes to attract shipping. To pay the Commissioners' debts in London more than £200,000 was granted by the British Parliament, but with this grant the experiment in systematic colonization came to an end. South Australia was brought completely under Colonial Office control, a Crown colony like its neighbours.

The economic crisis in South Australia was followed within a few months by depression in the neighbouring colonies. Each took the same course. British investors withdrew support, land sales collapsed, immigration was checked, falling prices and unemployment drove labour into the country. In New South Wales the slump was made worse by the end of transportation. This shut off supplies of cheap labour and the large income that Britain supplied each year to maintain the penal establishment.

Van Diemen's Land got more convicts but no gain, for the penal system was changed. Probation replaced assigned service. Assignment to private employers had long been condemned as an unequal, uncertain form of punishment that neither encouraged reform nor deterred crime. Probation was designed to correct these faults. Prisoners now had to work in convict gangs for at

PLATE VII

(*a*) King William Street, Adelaide, 1885

(*b*) King William Street, Adelaide, 1968

PLATE VIII

(*a*) Queen Street, Brisbane, 1883

(*b*) Brisbane today

PLATE IX

(a) Merino ram, 1882

(b) Merino ram, 1910

(c) Merino ram, 1958

PLATE X

(*a*) Panning gold

(*b*) A Bush inn, Willunga

least a year before they were given probation passes which allowed them to seek private employ in the country. To offset the loss of assigned servants in 1840, large sums were spent on immigration. When the free immigrants did arrive, they found themselves in competition with probationary pass-holders whose fixed, low pay depressed all wages. Work was scarce too, for one aim of probation was to cut the cost of the penal stations by making prisoners grow their own food. The plan worked too well; convicts fed themselves and grew a surplus for sale. This greatly reduced the British grants, while free settlers were left to compete with their former servants in a smaller market. To make matters worse, Van Diemen's Land suffered permanently by settling Port Phillip. Many of the best men and over £1,500,000 in sheep and goods went across Bass Strait, too much for the island's business which was ruined when prices collapsed.

Isolated in their separate communities, few people could tell when the depression began to lift. Nor did they see that the slump did more good than inflation for Australia as a whole. The continent's most accessible resources were not in the towns, but in the near-by country. Gradually primary production increased as families left the towns and braved the dreaded 'bush'. At first, farmers were poor and slow to adapt themselves to new conditions. Their fencing and clearing were as crude as their implements, although they contrived to grow enough for local needs. The best progress was made in South Australia where climate and soil favoured wheat growing. On the lightly timbered plains close to Adelaide, farmers were soon provided with labour-saving devices. The miller John Ridley produced a stripper capable of harvesting six acres a day. Although smallholders could not afford his machines, he and other big land-owners planted large areas. By 1850 South Australia had 2000 farmers, whose total of 40,000 acres under wheat made a secure foundation for future expansion. Around Hobart and Melbourne more acres were cultivated and more varied crops were grown, but irregular seasons stopped agriculture from flourishing in New South Wales. Although the continent no longer relied on imported food, subsistence farming remained the general rule. While the export of breadstuffs remained a costly risk, farmers were described as 'a needy, struggling and despised class of people'.

By contrast, pastoralists escaped from depression to enjoy great prestige. The slump did not greatly affect wool values, but sheep prices tumbled from 30s. a head to a few pence. It was not uncommon for a large flock to be sold at 1s. 6d. a head with the station, drays, bullocks, hurdles and utensils thrown in. Graziers found that it paid to boil down their surplus stock for tallow. This expedient was used chiefly in New South Wales where the fat from hundreds of thousand sheep and cattle slaughtered during the 'forties was shipped oversea to be made into soap and candles. In the other colonies squatters spread into unoccupied land with their cheap sheep. By 1850 the Port Phillip District had spurted to the lead in woolgrowing, with a clip worth more than the combined output of the continent in 1840. More important, Australia now triumphed over Spain and Saxony as England's chief supplier of raw wool. This impressive achievement brought renewed British investment, which helped to lift the depression and hastened political reform.

In 1843 the Legislative Council of New South Wales was changed. Twenty-four elected members were added to the nominees appointed by the Colonial Office. This beginning of representative government in Australia did not satisfy many people. Electorates were unequal, and voters and candidates had to have high property qualifications. Most of the seats were won by pastoralists and their friends. With the wealthy government nominees they hopelessly outnumbered the few members who wanted more reform. Townsmen in great annoyance found themselves with even fewer political rights than they had in England. There were other complaints. Only six seats were given to the Port Phillip District where settlers had hoped for complete separation from New South Wales. Their members had to travel 600 miles to attend the Council in Sydney and few could afford the time or expense. People in Melbourne thought that kind of representative government a bad joke and refused to take the elections seriously. They even elected the Secretary of State for the Colonies as one of their members. Other colonies thought themselves worse off with no representation at all. The nominated Legislative Council in Van Diemen's Land remained unaltered, and another like it was created in South Australia.

The various constitutional changes in 1843 left the Colonial Office in control as firmly as ever. Although pastoralists welcomed the grant of political power, they were no better placed to get land on their own terms, and that was what they wanted most of all. This brought them into conflict with the British Parliament which, in addition to making political changes, also passed the Australian Colonies Waste Land Act. This important Act of 1842 fixed a uniform minimum price of 20s. an acre for all Crown land in each colony and reserved half the land revenue for emigration, to be controlled by Commissioners for Land and Emigration in London.

When this Act reached Sydney it became a 'monster grievance', for it did not transfer the control of land to the colonists. Some prophesied that the high price of 20s. would deter moneyed settlers from coming to Australia and prevent working-men from buying their own farms. Others objected to the emigration provisions; they preferred a bounty system that rewarded with land those who brought out their own labourers. Pastoralists laughed at a law designed to save the faces of systematic colonizers whose experiment in South Australia had failed because too high a price was charged for land in the first place. Who expected squatters to buy what could be had for a £10 annual licence? Their laughter was soon stopped by new squatting regulations.

Governor Gipps admired the men who braved the wilds, but he disliked their contempt of the law. In 1844 he decreed that an annual licence had to be taken for each flock of 4000 sheep, and its owner had to buy part of his run after five years if he wished

4-2

to hold his pastures. As Gipps expected, the squatters were furious. Some predicted ruin, others talked of rebellion. Newspapers called Gipps the worst Governor the colony ever had. Squatters' defence committees held public meetings and launched petitions. One prominent pastoralist hurried off to England vowing that he would have the Governor dismissed. He enlisted wool-buyers, manufacturers and ship-owners, and made a great stir, but Gipps stayed on. The regulations were not changed until 1847 when new orders from England allowed squatters to take fourteen-year leases in the outlying districts, with the right of renewal; they were not compelled to buy land, though they could do so if they wished. With these valuable concessions the squatting problem seemed to be solved. Woolgrowers were now secure with cheap rents and lawful right to their pastures. They were also able to borrow money more easily.

In 1843 the pastoralists in Sydney's Legislative Council passed an Act allowing livestock to be mortgaged and loans to be raised on wool before it was delivered into Sydney stores or even shorn. The Act was entirely contrary to British law and custom, but squatters were quick to use it. By 1850 similar Acts were passed in other colonies and large sums were soon borrowed on wool and stock. But although Legislative Councils were quick to help woolgrowers, they had no enthusiasm for laws designed to benefit farmers and townsmen.

The squatters' special privileges aroused the envy of less favoured colonists who were already clamouring for civil rights. Each year public meetings and newspapers became more outspoken. When petitions were ignored they became more noisy and turbulent. Even sedate, respectable colonists were persuaded to join the ranks of reform. Soon they were defying the government and refusing to pay taxes on drays and land. One troubled observer said that 'people came from England in no wise radical or bitter against authority; after a short apprenticeship in colonial agitation, they became abusive, disloyal, democratic, in short, colonial'. The discontent, however, was not as widespread as it seemed. Wage-earners, busy scraping together a hard living, left politics to their betters. Most of the agitation came from townsmen and near-by small farmers, each with his own complaint to be exploited by irresponsible editors eager for notoriety. There were no parties and no programmes. Each man argued for what suited him best, but all believed that everything could be set right by self-government.

Faith in Parliament had been carried by the colonists from England, but it made a great difference which kind of parliament they remembered best. In New South Wales the leading 'ancient' families, who had arrived before Waterloo, loved to quote Edmund Burke and shared his suspicion of reformers. Men of property, they said, must guard political rights from autocrats above and democrats below. On the other hand, latecomers in the towns and younger settlements thought only of the great Reform Act of 1832. Hundreds of them had joined the fight for it, and emigrated because their hopes of it had not been completely fulfilled. Their hatred of monopoly and favouritism came with them. No special privileges must obstruct a fair field for all in their new country.

These differences split the colonists into angry factions, while they waited impatiently for self-government. They hired parliamentary agents in England and sent deputations, petitions and letters to anyone likely to help. A small Colonial Reform League was recruited and Westminster was reminded of Australia more during the 'forties than ever before or after; but the British Parliament had enough to do without sifting the colonists' conflicting requests. Such questions were usually referred back to colonial Governors. They, with their small courts of officials and wealthy land-owners, were not often able to measure public opinion, nor could they act without orders from London. By the time new laws were prepared it was usually too late; mails could not keep pace with quick colonial changes and each delay created new grievances.

One vexed question was immigration. The Commissioners for Land and Emigration sent very few migrants' ships to Australia

until 1847. Even then they gave no passages that were completel
free, for too many complaints had been made about the earlie
'shovelling out of paupers'. As each adult male now had to pa
part of his passage money according to his occupation, those wh
came were not all desperately poor or useless. The new rules wer
upset for a time by English philanthropists who still though
Australia should take Britain's destitute poor. Societies wer
formed to raise money and send out Ragged School children
orphan paupers, Irish workhouse girls and even lads from Park
hurst Reformatory. These newcomers were not welcome. Colonist
were not hard-hearted, but they did not want Britain's unemploy
ment problems thrust on them. They complained bitterly and a
the same time formed voluntary committees in each colony to fin
shelter and work for the new arrivals. Much of this benevolenc
was inspired by Mrs Caroline Chisholm who thought it wicked t
separate children from parents, especially in Australia where eacl
family could have a small farm. In six years this devoted woma
looked after the welfare of 11,000 immigrants.

Labour was scarce in all the colonies before immigration wa
resumed. After transportation was stopped in New South Wale
the number of convicts dwindled rapidly. By 1847 there were les
than 7000. To replace them, squatters brought in hundreds o
Chinese coolies, but the Colonial Office frowned on this immigra
tion. When Earl Grey became Colonial Secretary in 1847 h
stopped it altogether and declared that 'the population of th
Australian colonies should continue to consist in every class o
persons of European race'. Instead of coolies he wanted th
colonies to take convicts with conditional pardons. Prisoner
sentenced to transportation were now to go through a differen
probation. After hard labour at Gibraltar or Bermuda they wer
to be given an opportunity to reform under conditions that woul
discourage further crime. They were not to be called convicts, bu
'exiles'. Pastoralists could have their labour and isolated shee
stations would be nurseries for moral reform. Squatters wante

the exiles, but urban workmen feared competition with convicts, and settlers refused to expose their families to 'moral malaria'. Opposition increased to transportation in any form. When a ship-load of exiles arrived in 1849, angry citizens in Melbourne refused to let them ashore. They went on to Sydney to be threatened with the same treatment. They were landed at last at Moreton Bay and hurried into the pastoral districts. The only colony to take exiles willingly was Western Australia. The settlers there were desperate for labour, and with their small land revenue had no hope of getting free immigrants. From 1850 to 1868 some 9500 exiles were sent to Perth. Although its self-government was thus delayed, the colony reaped much benefit from their labour and Britain's grants to the penal establishment; but in the eyes of its neighbours, Western Australia became even more isolated by the convict stigma.

Van Diemen's Land's answer to exiles was an Anti-Transportation League. Soon it had branches on the mainland. No British convicts were to delay colonial self-government. Transportation must stop. In Melbourne, Leaguers pledged themselves to employ no convicts and to use every lawful means to resist their coming. In Sydney public men talked of separation from Britain if her authorities insisted on making Australia into a gaol. The battle was finally won in England. While Earl Grey remained in office he would do no more than exempt the eastern colonies from taking exiles. This was not enough and colonial agitation went on. In 1852 the Tory, Sir John Pakington, became Colonial Secretary and announced the long-awaited end of transportation to Van Diemen's Land. Soon after the arrival of the last convict transport, the island's name was changed to Tasmania. Meanwhile constitutional reform had arrived. The long-promised Bill reached the House of Commons in 1849. It provided for more representative government, and for a Federal Assembly with members from each colony to guard against inexperience and reckless laws.

After its first reading the Bill was sent to the colonial Governors for comment. The South Australians and their influential London friends objected to the Federal Assembly. They feared that New South Wales would dominate it and reduce the minimum price for land, so the Federal Assembly was omitted. When the Australian Colonies Government Act was passed in 1850, New South Wales gained little; instead it lost the Port Phillip District which was made into a new colony. Victoria, South Australia and Tasmania were given partly elected Legislative Councils like the one already established in Sydney. In all four colonies votes were given to householders paying £10 rent a year. The Act was greeted in Melbourne with tumultuous celebrations, and elsewhere with disappointment because complete self-government had not been granted. Nevertheless it was only a temporary Act, designed to allow each colony to make its own constitution when the time was ripe.

Before the old Councils were dissolved they arranged the electoral districts for the new representatives. Victorian electorates were fixed by the Council in Sydney. Pastoralists and land-owners were thus able to secure a generous number of seats for themselves. Fewer than one in three adult males had the necessary property qualifications to vote, and much higher qualifications for members shut out most reformers. In each colony, the new electorates gave more seats to country districts than to towns. When the nominees were added, land-owners and pastoralists had nothing to fear from any democratic opposition. But before elections could be held, the colonies were ringing with news of gold discoveries.

Mineral wealth was not unknown in Australia. Rich coal mines at Newcastle had been profitably worked for years, and amateurs had tried to smelt iron ore in various places. Silver lead from a mine close to Adelaide in 1841 had given the continent its first export of precious metal, and produced a tidy income for the family who owned it. Copper found further afield at Kapunda in 1842, Burra in 1845 and other smaller mines yielded nearly £750,000 in five years. The original £5 Burra shares rose to more than £200 on the London market as regular dividends of 200 per cent were paid each quarter. For a time new towns, new wealth and new jobs attracted more immigrants to South Australia than to any other colony. Farmers benefited from the wider market, ships came for copper ore and brought other trade. Land sales boomed, and Adelaide enjoyed a brief heyday as the most prosperous of all the Australian capitals.

There were rich profits in coal and copper, but they were best made by companies. Penniless adventurers were not attracted by mineral wealth until news of gold drew a few thousand from Australia to California in 1849. Some returned to tell of fortunes in alluvial gold. Nuggets could be picked up and dust washed from river sand. Already small pieces of gold had been found in the eastern colonies. They came from ancient rock strata worn away and scattered by centuries of erosion, yet few people knew how to prospect for precious metal or how to separate it easily from the surrounding soil. The authorities had not tried to avoid publicity about gold; by 1850 locally found nuggets were being shown in shop windows in Sydney and Melbourne, and all kinds of rumours were rife.

Among the gold-seekers who proved the value of a visit to California was Edward Hammond Hargraves. He returned to Sydney in 1851 and went to the Bathurst district where he knew gold samples had already been found. Other ex-Californians were already prospecting there, but Hargraves was out to win a government reward for finding a payable Australian goldfield. He soon found traces of gold in different streams over a wide area. Before he returned to Sydney with his report, he showed his assistants where to dig and how to make a miner's cradle for washing the alluvial clay from the heavier grains of gold. From this cradle there emerged what the excited Colonial Secretary called a golden baby. On 7 April 1851 Hargraves's pupils actually won three ounces of precious metal. The payable field was found, and they called it Ophir. As a reward the government later gave the three assistants

£1000 to be divided among them; Hargraves received £12,000 and £250 a year for life.

News of Ophir spread rapidly. There was immense excitement but no immediate rush to the field. Bathurst was 150 miles from Sydney, on the western side of the Blue Mountains. The first reports, though often exaggerated, were not of fabulous wealth but of daily winnings equal to very good wages. Small farmers and townsmen were sceptical at first; the onset of winter deterred others who had no experience of the bush. The unsettled and unemployed were the readiest in Sydney to venture to the diggings especially when they learned that gold could be won with no more than a shovel and a tin dish. By the end of May a thousand diggers were washing for gold in the streams around Ophir. When it was reported that food and tools were bringing fantastic prices, Sydney merchants responded eagerly. Their drays and carts eased the difficulties of travel to the diggings. By the middle of June Bathurst storekeepers were underselling Sydney. By that time new discoveries were taking attention away from Ophir, first to near-by diggings, then to fields far to the south. The year ended with more than 5000 diggers in New South Wales, and a total gold export of about £500,000.

In May news of Ophir reached Melbourne. The Port Phillip District was on the eve of separation from New South Wales. Some Melbourne employers, suspecting that the parent colony was using Bathurst gold as a bait to catch their labourers, offered a reward for the discovery of a payable goldfield within 200 miles of Melbourne. Next day it was claimed for gold found twelve months before on the River Lodden. In July rich alluvial fields near Mount Alexander (Castlemaine) were found. A month later came news of discoveries at Ballarat and in December at Bendigo. Soon it was clear that Victorian fields were richer than any in New South Wales. Gold fever gripped the new colony. Ships loaded with cargo were deserted in the ports. Work on farms and sheep stations came to a standstill. Business in town was paralysed. The civil service almost ceased to exist. From newcoming immigrants to staid old colonists the whole community came under the spell of gold. Even the Governor's aide-de-camp spent his leave at the diggings.

As reports reached neighbouring colonies the excitement spread. Men flocked from Sydney in thousands as though Bathurst did not exist. In Tasmania the male population, bond and free, burst through the Governor's prohibitions and crowded the tiny steamers headed for Melbourne and Geelong. From Adelaide every available ship went 'direct to diggings'; then an overland route was opened and South Australia was emptied of its men and vehicles. Before the first gold-seekers arrived from oversea over 50,000 men had joined the rush to Victoria.

The yellow fever showed no signs of easing during 1852. Small finds were made near Fingal in Tasmania and Echunga in South Australia, but neither weakened the magnetism of Victorian fields where the chain of new discoveries seemed endless. Wherever there were traces of colour the prospectors led the way. At their heels came the restless adventurers, stripping the soil from quiet bush gullies shadowed by stringy bark trees. Men came and went as reinforcements poured in with rumours of even newer fields. Claims were staked and sold and sold again until more persistent miners drove deep shafts and tunnels. Shearing, harvesting and water shortage might drive many diggers home in the summer, but with the first winter rains the roving brigade returned. Their work was rough and hard, their food coarse and uninviting, their shelters crude and primitive. Rheumatism racked the weak and typhoid took its toll, but the glint of gold and boisterous companionship were sufficient rewards for every discomfort.

By the end of 1853 rich nuggets and new discoveries became less common. Gold production continued to rise, but miners from oversea were crowding in to share the spoils. Storekeepers, butchers, police and gold-buyers came too. Wives and families followed to transform the rude masculine camps of the pioneers.

The carefree happy-go-lucky open air freedom of the diggings was gradually replaced by the serious business of making a living. The roaring days soon passed, yet in those two early years thousands of men first tasted the joys of independence, and even more important, lost their fear of the bush.

A few diggers made large fortunes, but average earnings were not very high. Out of every forty miners at Mount Alexander, one was said to be making over £100 a week, seven as much as triple wages, seven fair wages and the rest scarcely enough to pay for sharpening their picks. Gold was supposed to go as easily as it came. When lucky diggers went to town, they often squandered their winnings. Every field had stories of horses shod with gold, of pipes lighted with five pound notes, of bread and butter sprinkled with gold dust. Lucky diggers often had showy weddings and boasted that their brides were better dressed than the Governor's lady. These tales of wild spending and drinks-all-round must be weighed against official reports of the orderliness of camps and the absence of crime. Church services were held more regularly than prize-fights, and no publicans' licences were granted on Victorian fields until the end of 1853. This did not stop the diggers' sprees; camp-followers were always ready to relieve miners of their precious dust. Gold-buyers at Ballarat in January 1852, for example, were offering less than 52s. an ounce, although the Bank of England's price was 77s. 10d. To stop this hard bargaining the authorities provided police escorts to take the gold to Melbourne. The government in Adelaide wanted diggers from South Australia to send home their winnings; an assay office was opened where crude gold was bought for 71s. In this way one-fifth of Victoria's gold output for 1852 went to South Australia although the colony sent only one-twelfth of the diggers.

In 1854 gold fever was stopped by a mild depression and a serious drought. In two years more than 150,000 immigrants had come from Britain alone and with them came heavy supplies of goods. Markets were glutted, unemployment followed, wages and prices fell, speculators faced disaster. The depression was soon over but it sobered the whole community. Thousands who had divided their time between their homes and the diggings went back permanently to their families and old jobs.

Gold exports from Victoria reached a peak in 1856 and thereafter steadily declined. The number of diggers was highest in 1858. By then average earnings were less than 25s. a week. Most miners were still independent and many still used primitive tools, but partnerships were becoming common because many hands were needed for more efficient sluice-boxes. Others still more efficient turned from alluvial gold to the precious metal in quartz reefs. These mines needed steam engines and regular supplies of water, so pumps had to be installed and long water-races constructed. Such work called for wage labour and the promotion of companies. On old fields gold mining became a business instead of an adventure, and miners found that it paid to work for a boss. But whenever new fields were discovered, independent miners were always ready to flock to them. Some crossed the sea to New Zealand in 1861; others marched north to New South Wales and far afield into Queensland.

During the 'fifties Victoria exported more than twenty million ounces of gold. With three million more from New South Wales the total was nearly 1000 tons, a worthy start to the 5000 tons that were to come from Australia in the next century. It is tempting, therefore, to attribute all the changes of the 'fifties to gold, but most of its influence was indirect. Population rose rapidly, yet half the newcomers had to be assisted. Many were single females who helped to balance the disproportion between the sexes by 1859. Fewer than one in ten of the immigrants returned to Britain. A majority of the others settled in Victoria, but other colonies also shared the increase of numbers.

It is not possible to say how many foreigners were attracted by gold. The recorded arrivals in Victoria from non-British ports were 45,000, while 27,000 left for foreign destinations; both groups were

97

mostly males. Every nation on earth was said to be represented on the goldfields except Persia and Japan. The Chinese were the largest alien group and numbered 36,000 by 1857. But foreign gold-seekers were too few to upset the predominance of Anglo-Saxon stock in the population.

Gold did bring great prosperity and increased purchasing power. In 1853–4 alone sales of Crown land in Victoria rose to nearly £3 million, in South Australia to £675,000 and in New South Wales to £530,000. By 1858 wages were only about one-third above the pre-gold level, but goods were more plentiful and markets were bigger. Imports into Victoria alone averaged £19 per head, where they had been £8 in the 'forties. As most goods came from Britain, the mother country shared in the prosperity. Imports and heavy immigration encouraged regular and reliable shipping. Australian exports flowed back to England and the huge influx of gold helped British trade throughout the world.

By helping the colonies to pay their own way, gold also hastened the coming of self-government. At the same time it revived the problem of imperial control of land. When copper was found, the Commissioners for Land and Emigration had proposed that each owner should pay a royalty to the Crown on any minerals taken from his land. This rule was applied in South Australia in 1846, after the best copper land had been bought. The royalty was small and the courts soon declared it illegal, but it left bitter resentment against 'government from a distance' and strengthened the forces of democratic reform. Taxes on gold-diggers brought the same results.

The diggings near Bathurst were mostly on Crown land, fit only for grazing cattle. What was Sir Charles FitzRoy to do? He had been made Governor to conciliate the colonists after Gipps's stormy rule. Some of his advisers said mining should be stopped, others that a royalty should be imposed. Since diggers were already at work, and the Legislative Council in Sydney said land was not its business, FitzRoy took a risk with his own plans. To maintain order he put a Commissioner and police on each goldfield.

For this protection and as a royalty, diggers had to pay a licence fee of 30s. each month. The regulations were unpopular, yet they were applied in Victoria and approved by the Colonial Office. Goldfield police, however, were hard to recruit and many ex-convicts were pressed into service. At first the roving diggers easily evaded the fee; gradually authority caught up with them. Regular monthly hunts for licences by officious police caused angry protests. Unlicensed diggers were herded like cattle into government camps and fined without trial. Diggers had to pay the fee whether they found gold or not. As few of them had a vote, they claimed they were being taxed without representation. Soon the licence system became a political question and the miners appealed to the Victorian Legislative Council. In August 1853 the fee was reduced, but armed police still tyrannized the diggings. Anyone who protested was marked out for vengeance.

When Sir Charles Hotham became Governor of Victoria in June 1854 the diggers thought they would have better treatment. Hotham visited the goldfields and listened patiently to complaints, but by October drought and depression sent many sober-minded miners to their homes. A few Chartist reformers, Irish rebels and continental revolutionaries urged the diggers to take the law into their own hands. Licences and police hunts were still the major grievances, but when a hotel-keeper was arrested for murdering a miner and acquitted, an angry mob burnt his hotel. Troops were brought in to restore order, and three men were arrested for starting the fire. Thousands of diggers met to demand their release. Hotham was used to naval discipline and refused to listen to 'demands'; he knew the police were arrogant, but the diggers must send a respectful petition. This answer infuriated Ballarat. A fortified stockade was made at Eureka and 2000 men began drilling there. The Governor's answer was prompt and forceful. Early on Sunday 3 December 1854 troops stormed and carried the stockade. Two soldiers and twenty miners were killed and one hundred and twenty-five prisoners were taken.

At the time Eureka was overshadowed outside Victoria by news of the fall of Sevastopol. Since then Victoria's 'little rebellion' has had much publicity in story, film and political propaganda, yet it was not as important as some would like to believe. It was not the first or last time that blood was shed in Australia for independence. The diggers certainly made some gains; monthly licences were replaced by Miners' Rights which cost 20s. a year and entitled diggers to prospect, mine and hold land in defined areas, and to vote. An export duty of 2s. 6d. an ounce was also levied on gold, and unlucky miners were thus freed from taxation. But Eureka had no effect on the colonial constitutions of self-government which had already been drawn up. Such democracy as they contained was the product of older conflict.

The Legislative Council elections provided by the Australian Colonies Government Act of 1850 were not held in the three eastern colonies until gold fever had weakened the town electorates; only South Australia had its election before the rush to the diggings commenced. The chief electoral issue was government aid to religion. For four years grants had been given to some churches in spite of bitter opposition from Nonconformists who were strong in Adelaide. Small farmers and town democrats threw their weight behind the Nonconformists in exchange for promises to support vote by ballot and a wider suffrage. Hard work by their candidates brought nearly every elector to the poll and the anti-grant party won by a small majority. When the new Legislative Council met, government aid to religion was stopped and South Australia became the first colony in the Empire completely to separate church and state. The reformers also wanted to be first with a new constitution, but Earl Grey ordered that the 1850 Government Act was to be given fair trial before any changes were made.

In 1852 the new Colonial Secretary, Sir John Pakington, wrote to congratulate Governor FitzRoy for keeping order in the goldfields; as a proven law-abiding colony New South Wales might now prepare its constitution. But if colonists wanted to control their waste land Pakington insisted they must have a nominated upper chamber to check the elected lower house. Although this important dispatch was meant chiefly for New South Wales, copies of it were also sent to the Governors of the other colonies. A month later the coalition government of Lord Aberdeen was formed with the Duke of Newcastle as Colonial Secretary. In his first letters to the Governors, Newcastle confirmed Pakington's dispatch and withdrew its one restriction. The colonists might frame their own constitutions; nobody was better able than the local legislatures to decide what form of government best suited their conditions.

The way was now open for constitution-making to begin in earnest. In New South Wales the conservative old families, led now by William Charles Wentworth, had two aims. Their new Parliament must have complete control over all colonial affairs, and that control must rest with men of property; if colonists wanted an Assembly elected by the people, there must be proper safeguards. First, electoral divisions favouring the land-owners should not be altered. Second, no change should be made in the constitution except by a two-thirds majority. Third, the upper chamber should be elected by the leading families of the colony, raised for the purpose into a titled aristocracy. Without these safe-guards, Wentworth prophesied that the cream of society would leave New South Wales; with them, it would become 'a glorious country' free from 'democratic and levelling influences'. The proposal to make a colonial aristocracy was not new and as usual it was laughed to scorn, but the first two of Wentworth's safeguards were accepted; the third was replaced by an upper chamber nominated for five years. The Legislative Council had followed Pakington's advice. The completed constitution was sent to the newspapers. Public opinion was invited, freely given and as freely ignored. The constitution went to the Colonial Office unchanged.

In South Australia the Governor held back Newcastle's dispatch

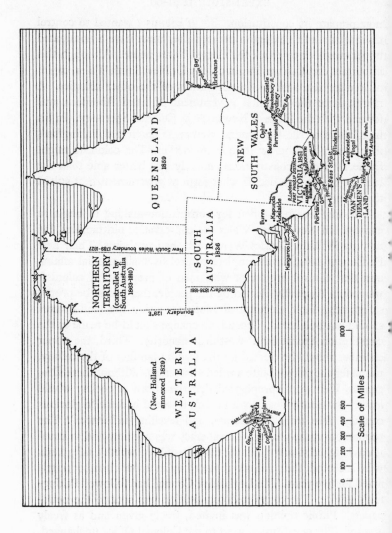

Moreton Bay
Brisbane

QUEENSLAND
1859

Newcastle
Hawkesbury R.
Sydney
Ophir
Botany Bay
Bathurst
Parramatta

NEW
SOUTH
WALES

NORTHERN
TERRITORY
(controlled by
South Australia
1863-1910)

New South Wales boundary 1788-1827

SOUTH
AUSTRALIA
1836

Burra
Kapunda
Adelaide

Port Phillip
Ballarat
Melbourne
Geelong
VICTORIA 1851

R. Loddon
PORT PHILLIP DISTRICT

Bass Strait
Flinders I.
Launceston
Fingal
Tasman Penin.
Port Arthur
Macquarie
VAN
DIEMEN'S
LAND
Hobart

Portland

Boundary 1836-1861

Kangaroo I.

Boundary 129°E

WESTERN
AUSTRALIA

(New Holland
annexed 1829)

DARLING
Garden I.
Perth
Fremantle
Cockburn
Sound
Pinjarra
RANGE

Scale of Miles

0   100 200 300 400 500   1000

and persuaded the Legislative Council that no constitution would be accepted unless it included a nominated upper chamber. When that was done the constitution went off to London in spite of strong public disapproval. In Victoria the population grew so rapidly that the Legislative Council had to be enlarged in 1853. The new members were a little more liberal than the old land-owners. They chose to be guided by Newcastle's dispatch and decided on an elected upper chamber with high property qualifications for its members. The three constitutions reached England too late for the 1854 session of Parliament, and were sent to the Crown Law Officers who decided that the colonies had exceeded their powers. By limiting the rights of Governors to reject certain laws, the constitutions invaded the royal prerogative.

In Tasmania the Legislative Council was slow to make its constitution. Members did not decide to follow Victoria's example until late in 1854. By that time news reached Hobart of the Law Officers' decision and the offending clauses were quickly removed from the Tasmanian constitution. It arrived in London in May 1855 and was soon confirmed. Thus Tasmania was the first Australian colony to receive self-government. A few days later the amended constitutions of New South Wales and Victoria were passed by the Imperial Parliament. The Waste Lands Act of 1842 was then repealed and the control of land passed to the colonial Parliaments.

The South Australian constitution was treated differently. Early in 1854 returning diggers had been disgusted by the way in which the Governor had forced a nominated upper chamber on the colony. More than 5000 people petitioned Westminster to reject the constitution and to give the colony two elected Houses. The Colonial Secretary decided to return the constitution to Adelaide for review, and a freshly elected Council, strong in democratic reformers, revised it completely. The new upper chamber was to be elected with low property qualifications for voters and members. The Assembly was to be elected by male suffrage and vote by ballot. Electorates were to be based on population and parliaments were to be changed every three years. These radical proposals were approved in Westminster without alteration.

In the other colonies land-owners soon found that their constitutions did not satisfy a population enriched with gold. In the towns not many houses could now be rented for less than £10 a year. The democratic vote was thus increased and some of the land-owners' safeguards were soon swept away. By 1860 radical members in New South Wales and Victoria had won vote by ballot, manhood suffrage and more equal electorates. Another colony came into existence when Queensland was separated from New South Wales. After 1840 when transportation to Moreton Bay ended, settlers moved in and land sales commenced. Exploration soon drew squatters farther north with their flocks. Brisbane grew slowly and free settlers often asked for separation, but their numbers were small and the boundary was hard to fix. In 1859, however, the 24,000 people north of the 28th parallel were given independence and a reformed constitution like that of New South Wales.

In 1840 colonists had fretted under the control of the remote Colonial Office. Twenty years later they had five parliaments and political reforms in advance of the mother country. Government from a distance was at an end, but the long struggle between advocates of the great Reform Act and disciples of Edmund Burke had ended in compromise. What had emerged was a democracy of the middle classes, not of the wage-earners. However radical the new Assemblies, the privileges of conservative land-owners in the Legislative Councils remained as an effective check on popular government.

CHAPTER 6

TRANSITION: 1860–80

Gold and new constitutions set colonists free to shape their own destiny, but the social structure based on wool was hard to change. Long opposition to Colonial Office rule was not the best training for political independence, and no one knew clearly what was wanted. Some thought of equal opportunity for all to better themselves, others only to avoid the paralysing poverty of the old world. Their ideas became more distinct after 1880, chiefly because of lessons learnt in twenty important years of experiment.

The first years of transition were difficult and unsettling. Distant new goldfields lured fewer restless diggers as other ways were opened to get rich quickly. Each new promise brought its scurrying movement of people. The eager rush and bustle made everything seem temporary and makeshift. Speculation seemed to gain more prizes than hard work, for the land was niggardly with its favours. Those who stayed to struggle were as often disillusioned as those who moved to fresh ventures. Independence was not easily won, yet the vision persisted to comfort and inspire the families that yearned for places of their own.

Against this background of individual enterprise and shifting populations, the years of transition brought more rivalry between the colonies. Their competition was no tame game of follow the leader. Victoria had forged ahead in wealth and population. Its independent advance was hard to match even after its gold-fields passed their peak. Less favoured colonies had to bid boldly for men and money. To the outside world Australia appeared as a boastful country with its extravagant promises of unlimited opportunity. Inside the continent, local pride was a sharp spur to regional progress.

In the eastern mainland expansion was irregular throughout

most of the 'sixties but more rapid and certain in the 'seventies. In 1880 Victoria was still ahead in population, but New South Wales with its larger territory had regained the lead in wool growing. South Australia, although outstanding in wheat, was being challenged by Queensland for third place in the colonial race. Tasmania lagged behind, while Western Australia, still isolated and a Crown colony at its jubilee, was about where New South Wales had been in 1823.

By 1880 the population passed 2,250,000, with the colonial-born in a majority. Ties with Britain were different and stronger as reason took the place of restraint. The constitutions had not given complete independence and isolationists were slow to lose their suspicion of the mother country. They became less intolerant as Westminster met their demands with concessions. By 1861 Chinese immigration, for example, was restricted in Victoria, South Australia and New South Wales by laws that ran counter to Britain's treaties with Peking. In 1870 the withdrawal of imperial garrisons put an end to a very vexed question and left the colonies responsible for their own military defence. In 1873 Britain abandoned the right to control the colonies' trade with the Empire although freedom to make commercial treaties with alien nations was not granted or needed for another twenty years. Another important concession was the Colonial Laws Validity Act passed in 1865 to save South Australia from a Judge who persisted in challenging local Acts that he claimed were repugnant to the laws of England. The Validity Act made the legal position clear and remained as the charter of Empire until the Statute of Westminster in 1931.

These extra rights confirmed the colonies in their separate ways, though they had much in common. Their Governors were still appointed by the Crown and still required to disallow certain legislation or reserve it for royal assent. Their new Parliaments now controlled the civil service, and not many of the old officials nominated by the Colonial Office were left in charge of their departments. As new men were often more eager than able, administration suffered. The Parliaments themselves were not much better. Until political parties emerged to subdue personal rivalry, governments were formed and broken on every important question. In forty years South Australia had forty-one ministries, New South Wales twenty-nine and Victoria twenty-eight. On the hustings, leather-lunged candidates made impossible promises and when elected scrambled wildly for places of power. Newspapers and political associations clamoured continually for reform, but opinions were always sharply divided. Conservatives looked to the Legislative Councils to uphold the rights of property while democrats pinned their hopes to the popular Assemblies. In each Parliament the two chambers fought for precedence, but neither conservatives nor democrats could claim a clear victory. The major triumph went to the successful merchants and aspiring professional men who at first represented the towns and farming districts. These middle-class townsmen called themselves Liberals and talked much of social equality. They would have no upper class above them. They hated the privileged 'ancient' families who had feathered their nests with convict labour and free land grants. Good government, they argued, gave no such favours; each man should depend on his own elbow-grease and thrift. No two Liberals, however, could agree in applying these principles; they knew best what they did not want. Each year politics became more confused. The colonies drifted farther apart as each attempted to solve the problems of expansion in its own way. In the process, country land-holders steadily lost influence and the towns gained a larger share of investment and population.

The squatters' special privileges were the first to be challenged. Although sheep numbers reached 65 million, and wool yielded a million bales by 1880, wool never regained the outstanding prominence it held before the gold rush. One reason was land reform.

The squatters' long leases granted in 1847 were unpopular and hard to enforce. Few were taken in Victoria and not many were surveyed in New South Wales. Most squatters still relied on annual licences for their grass and water. With support that the banks denied to others, they were often able to outbid farmers at government auctions of unoccupied acres in the settled districts. The clamour for new land laws began long before colonists mingled on the goldfields and shared their hopes and grievances. Was Australia to be one great sheep run? Were smallholders never to fulfil their dreams of independence and security? The protests became louder as successful diggers looked for farms and the unsuccessful looked for employment. Land-hungry settlers and urban democrats joined forces to demand reform. Many middle-class Liberals supported them because the cities could not thrive on wool alone. Victoria's first land Bill was passed by the Assembly but met defeat by the Legislative Council. Although an angry crowd stormed Parliament House and a second Bill was passed, so many changes were made by conservatives that it proved unworkable.

New South Wales had quicker success with land reform because its leaders had paid for their acres and resented the squatters' attempt to turn leases cheaply into permanent ownership. The Premier, John Robertson, and some of his ministers were wealthy freeholders with farming tenants. His land laws of 1861 caused a political crisis but they were passed when newly nominated members filled the Legislative Council. The new system was called free selection. Except where land was already sold to graziers, selectors were free to choose blocks of up to 320 acres, even on squatting leases, and buy them on terms at £1 an acre subject to conditions of residence and improvement.

The new law had mixed results. Too many selectors started without enough money. Much land was taken, worked out and abandoned. Some selectors were honest and experienced, some were the tools of speculators, some were rogues and some made 'earnings proportionate to their exertions'. In a few coastal districts too wet for growing wool, selectors started dairying and market gardens, but often had to buy out their neighbours to get

enough land. In other areas farming and grazing were combined
with some success; small selections in the pastoral districts in-
variably failed. Threatened with loss of their pasture, some squatters
used their children and faithful servants as dummies, and in their
names took small selections around the water and other choice sites
on their runs. Others bought out the unscrupulous selectors who
preyed upon them. The conditions of residence and improvement
were often ignored as squatters and selectors fought each other
with threats, blackmail, fraud, marauding dogs and trespassing
stock. The squatters usually won, thanks to the banks and merchants who for years had lent money on sheep and wool. By 1880
some thirty million acres of Crown land were sold in New South
Wales. Much more was still held by lease but fewer than one in
eight of the 190,000 selectors remained on their land. Instead of
creating independent yeomen, Robertson's Acts had turned many
leaseholders into big freeholders. Although most of them were
little more than managers for urban and oversea moneylenders,
their hearts were cheered by the crumbling huts and decaying fruit
trees of selections that once dotted their runs.

In Victoria land reformers tried to avoid these mistakes by
offering selectors only those areas of squatters' land that were
suitable for farming. Duffy's Land Act of 1862 threw open vast
districts, forbade dummying and altered the terms of squatting
leases. Within one week 800,000 acres in the rich Western District
were selected; within three years they were all owned by a handful
of squatters. Such abuses brought a change in the law. Under
Grant's Act of 1865 each selector had to prove his good faith by
living and working on his land for three years at a modest rent,
before claiming his freehold. These terms were accepted by some
30,000 selectors, but distance from markets, bad seasons and inexperience left many unable to pay their rents. Hundreds forfeited
their land and lost the value of their improvements. By 1870 more
than half of the colony's best farm land was in the hands of sheep-
owners; only 12,000 had been added to the smallholders' ranks.

In South Australia land reform was delayed. The colony's squatting problem was different; most leases were in the remote dry north where no smallholder dared to venture. As explorers opened the interior, pastoralists in the Legislative Council easily won favourable terms for more vast runs. With large areas of cheap pasture, grazing boomed, but whole herds of cattle died when drought blistered the northern runs in 1864. The squatters appealed for lower rents and the Surveyor-General, G. W. Goyder, was sent to investigate. Travelling north he found no signs of drought until he reached saltbush country. His report on this line of rainfall produced rash claims that all land south of it was suitable for farming, so Goyder was sent to examine selection in Victoria. He was greatly impressed and South Australia ventured into land reform. Many pastoral leases were surveyed and thrown open for purchase on credit, with residence and cultivation conditions. This system, introduced by Strangway's Act in 1869, was amended fifteen times in as many years and still did not avoid abuses. In twelve years some four million acres were taken up, but purchases were completed by less than 6000 selectors, and half of them promptly sold or transferred their land, mostly to sheep-owners.

Although reformers boasted that selection had not entirely failed, the best parts of the public estate in each colony were now privately owned and beyond the reach of radical governments. Much land was still leased and many southern squatters had found new runs in Queensland, there to defeat the half-hearted attempts at free selection. By 1880, the northern colony had sold 460,000 acres, but 200,000 squares miles were leased. Until artesian water was tapped Queensland squatters were always pressed for pasture. Their cattlemen, with less difficult stock routes, spread into the Northern Territory before the South Australians who had annexed it in 1863. Neither colony gained much benefit from the Territory. Indeed, South Australia found it a costly incubus. The great distances that separated its areas of good country from each other and from coastal ports increased the costs of labour and transport. Enthusiastic land speculators and tropical farmers quickly lost their money, while early government officers also lost their reputations. A few hardy pastoralists struggled on, but the Territory, unprofitable, lonely and neglected, lapsed into fitful depression, lifted only by small gold discoveries and occasional rises in the cattle market.

Although wool prices fell steadily after 1870, freeholding graziers in each colony began to improve their runs. Shepherds with movable huts and hurdles were replaced by boundary riders as wire fences enclosed thousands of paddocks. Earthen dams caught surface rainwater and windmills became common as bores tapped underground streams. The dead limbs of ringbarked trees dominated every skyline as owners tried to increase their sheep-carrying capacity. As well as bigger numbers, they aimed at bigger yields of wool. More care was given to breeding and new types of merino sheep were imported. Marketing improved too. Sheep washing and wool scouring were slowly displaced as 'greasy' fleeces went straight into bales at the great shearing sheds on each station. The men's huts near-by were squalid, but substantial new homesteads proclaimed that social patterns had changed as well as land tenure. Carters, contractors, shearers and wage-earners might camp on the runs; station affairs might be managed by overseers, book-keepers and genteel 'jackeroo' apprentices; but the homestead was a place apart where only land-owners and professional men enjoyed the hospitality of the owner and his family. This social gulf did not disturb masterless, migratory bushmen; their ambitions and shyness were buried in spells of contract work and bouts of hard drinking. Struggling selectors, however, often resented the squatters' lordly ways.

Bushrangers found this resentment useful when they varied highway robbery with raids on station stock and homesteads. Frank 'Gardiner' and his henchmen John Gilbert and Ben Hall made New South Wales ring with their exploits; like their successor, Frank Ward (Captain Thunderbolt), they were long shielded from the police by selectors. So was Victoria's great bushranger, Ned Kelly. From horse and cattle stealing he turned to holding up banks in small towns. Fierce hatred of policemen made him attempt to wreck a trainload of them. The plan failed and his gang was surrounded. Trying to break through in an armour of ploughshares he was captured—the last of the bushrangers. The legend lives on in such fanciful tales and films as *Robbery under Arms* that reflect the romance of wild frontiers already changing when Kelly was executed in 1880. Another picturesque and more useful feature of the outback was Cobb and Co. Its first coach ran from Melbourne to Bendigo in 1854. Freeman Cobb soon returned to America and his business passed to a fellow countryman. By 1870 the great leather-slung coaches were rumbling each week over thousands of miles of unmade bush track in New South Wales and Queensland with mails and passengers. As railways spread, Cobb's coaches were driven far afield. They kept running until 1924. A few survive as museum pieces, dim reminders of brilliant drivers, grand horses and worthy enterprise.

By 1880 wool and mines still provided most of Australia's export income, but most of Australia's people lived in towns and on the farms that fed them. The progress of agriculture, like everything else, differed in each colony. In twenty years of land reform the area under crop doubled in New South Wales and multiplied six times in Victoria and South Australia. Far behind, Queensland and Western Australia slowly gained on Tasmania. As an exporter of wheat South Australia was well in the lead. One in four of its breadwinners were farmers and their wheat exports earned more than the colony's wool and copper. There were many reasons for this success.

One was the Real Property Act of 1858. Until Strangway's Act brought time payment for selectors, most new farmers had to buy land on ruinous terms from private owners. As carefree speculation and subdivision in the early settlement had made chaos of land titles, the transfer of deeds often cost more than the land, while mortgaging was risky and expensive. Of the colony's land titles fewer than one in twenty was properly valid. Reformers argued for years until R. R. Torrens, son of Wakefield's most difficult disciple, blended their plans into the Real Property Act that made land transfers simple, cheap and efficient. Instead of deeds, each buyer was given a copy of his certificate in the official register at the Lands Titles Office. No lawyer's fees or searching of titles were needed; the government guaranteed each certificate and the subsequent transactions recorded on it. Torrens himself after twenty years' service under the Colonial Office was able to clear his own doubtful titles, sell his land and return to England with fame. Others benefited too. With secure titles private land sales boomed and mortgaging became safe at reasonable rates. The Torrens title system was copied in neighbouring colonies, and many more farmers were able to borrow money on their land.

Other help came from mechanical inventions. By 1860 John Ridley's strippers were being used to harvest half the wheat crop. Steam flour-mills became common. Two-, three- and four-furrow ploughs were used wherever draught horses were available. As farmers spread farther afield they learnt the value of fallow, conserving moisture and sowing after rain. Settlement was barred in many places by dense mallee scrub. The land was good, but the stunted eucalypts grew in stools and their roots were hard to grub. The conquest of this mallee was to become one of Australia's best success stories; it brought millions of fertile acres under wheat that helped to feed the colonists and the old world as well. A century later the mallee farmers' methods and implements were taming tropical jungles in many parts of South-east Asia.

One of the first mallee conquerors was Charles Mullen. Born of poor Irish immigrant parents, he wanted a home for his family and bought some scrubland for a song. His only tool was an axe; he cut the mallee and his children carted it into the Gawler smelters for firewood. With a home-made harrow he scratched his small clearing between the stumps. His successful crop paid much better than firewood and he looked for bigger crops. At the smelters he found an old engine boiler; drawn by bullocks it readily rolled down the scrub for burning without risk of bush fire. His method was quickly imitated, often with heavy logs; but whatever the device it was always called a 'Mullenizer'. Within five years the Smith brothers and J. W. Stott separately devised ingenious new ploughs. On striking a root or stone their shares could rise, clear the obstacle and return to the furrow. By using wrought iron instead of brittle cast iron for the shares, John Shearer improved the stump-jump plough. By 1880 he was making them in large numbers at his Mannum factory and finding ready Victorian buyers farther up the River Murray.

Improvements in transport also helped agriculture. When eastern farmers flocked to the goldfields, many South Australians stayed at home to grow food for the diggers. Large shipments of flour were sent to Melbourne where wild speculation made prices fluctuate sharply. Adelaide millers looked for other ways to reach the diggings. This was easy with the River Murray near-by. The first steamboat on the river was launched in 1853. It was a crazy affair with a boiler bound by heavy chains, yet with other boats it did carry flour and stores through Victoria's back door. Before long paddle-steamers were plying as far as Bourke on the Darling and Albury on the Murray. By 1870 several companies were competing for the river trade. Only a small part of it was flour, but South Australian breadstuffs had followed the gold-diggers into New South Wales and Queensland, and found new markets in England.

The problem of haulage was never serious for South Australians near the coast. Harbours were plentiful and horse-drawn tram-ways gave easy access to jetties in the sheltered gulfs. Inland districts were harder to open and less profitable although they were well served with railways by 1880. By contrast, railways set agriculture on its feet in Victoria where the best wheat land was north and west of the Dividing Range. When railways reached Hamilton, Horsham and Wangaratta, the area under crop doubled within three years, and Victoria became a wheat exporter. Better results were to follow; meanwhile railway building created new problems for the colonial Parliaments.

From 200 miles in 1860, Australia's railways increased by 1880 to 4000 miles, with more than half of them in New South Wales and Victoria. The first sod was turned in Sydney in 1850, but work was delayed for five years by gold fever. The first track, between Goolwa and Port Elliot in South Australia, was completed in March 1854, but labelled a tramway by Victorian rivals whose line from Melbourne to its port was opened five months later. More serious rivalry came from railway gauges. England had its uniform gauge of 4 ft. 8½ in. and Ireland its 5 ft. 3 in. The Colonial Office wanted the colonies to use the English gauge, but gave way when the Sydney Railway Company persuaded authorities in New South Wales to adopt the Irish gauge. A few months later the Railway Company changed to the English gauge. This alteration came too late for Victoria and South Australia: they had already ordered rolling stock and crossings for the wider track and refused to change them. Although Tasmania and South Australia at first adopted the wide gauge, they also used the cheaper 3 ft. 6 in. track later adopted by Queensland and Western Australia. Thus all the colonies had the confusion of different gauges, later to become an expensive tribute to regional loyalties.

Many of the first railways were started by private companies, but before long most of them were taken over by governments. The capital cities were first served and most of the country lines radiated from them. Liberal townsmen in Parliament had little mercy on smaller ports. Each metropolis wanted all the trade of its own colony, as well as what could be taken from its neighbours. While railways from Sydney were struggling to cross the Blue Mountains, Victoria's lines spread north on easy gradients to tap the River Murray trade, in addition to the wealth of its own rich farm lands. By 1878 Adelaide was running several trains each day to Morgan on the Murray, in answer to competition from Port Elliot, while a hopeful transcontinental line started north, to languish once it tapped the stock routes from western New South Wales and Queensland. Brisbane, Hobart and Perth, less favourably placed, made slower progress with their monopoly of trade.

Metropolitan growth was also helped by posts and telegraphs. Each colony had its own money orders, stamps and postal contracts. All oversea mail and most colonial mail went to the capitals for distribution. The systems were generally efficient, if somewhat unequal. Letters and newspapers meant much to homesick expatriates, but whereas cities had daily home deliveries, isolated settlers thought themselves lucky to be within reach of a monthly pack-horse service. The capitals also gained most from telegraphs. They were first used to bring the latest shipping information from the ports to city merchants. From these small beginnings, Sydney, Melbourne and Adelaide were linked by 1858 and joined to Brisbane three years later. A submarine cable was laid to Tasmania, but the connection broke down through faulty material. The island had to wait for ten more years before another cable brought permanent communication with the mainland. Before long a transcontinental telegraph was being built. It was used before work was completed. The first message sent from Darwin in June 1872 had to be relayed by horsemen in places and took a week to reach Adelaide. Once the land line was joined by cable with Java, messages from London came through regularly. Five years later Adelaide was linked with Perth. Meanwhile the network of wire was spreading in all the colonies. By 1880 Australia could boast 25,000 miles of telegraph, with one-third of them in New South Wales.

Although communications and transport were necessary, they were always costly and seldom well planned. They owed their existence to politics more than to hopes of public profit. Whatever

PLATE XI

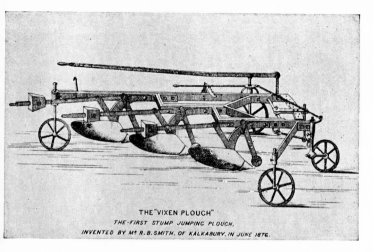

THE "VIXEN PLOUGH"
THE FIRST STUMP JUMPING PLOUGH,
INVENTED BY MR R.B. SMITH, OF KALKABURY, IN JUNE 1876.

(*a*) The first stump-jumping plough, 1876

(*b*) Murray steamer and barge unloading stores, about 1900

PLATE XII

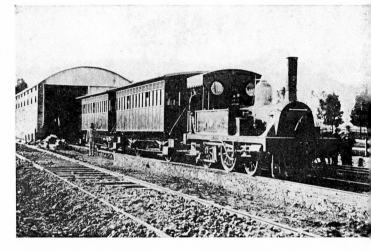

(*a*) Railway engine and carriages, 1873

(*b*) The 'Overland' express between Melbourne and
Adelaide, 1960

PLATE XIII

(*a*) Sheep shearing, 1870

(*b*) Sheep shearing, 1959

PLATE XIV

(*a*) Farm land in southern New South Wales

(*b*) A typical scene near a station homestead

Liberals felt about private thrift did not apply to the public purse; they could dip into that happily and borrow more to ensure the progress of their colonies. By 1880 their public debts totalled £66 million, which was more than the value of the year's exports; the annual interest on these loans was more than the combined earnings of railways, posts and telegraphs. The oversea debts and interest charges of private borrowers were also mounting steadily.

The colonies' loans were not equal in size and not used in the same way. Victoria had the biggest debt; with a small area, large population, gold and rich lands it could afford to do more than its neighbours. Most of its borrowed money was spent, as elsewhere, on railways, but the metropolis got more than its share. Melbourne's roads, bridges, harbour, gasworks, water supply and public buildings were on a grand scale. They helped to give an air of permanence and stability to what had previously been improvised. The other capitals also put on bold fronts that made country visitors marvel, but newcomers from England were sometimes scornful of the garish display and noisy pride. What they called 'colonial character' was in evidence everywhere, though it made up in youth and vigour for what it lacked in tradition.

Measured per head of population Victoria's debt was only half that of Queensland where a late start and sparse settlement left everything to be done in a hurry with a very small income. Above all, Queensland needed people. Like other colonies it looked to the Colonial Land and Emigration Commission in London for its immigrants. The Commission chartered ships while its scattered agents selected the kind of workmen that the colonies asked for, and made travelling arrangements for the families nominated for free passages by their colonial friends and relations. The work was well organized and the colonies did little more than pay the bills. Queensland, however, was soon dissatisfied with its share of assisted immigrants. Long before the Commission closed in 1872, the northern colony changed to a more vigorous policy. Its own recruiting agents were sent to Britain and Germany. Their lectures, pamphlets and advertisements promised free passages to the poor, and generous land grants to all who cared to come at their own expense. In return for land, ship-owners were also persuaded to carry immigrants free of cost to government. On these schemes Queensland spent more than it could afford, and gained one in three of the newcomers to Australia. This was a plucky achievement. Older colonies were more timid and used very little loan money for immigration even in hard times. Their recruiting agents competed wildly in England but were often left without funds. After 1867 bad seasons and a temporary collapse of the London loan market caused assisted immigration to be stopped for six years in South Australia and greatly reduced in other colonies. Only in Queensland was it unchecked. Free passages returned with prosperity, but by that time Victoria had entirely withdrawn government assistance to immigration.

The rate of immigration from Europe was irregular and much lower than in the 'fifties. Between 1860 and 1880 some 400,000 came and 80,000 left. This gain in population was doubled by natural increase. The colonies' populations were also greatly affected by migration within the continent, for people were constantly on the move.

More than half the newcomers from oversea received assistance of some kind. Some became smallholders, and some joined their friends and relations, but most were left to fend for themselves on arrival. Rural work was usually easy to find; although immigrants were often scorned as inexperienced new chums, they were readily employed. Railway navvies, farm labourers and domestic servants were always in demand. They found working conditions rougher than those they left behind, but wages were higher and food more plentiful. Independent life in the bush, however, did not attract many town-bred immigrants. Most newcoming families preferred to stay in the cities where, in 1880, they still outnumbered the colonial-born.

The most important industry in each capital was building. The increasing demand for public buildings and houses gave work to bricklayers, carpenters, timber yards, limeburners, quarrymen, carters and a host of other trades. Homes were usually plain and cheap. Whether stone or timber, most were adorned outside with galvanized iron skillions, sheds and stables. Although the rich had ostentatious old-world mansions, or spacious colonial bungalows, rent-payers had to choose between squalid crowded tenements and separate single-storey dwellings with small-windowed rooms boxed around a dark passage. As most families, wanting homes of their own, had to depend on loans from banks or co-operative societies, the building trades fluctuated with every change in the money market. In each bout of unemployment, urban workers made strong appeals to stop the flow of immigration. They were successfully opposed by employers who wanted to see more men than jobs. During the years of transition wage-earners won little sympathy; their best friends in the Parliaments were immigrants who brought new ideas of reform from Britain.[1]

Each colony had ambitious political leaders. Some won knighthoods but few were outstanding. At first the Parliaments were dominated by men who had helped to frame the colonial constitutions. Many of these ageing patriots thought every new democratic proposal was part of a sinister plot to cut the ties of empire and turn Australia into an independent republic. Until this peppery generation died out, reformers were never sure of success. To make headway at all they had to pose as liberals and became so accustomed to defeat that they often lost their radical vision.

One leading reformer was Henry Parkes, a self-educated labourer who was several times Premier of New South Wales. As an avowed Chartist he came to Sydney in 1839, and quickly found the country less to his liking than the city. By 1850 he owned the *Empire* and its outspoken editorials soon won him a place in Parliament. Two jobs were more than he could manage. Parkes worked day and night but the *Empire* went bankrupt. His seat was easier to hold and he stayed in politics until 1894. Like other Australian politicians he published an autobiography explaining his public career; even then working-class supporters did not always understand his changes of front. Zeal for land reform and exclusion of Chinese seemed inconsistent with enthusiasm for free trade and uninterrupted immigration. Nevertheless, Parkes could always claim to be a champion of popular rights; a long vain fight against conservatives in the Legislative Council led him to believe that their power could only be broken by federation of the colonies.

South Australia's political giant was Richard Davies Hanson. He had helped Lord Durham report on Canada, advised Wakefield and guided New Zealand councils before he came to Adelaide in 1846. He was too far ahead of his time to be popular, yet his home was a rendezvous for all reformers. Most of the laws that gave South Australia a progressive reputation were his handiwork, but appointment as Chief Justice in 1861 robbed the colony of his political genius.

In Queensland and Victoria the ablest leaders were gold-rush immigrants. One of the best was George Higinbotham, an Irishman who came to Melbourne in 1854. At first he practised law, then helped to win the *Argus* a worthy title as the *Times* of the antipodes. Before long Parliament had the benefit of his learning, sincerity and persuasive oratory. In paving the way to democratic reform he secured many notable achievements. The greatest was his firm stand against interference by London in colonial matters that were not of 'imperial concern'. For this Higinbotham was thought disloyal, although he aimed only at removing one of the rankling grievances that caused disloyalty. Like Parkes he fought resolutely against the Legislative Council and like Hanson he was withdrawn from politics to become Chief Justice.

Compared with other colonies, Victoria's public men were more vigorous, partly because they were strengthened by the democracy of the goldfields. In spite of a falling gold yield, the mining communities remained large, robust and closely knit by common interest. They also had fine towns—Ballarat was Australia's fourth largest in 1870—and their miners and tradesmen took politics seriously. When allied with Melbourne's clamorous reformers, not even Parliament could ignore them. Their joint influence was not limited to unlocking the land for smallholders or to resisting the immigrants who threatened their living standards. Their insistence on other reforms kept politics in ferment for twenty years and made Victoria the leader in social legislation. Queensland was seldom far behind; other colonies followed more slowly.

One important measure pioneered by Victoria was the exclusion of Asians. Although the chief motive was colour prejudice, other reasons were usually given. On the goldfields the Chinese were disliked because they kept to themselves, lived differently and sometimes succeeded where other diggers failed. Ugly racial riots took place first in Victoria, then in New South Wales and later in Queensland. In 1855 Victoria took the lead in checking Chinese immigration and was soon followed by South Australia and New South Wales. As alluvial gold petered out many Chinese went home. Some who remained took contracts for fencing, ring-barking and railway work; others opened market gardens or made furniture in the cities. Although their work was mostly menial, they were supposed to menace colonial living standards; they were often persecuted and sometimes denied the right to follow their trades. When gold was found in Queensland, many Chinese drifted north and others immigrated. On the Palmer diggings in 1877 they outnumbered Europeans by more than ten to one. Next year Queensland had restrictions against Chinese immigrants and their employment as seamen. This was not enough for many Queenslanders who also wanted to exclude the Polynesians employed on coastal sugar plantations.

The Polynesian Kanakas were brought first in the 'sixties and proved useful in the canefields. Plantations in Queensland and

Fiji were soon competing strongly for island labourers. The recruiters who scoured the Pacific were called blackbirders and often accused of kidnapping and murder. As the complaints grew louder, Queensland tried to check abuses but had no power beyond its coastal waters. Nor would the British navy prevent atrocities until Fiji was annexed to the Empire in 1874. Even then the blackbirders were hard to control. In Brisbane, Liberals in Parliament denounced the planters as slave traders, while Conservatives claimed that only Kanakas could work in the tropical heat. Although no agreement was reached by 1880, it was becoming clear that exclusion would triumph. No coloured labour was to threaten the jobs of colonial wage-earners, or what Parkes called 'the British character of the colonies'.

A second policy pioneered by Victoria was protection. In 1850 the colonies were given the right to fix their own customs tariffs provided they did not discriminate against their neighbours or the mother country. Their early duties were high enough to yield a useful revenue and low enough to permit imports. No special favour was given to the hundreds of small workshops run by struggling families, even after shipping costs and distance failed to protect such bulky goods as bricks and beer from competition with the imported article. To most liberal merchants and shopkeepers the best plan was to buy in the cheapest market and sell in the dearest. For this reason there were few protests when Victoria was flooded with oversea goods during the gold rush. Opinions gradually changed as the falling gold yield brought lower wages, unemployment, and less spending. Many skilled tradesmen had come to the goldfields; were they to be allowed to drift away? Was Victoria with ample money and a big local market to depend on factories and mills 12,000 miles away? Was cheap oversea labour to prevent Victorians from using their skills?

Many thought the answer to these questions was a customs tariff high enough to protect local manufacturers. Of course goods would be dearer, but every purchase would help to keep a Victorian in a job. From an argument protection became a crusade. One of its strongest advocates was David Syme, a Scottish immigrant who turned from mining to make the *Age* into the most widely read newspaper in Australia. His powerful pen overwhelmed the most learned free-traders and helped to win a majority for his cause in the elections of 1864. Next year Victoria had new customs duties designed to encourage local production of a range of goods from boots to machinery. This did not satisfy reformers who fought for another ten years before they had a tariff high enough to justify their boast that protection was the policy of the colony. The benefits were hard to measure. By 1880 Victoria did have a greater variety of industries and more factory workers than any of its neighbours, but New South Wales, with its rich coal supplies and free trade, was catching up. Meanwhile fierce quarrels over border customs embittered colonial rivalry and forced the smaller colonies to venture timidly toward protection in self-defence.

A third Victorian innovation was payment of members of Parliament, sometimes called the keystone of democracy. After long years of argument it was given a trial in 1870. Members were allowed £300 a year. With less generous payments, this step was quickly followed by Queensland and more slowly by other colonies. Although it later gave great help to the Labor Party, it brought few immediate changes. Before the Victorian Act was made permanent in 1880, it provoked a deadlock in Parliament. This friction between the two Victorian houses was not new. The Assembly constantly complained that the Legislative Council had too much power, even when the grievance was not wholly justified. The Councillors were conservative and did represent property, yet their duty in the upper House was to prevent rash legislation. In Victoria, as in the other colonies, they had early agreed to make no changes in the annual Appropriation Bills that the Assembly alone could introduce to provide money for government. The misuse of this privilege by the Assembly caused as much confusion as any obstruction by the Legislative Council.

Victoria had its first serious deadlock on the question of protection. Guided by Higinbotham, the Assembly tacked its new customs tariff to its Appropriation Bill of 1865, in an attempt to force acceptance by the Council. The Councillors, unable to separate the tacked clauses, rejected the whole Bill, leaving the government without funds. By persuading a private bank to provide money the Premier was able to carry on until financial crisis and a host of law-suits forced the two Houses into a short truce. Trouble started afresh when Graham Berry became a Liberal leader. An English immigrant of 1852, he established himself as a merchant and newspaper owner before he won a large political following. Conservatives thought him ruthless and dangerous, for he increased protection and imposed the first tax on big land-holdings; above all Berry was intent on reforming the Legislative Council. To force a deadlock he tacked payment of members to his Appropriation Bill in 1877. The Council promptly rejected it. On 8 January 1878—'Black Wednesday'—Berry dismissed many senior civil servants. In the panic that followed he persuaded the Governor and the Assembly to meet the costs of government. These irregular actions soon brought the Councillors to terms. Within two weeks the deadlock was broken and within three years the Legislative Council accepted more members and a lower franchise for its electors.

Another important step first taken by Victoria was secular education. The long-debated subject of schools was closely linked with state aid to churches. Each religious denomination claimed equal right to have its own schools, but while some churches looked to the state for money, others refused any kind of government support. To settle these differences, some reformers wanted 'National' schools, aided by the state to provide unsectarian teaching in the common truths of Christianity as part of a general education. Although the national system was denounced by Catholics as a Protestant plot, it was introduced in South Australia by Hanson after state aid to churches was abandoned, and in

Queensland after separation. Meanwhile in New South Wales and Victoria a dual system was used. Two separate Boards—one denominational, the other national—distributed government aid. Their competition proved clumsy. Some districts had too many schools and others had none. In 1862 Victoria changed to a single Board, and Parkes led New South Wales into a similar change four years later. In spite of continued grants to church schools, the single Boards were not successful. In town and country large numbers of children remained untaught; parents were reluctant enough to pay fees, but they refused outright to contribute to school buildings. While Parliaments wrangled over school fees and compulsory attendance, gangs of young larrikins roamed the city streets. Queensland led the way with free education in 1870, by which time all the eastern colonies had withdrawn state aid to churches, but many church leaders still protested against undenominational teaching in the Boards' schools. To many Victorian Liberals these old-world controversies seemed out of place in a new country. The state, they claimed, had no right to decide religious differences, but it did have a duty to provide secular education for every child within its borders; if churches disagreed, they must manage their own schools without state assistance. In the election of 1872 the secularists triumphed. Education was made compulsory and Victorian state schools became free and secular. Three years later Queensland and South Australia adopted the secular system and New South Wales followed in 1880.

The most significant changes in the years of transition were these new social laws. They had little effect by 1880, but proved that new attitudes were emerging. After the excitement of gold and new constitutions, land reform had brought disappointment. To the colonial-born who hated to be pushed around, governments seemed to be only a tool for wealth and property. The vigour of colonists was sapped by pessimism until urban immigrants with fresh ideas revived the hope that government could also be an instrument of the people. In turn, immigrants quickly caught from the colonial-born an aggressive independence that annoyed employers and upset class distinctions. Although it did not bring social equality, it made men sensitive about living standards and material well-being. As reforms weakened the political power of the rich, electors slowly began to see government as a friend and provider that could turn each colony into a paradise for working-men. For good or ill, these new attitudes were to do more than wool or gold in shaping modern Australia.

CHAPTER 7

READJUSTMENT: 1880–1900

Transition went on long after 1880. The next twenty years brought many new experiments, some reckless and ill-considered, others designed to give more equal opportunity. The new changes aimed at correcting old mistakes and strengthening the promise of a southern utopia; but in spite of common aims and closer links, the colonies still cherished their separate policies. The penalties of rivalry only became irksome when isolation within and from outside seemed to threaten the continent's welfare. Reluctantly the colonies agreed to yield some of their jealously guarded rights. In this great readjustment 'the indissoluble Federal Commonwealth' came into being, more through necessity than in faith.

The years of readjustment did not treat each colony alike and the restless movements of population continued. Fortune seemed to frown throughout on South Australia and Tasmania, while it smiled on the eastern colonies in the 'eighties, and left them in gloom in the 'nineties to shower its favours on Western Australia. The big intake of funds and families from Britain was not equally distributed, and when it stopped intercolonial migration increased. The century ended with a total population of 3,765,000, and new positions in the colonial race. New South Wales with a higher birth-rate regained the leading place in 1892 after a tough ten-year struggle with Victoria. Queensland passed South Australia in 1884, and Western Australia left Tasmania behind in 1900.

With three-quarters of the population colonial-born, the colonies lost their enthusiasm for government-assisted immigration. When Victoria with no assistance at all continued to attract most new-comers, its neighbours began to think that free passages were a costly luxury. Unemployment clinched the argument. In the 'eighties aid was withdrawn by South Australia, Tasmania and New South Wales; even Queensland reduced its heavy spending on immigration in the next decade. But enthusiasm for borrowing in London did not stop until British banks called a halt. In the 'eighties the colonies' public debts tripled to reach £150 million, with New South Wales owing one-third of it. Repayments and more sober lending kept the rate much lower during the 'nineties. As in the years of transition most loan money was spent on railways. A trunk line with a break in gauge joined Sydney and Melbourne in 1883, and four years later linked Brisbane and Adelaide. By 1900 the colonies had 13,500 miles of track, with Queensland, Victoria and New South Wales close rivals for first place and Western Australia ahead of South Australia.

While railways and other public works played the leading parts in the drama of expansion, another important role was taken by private British investors. By providing plentiful funds to colonial banks and moneylenders they set off a reckless spree of private speculation. Most of the money went into land in one form or another, for few other fields of investment seemed ready for expansion. Borrow and boom ended in bust, but brought immense development while it lasted.

To pastoralists the private loans were a merciful boon. At a time when oversea markets were falling, graziers were able to increase their flocks and improve their properties. The 'eighties brought new records in pastoral expansion. Some sheep spread into new country, but most development was on old runs. Fences and new water supplies were expensive and increased the graziers' debts, yet once improvements were made, they paid well in bigger flocks, better fleeces and lower labour costs. In the wool sheds old-world 'blades' were replaced by steam-driven machines that drowned conversation and helped to transform shearing from a friendly craft into an unromantic business. Railways reached out across the coastal ranges to displace the leisurely bullock waggons, slash the cost of transport and speed the bales to market. Many drovers were also displaced as stock and station agents in ugly railway towns took more of the graziers' business. The picturesque out-back life changed quickly, not only on the big runs. Each struggling selector had his sheep and cattle. Station managers might suspect the brands on his many lambs and calves, while he looked hungrily at the leases that big graziers still held, but would not improve because of temporary tenure. These vast leases were also a breed-ing ground for rabbits and other pests that ravaged the pastures of all landholders. Clearly the land laws needed revision to protect all classes of sheep-owner.

Closer settlement seemed the best solution. In New South Wales a reform in 1884 offered selectors blocks of four square miles in the rich central districts, and as each big lease expired the lessee was allowed to renew only one half of it, while the other half was resumed and thrown open for conditional purchase. The new law was carefully enforced and gradually proved effective. Sheep numbers increased rapidly as many selectors acquired more acres and bigger flocks with the aid of private loans. The government earned more from land sales than all the other colonies combined. Although cultivation did not increase, and New South Wales still had to import grain, the growing wool cheque brought the colony nearly half the continent's total trade.

The pastoral boom was also shared by Queensland. In the 'eighties its sheep trebled, and its cattle increased to half the Australian total. As in New South Wales much of this expansion came from artesian water and new land laws. Champions of closer settlement in Queensland were keen, but their problem was different. Because of uncertain seasons, graziers needed areas much larger than any selector could afford to buy, yet reformers in Parliament did not want to hand over the public estate to big owners. The new law in 1884 resumed portions of large leases, but offered them to new lessees, not to purchasers. This started the slow process of increasing the number of graziers and reducing the size of big runs.

Although wool provided more than half the export income for New South Wales and Queensland, other colonies were less dependent on sheep. Stockmen still ventured far north and west, but elsewhere new prospects were opened by refrigeration. At first it failed to attract oversea investors because preparation was slow and costly. Cattle and sheep could walk to coastal abattoirs, but dairymen and orchardists needed many local ice-works. New breeds of cattle and sheep were also necessary in large numbers. These changes were later to transform the continent's fertile regions, but they brought few quick results. Not until the 'nineties was there any spectacular export of Queensland's frozen beef, Tasmanian apples, Victorian butter and New South Wales's mutton.

The years of readjustment brought many changes in agriculture. In South Australia bad seasons followed the bumper harvest of 1880 to stop expansion. Settlement had spread too far afield and failed to prove that rain followed the plough. Grasshoppers, drought and water-shortage ruined farmers who depended wholly on wheat. As harvests dwindled and speculators became bankrupt, the land laws were revised. Stricken farmers were allowed to turn their unpaid selections into long leases, or to take new sections in safer areas at reduced prices. Although large areas reverted to sheep runs, disaster taught many lessons. Some farmers gained new respect for their land and tried to replace old hit-or-miss methods by better understanding of soil, seed and climate. The government opened an agricultural college at Roseworthy to train young farmers and make experiments; but scientific progress was slow while the colony laboured in depression. During the 'eighties a thousand miles of new railways helped South Australia to keep the lead in agriculture, but they also assisted urban factories to ruin the small implement workshops that had sprung up in each country village. Skilled workers drifted to the larger towns and hundreds of farmers left the colony. Many, including industrious German families, went to the Wimmera in western Victoria.

Further north in Victoria were fourteen million acres of mallee scrub, neglected by graziers and overrun by rabbits and wild dogs. In return for destroying these pests, settlers were offered the land in 1882; with the aid of Mullenizers and stump-jump ploughs they found that it grew good wheat. A rush followed with much speculation. Within ten years 60,000 people were in the mallee district and Victoria won first place in wheatgrowing.

Victorian farmers soon learned to improve on South Australian methods. At Dookie, an agricultural college bred new types of wheat that yielded better hay and resisted disease. At Ballarat, Hugh Victor McKay began to make combined harvesters that reaped and winnowed in one operation. South Australians had already invented several such harvesters but made very few of them. Quite independently on his father's farm, McKay had proved that a Ridley stripper and a winnower could be combined in one labour-saving machine; more important, he had the business sense to see its commercial value. Helped by tariff protection he was soon exporting harvesters to other colonies and had to move his factory to Sunshine near Melbourne.

On the River Murray the Canadian Chaffey brothers started an irrigation company at Mildura in return for land grants which they hoped to sell to settlers. The scheme began well, then ran short of money. George Chaffey went home but William stayed. His courage and resource at last won success for Mildura and for Renmark in South Australia, and proved that vines and orchards as well as wheat could be grown in the Murray mallee by irrigation. This was important for the rising wine industry, for vineyards elsewhere were being ravaged by the phylloxera insect. The pest was gradually brought under control, especially in Victoria where grape growing multiplied during the 'eighties. Northern cane growers also encountered pest problems and hard times, but by means of scientific research and more careful methods, sugar production steadily increased and spread from New South Wales far along the Queensland coast.

Unlike the pastoral boom, agricultural expansion attracted few oversea investors. It owed most to urban merchants and land speculators who also won the best pickings from the mining revival of the 'eighties. Victorian gold was still yielding over £3 million a year and the copper mines at Moonta in South Australia and Cobar in New South Wales were still profitable when startling discoveries provided more windfall wealth.

A boundary rider pegged the first leases at Broken Hill in 1883. He believed it was a mountain of tin; nearby silver miners in the Barrier Ranges scorned it as a mountain of mullock. A syndicate was formed, expert advice was sought and silver worth £30,000 was mined by two men in a fortnight. This seemed too big for a small syndicate to handle, so the Broken Hill Proprietary Company was formed. Its shares boomed and subsidiary companies were started as men and money flowed in from every colony. The population shot up to 20,000 by 1890, the year's output was worth £3,500,000 and the silver city was linked by rail with Port Pirie, where a British company opened new smelting works and soon developed new processes for smelting ore.

On Tasmania's rugged western coast, prospectors found Mount Lyell in 1883. They were seeking gold and the new find disappointed them. One early partner sold for £20 a share that thirteen years later was worth £1,500,000. Beyond the gold-bearing quartz was copper ore, hard to win without machinery, smelters and a railway. For ten perplexing years experts blundered and shareholders quarrelled. British investors helped to find the money that made the mine more accessible. Then in 1897 road labourers working for 6s. a day exposed a mighty copper lode. Proclaimed the richest copper mine in the world, it was yielding by 1900 the first of many handsome dividends.

Mount Morgan in Queensland was another old prospecting site. Renamed and opened in 1882 it seemed to be a hill of gold and copper. With a company to work it, its top was torn off to yield two million ounces of gold in fifteen years. This wealth and the output from a hundred lesser mines put Queensland into second place as a gold producer. Every colony shared in the mineral revival. Positions were soon to change, but in 1890 Victoria still led in gold, and South Australia in copper. New South Wales had most silver lead, while its coal, now needed for ships, railways, gasworks, industries and a big export trade, was beginning to be worth as much as its precious metals.

Most of the trade in wool, grain and minerals enriched the capitals which attracted an increasing share of population and investment during the 'eighties. As each city burst its old boundaries, speculation ran riot. It spread to country towns, particularly in New South Wales; most of all it affected Melbourne, where a great International Exhibition in 1880 brought a wild burst of optimism. Melbourne's influence reached far beyond Victoria's borders. Railways gave it control of the River Murray and Riverina trade. Protection helped it to provide most of the colonies with boots and clothing. Golden wealth attracted the continent's company promoters to its money markets. From farms and goldfields, the sons and daughters of selectors and miners flocked to 'Marvellous Melbourne'. Its size and population doubled in a decade as it sprawled unevenly over a hundred square miles. The rapid spread of straight streets and tin roofs brought new suburbs and municipal councils each eager to borrow and spend. Their reckless rivalry gave Greater Melbourne a network of suburban railways that forced up land values. With cable trams, electricity, elaborate shops, grand new buildings and even elevators, the price of city blocks soared above £2000 a foot, while suburban growth, stimulated by a host of new moneylending companies, outstripped provision for water and sanitation. Land and houses seemed to be fool-proof investments.

Speculation was momentarily checked in 1886 as the demand for houses began to slacken. Oversea market prices for wool and wheat fell alarmingly. Although Victorians produced more, their exports brought £4 million less, a drop of 25 per cent in one year.

The setback was even more marked in South Australia where banks and land companies were crashing and expansion had already passed a peak that was not to be regained for twenty years. In other colonies where house-building was less centred on the capitals, speculation was less wild and the fall in private incomes was offset by heavy government spending.

Victoria's quick recovery did not depend on public works alone. Melbourne's marvels were loudly acclaimed in London and brought a new flood of private investment from oversea. Incoming goods swollen by luxuries and liquor rose to twice the value of the colony's exports; new land and mortgage companies turned speculation into frenzy. Even the government threw caution to the winds and doubled its spending. With immense enthusiasm the celebration of Queen Victoria's Jubilee was followed by an elaborate Centennial Exhibition. The high tide of borrowed prosperity drowned all doubt. Every gamble seemed safe as many fortunes were made—on paper. The building trades flourished, railways opened great engineering shops and factories turned out increasing supplies of furniture, boots, farm implements and coaches; yet there were rumblings of discontent. Wages and living costs were reasonable, but cheap and plentiful labour was a constant threat to skilled workmen who were beginning to find a new faith in trade unions.

Urban unions had a record reaching back to the convict era. They languished in hard times and revived with prosperity. The eight-hour day won by building trades in Melbourne, Sydney and Brisbane in the 'fifties was slowly extended to other capitals and other industries. As the movement spread to miners and transport workers, the unions began to combine. From new Trades Halls, freshly formed Trades and Labour Councils clamoured for better conditions, factory acts and legal rights for unions. At Intercolonial Trade Union Congresses—the first in 1879 and five more next decade—delegates were urged to fight assisted immigration and competition from Chinese labour. Some unions wanted direct

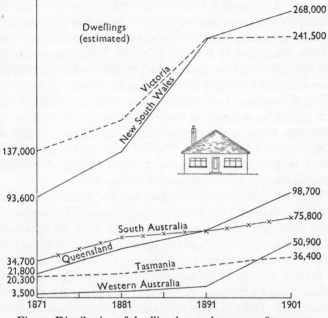

Fig. 2. Distribution of dwelling-houses by states, 1871–1901.

political influence and subscribed to pay their representatives in the Parliaments. A harder task was to reach a common loyalty and purpose. The tradition of independence was strong amongst wage-earners and new prospects of wealth kept unsettled men on the move. At first governments and employers were not unsympathetic and each year brought more unions. By 1880 the lock-out or strike that gave temporary unity against a single employer began to take wider effect. While employers slowly united in each colony, trade union organizers turned to semi-skilled labourers, shearers, and seamen. Disputes became longer and more serious as some employers tried to reduce wages by using non-union labour. To Trades Councils this challenged the whole principle of unionism;

to many old liberals it seemed that unionists were instructing employers how to manage their affairs. As each side prepared for battle, the opening skirmishes showed which was stronger. Ships' officers, threatened by a drastic wage cut, formed an association, but after three weeks were persuaded by ship-owners to withdraw from affiliation with other unions. When friction spread, moderates talked of conferences and boards of conciliation to bridge the gap that aggressive demands of hotheads on both sides was rapidly widening. Some concessions were made, but disputes continued. They came to a head in 1890. The Australian unions that had just joined employers in subscribing £37,000 to help the striking London dockers, now went on strike themselves.

The great maritime strike began when ships' officers again united with other unions. They were promptly dismissed by owners, and ships were laid up as seamen refused to work for non-union officers. Shearers were already on strike; in defiance of Pastoralists' Associations they persuaded the transport and waterfront unions to boycott wool shorn by non-union labour. In Queensland the strikers won a temporary victory, but in Sydney the employers fought back. Defence funds were raised, special constables sworn in and militia brought from Melbourne. Heads were broken on the wharves when 'black' wool arrived under police escort. The strike spread to Newcastle and Broken Hill where mines were closed and guarded by troops. Short of funds and weakened by deserters, the unions struggled for two tumultuous months before the strike collapsed. Many unionists had been arrested as trouble-makers and although some regained their jobs, the cause of compulsory unionism was discredited. Next year it suffered again in Queensland. The shearers who gathered at Barcaldine and other railheads flew the Eureka flag of freedom and made a brave show against non-unionists, until artillery, police, volunteers and a severe Peace Preservation Act damped their ardour. The union camps were soon deserted, but trouble revived each year as unyielding pastoralists rubbed salt into union wounds. Woolsheds were burnt and even a river steamer used by strike-breakers was destroyed, but everywhere the unions were beaten as governments helped the employers.

Some disappointed unionists rallied around William Lane, a utopian dreamer who planned to found a New Australia in Paraguay. Parties sailed from Sydney and Adelaide, but the scheme was a dismal failure. Other unionists overcame their suspicion of politics and planned to make the small Labor Parties strong enough to capture the reins of government in each colony. Their first representatives were not all working-men, for some urban Liberals had learned to respect the Labor voters who elected them. Although Conservatives professed to be shocked by this kind of political party, the Liberals were already sorely divided. The old clamour for independence and freedom from government interference had spent its force. Protective tariffs, government railways and public works seemed to make the state into a 'fine old milch cow' that anyone could milk. It was not only selectors who asked for land and cheap transport, or dairy farmers for a bonus on exported butter; big sheep-owners wanted help with rabbit-proof fences, and mine-owners with a bonus on coal. Free-traders and protectionists alike seemed willing to become dependent on the state whenever it suited them. Yet unequal privileges and class legislation still disturbed many Liberals and made some of them ready to join with the Labor Parties in extending reform. One common complaint was the voting system that disfranchised women and favoured the elector with property in more than one district. In spite of fierce opposition from the Legislative Councils, the 'Lib-Lab' alliances had some early triumphs. In New South Wales plural voting was abolished in 1893, and next year strong agitation by female reformers helped to win votes for women in South Australia. The alliances gained influence as their reforms spread slowly to other colonies. By 1900 the trade unions had regained their former strength, although some Conservatives still blamed their strikes for plunging the continent into depression.

More important causes were the fall in prices for wool and wheat, and the collapse of credit in London.

Prosperity was waning before the maritime strike. Melbourne was losing population, houses were becoming untenanted, unemployment was growing and foolhardy speculation was slowing down. One big building company had already failed and others were tottering. Fewer goods were being imported, although the export income was rising in spite of floods, drought and low prices. The Government was finding it hard to pay interest on its loans and harder still to raise more money in London. The crisis developed quickly when oversea investors began to withdraw their money. This left the banks short of cash. They had lent too much and could not recall enough when local depositors took fright and rushed to withdraw their savings. In panic bank after bank closed its doors. Each day brought its sorry tale of fraud, failure and unemployment. Public works and private building came to a standstill. For many families Melbourne's proud exhibitions were replaced by soup kitchens. Neighbouring colonies suffered less than Victoria, but depression was heavy everywhere. Thousands of families lost their hard-won savings as financial concerns collapsed and went bankrupt. Mercifully recovery was rapid. The colonists worked with a will and by 1900 regained some of their pre-depression standards. Some of the banks were reorganized and cautiously reopened. The money-market recovered in London and world prices improved, but the colonies were still starved for private investment.

Hard times had made the governments more attentive to social problems. The Lib-Labs tried with varying success to improve conditions by factory laws, to create boards of arbitration for preventing strikes and to tax personal incomes for such benefits as old-age pensions. Everyone looked to the Parliaments for help, but they still looked to land reform as the best solution to unemployment. Big estates were taxed and many leases were subdivided into working-men's blocks and group settlements. Though rabbits and dry seasons reduced sheep numbers, refrigeration now gave a mighty increase to frozen meat and butter. Victoria was still first in wheatgrowing but the yield from old land was decreasing. In New South Wales cultivation tripled as southern railways opened virgin farm land; after nearly a century of grain importing, the colony fed itself, had a big surplus for export and challenged South Australia for second place in the wheat race. In Queensland generous government aid multiplied the small sugar-planters and doubled output. Hundreds of families in each colony started life anew on small mixed farms and orchards, but thousands more refused to leave the cities. Regular town jobs were scarce. The building trade remained at a standstill and urban industry languished. Much use was made of female labour which was scandalously exploited especially by clothing manufacturers. While women slaved at sewing machines their menfolk looked for work. Some fossicked in old diggings and helped to raise the gold output each year in Victoria and in New South Wales, until discoveries in Western Australia brought a new rush.

Freed from its convict influx in 1868, Western Australia had advanced steadily to win its own constitution and responsible government in 1890. Its public debt was then the lowest in the continent and it had more sheep, horses and railways than Tasmania. Wheat lands south of Perth had attracted many South Australian farmers and, in the north, Western Australia had a busy trade in sandalwood, pearls and shell as well as cattle stations. Although Hargraves of Bathurst had doubted the existence of gold in the colony, a small field was opened in the Kimberleys in 1886. Other discoveries followed in widely separated places. Two travelling prospectors camped by a native well at Coolgardie where they found 500 ounces of gold in a few days. The news spread quickly and brought a rush. In June 1893 Patrick Hannan lost his horses and found Kalgoorlie; then came the Golden Mile. The whole area seemed to be studded with nuggets and reefs, a golden magnet which attracted more than eighty thousand people in the next seven years. A hardy few crossed the desert on camels, but most came by sea from Melbourne and Adelaide. Many brought their wives and families. Perth's population multiplied tenfold. Towns sprang up like mushrooms on the goldfields. Farmers neglected their crops to make small fortunes by carrying food and water until displaced by a railway and a mighty pipeline that brought Kalgoorlie five million gallons a day from the coast three hundred miles away.

The gold brought a few immigrants direct from England and much gambling investment. While speculation in mines ran riot, the new government in Perth borrowed heavily in London. Goldfield services were costly and much else had to be done if diggers were to be turned into permanent settlers. A proper harbour was needed at Fremantle and other ports clamoured for attention. Land granted to a private railway from Perth to Albany was needed for farmers at reasonable rates; with the railway it had to be resumed by government at great cost. Other land had to be cleared before farmers would buy it. By 1900 Western Australia's public debt per head of population was twice as high as in any other colony. Nevertheless its gold had helped the whole continent to recover from depression, while the diggers, as 'tother-siders', helped to destroy the westerners' isolation and to bring them into the Australian federation.

The idea of federation was not new. After Earl Grey's plan for a Federal Assembly was rejected in 1849, other proposals were made by retired Governors and ageing theorists. In far-off England, Australia's federation seemed a simple cure for the ills of separate colonies, but practical colonists were not so easily impressed. Busy with local affairs, and jealous for local power, they saw no need for central control of land and quarantine, or even for a central court of appeal. If problems did arise, let them be solved by intercolonial conferences; federation could wait until the colonies asked for it.

While Parliaments quarrelled over railways, boundaries and customs duties, a national feeling began to stir the colonial-born.

From Victoria their Australian Natives Association spread to give new purpose to the little groups that met for lectures and debates in Mechanics Institutes and Schools of Art in cities and country towns. Colonists long bound by British traditions in poetry, prose and painting slowly turned to livelier styles more suited to a young and vigorous people. Their Australianism captured in story, verse and picture touched deeper chords than politics could reach. Its tone was often crude and truculent, and sometimes fiercely isolationist towards the outside world. To some it spoke of good old days and to others conjured up a glorious future. Most of all it exorcized the apologetic spirit that made men hesitate to take pride in their native land. Some of their praise was as shy as this quatrain by Dowell O'Reilly:

> When Nature's heart was young and wild
> She bore in secret a love-child;
> And weeping, laughed—too glad to dress
> Its lawless naked loveliness.

Others like Henry Lawson rebelled more frankly:

> Though the bush has been romantic and it's nice to sing about,
> There's a lot of patriotism that the land could do without.

Much verse of this kind found its way into the weekly Sydney *Bulletin*, first published in 1880 to preach 'Australia for the Australians'. As the 'Bushman's Bible' it swept across all colonial boundaries; by 1900 its arrival at Kalgoorlie was a signal for miners to take a day of rest.

While the new school encouraged nationalism and scorned old-world shams, other forces were at work to bring the colonies together. Every threat of coloured immigration drew attention to the empty north and its near-by islands. A few enthusiasts wanted to settle the eastern part of New Guinea unclaimed by the Dutch, but missionaries, pearlers, prospectors and colonizers were all suspicious of each other and the Colonial Office frowned on annexation. In 1883 rumours of German plans to occupy New

Guinea roused the Queensland government to plant its flag at Port Moresby. This action brought reproof from the Colonial Office even though Queensland proposed to foot the bill for the new territory. In spite of London's bland assurances, Germany next year did take possession of north-eastern New Guinea, and resentful colonists loudly complained of betrayal by the imperial government. In Victoria, where missionaries had reported French threats of island annexation, plans were made to send an occupation force to the New Hebrides. Although France soon agreed to leave those islands independent, its convict settlement of New Caledonia brought fresh fears, this time of deluge by the escaped criminals of an alien power. National feeling ran high; republicans clamoured for separation from the Empire and even sober loyalists denounced England's negligence in the face of foreign aggression. One thing seemed clear: the separate colonies must speak with a united voice.

Led by Victoria, a conference at Sydney decided to form a Federal Council. Though its powers were very strictly limited to allay regional fears, it was called 'the first beat of a national pulse'. Before the Federal Council met in 1886, however, New South Wales and South Australia pronounced it a Victorian invention and refused to attend. Without their aid, the other four colonies passed a few Acts on naturalization and northern pearl fisheries, but the Council had no power to enforce its laws. Each year its pulse beat more faintly and no one mourned when it stopped altogether in 1899.

Meanwhile patriotism gained strength. A New South Wales contingent went to Britain's aid in the Sudan and a formidable bevy of colonial leaders attended Queen Victoria's jubilee. At the London Colonial Conference the Australians agreed to share the costs of a special British naval squadron stationed in their waters. Next year, an expert British strategist came to examine the military defences of the colonies. The danger of divided forces and the need for a central authority were emphasized in his report. It stirred Sir Henry Parkes to appeal for a Federal Convention. Attended by the leading lights of each colony it gave much promise of success. Memory of the New Guinea fiasco still rankled, but the republican element was weak; even the proposed title of 'Commonwealth' was suspect. Intercolonial rivalry was strong. Few of the delegates had ever met and some looked on their neighbours as foreigners. A single central government was clearly not wanted. The colonies were too jealous to surrender all their separate powers, but problems of defence, coloured immigration and customs tariffs did call for united action, and some adequate form of joint government was obviously needed. Canadian and American federations were freely ransacked for ideas and in 1891 the Convention appointed a committee to draft a constitution that was to give the central authority adequate powers and at the same time safeguard the colonies' separate rights. The constitution was chiefly the work of Sir Samuel Griffith, but unfortunately this scholarly lawyer was soon lost to the federal cause by his appointment as Chief Justice in Queensland. Other leaders dispersed to seek the approval of their Parliaments for the proposed new government.

Financial depression intervened. For a time it seemed that interest in federation had lapsed. New Zealand and Fiji would not join. The new Labor Parties thought social reform more important, and free-traders in New South Wales were bitterly opposed to compromise with their protectionist neighbours. Queensland, fiercely divided over coloured immigration, talked of dividing its tropical north from its more temperate south. Years passed before planters were convinced that federation promised them a wider and more profitable market for sugar grown only by white labour. South Australia took offence when Sydney planned a trans-Pacific cable to compete with its overland telegraph connection with the old world. Each colony seemed to suspect its neighbours of malicious designs.

The subject of federation was kept alive by such enthusiasts as the Australian Natives Association and numerous Border Leagues.

When the Federal Convention was reopened in 1897, only Queensland was unrepresented. Among a host of brilliant delegates, most of them colonial-born, one of the ablest was Alfred Deakin of Melbourne. Son of a Cobb and Co. accountant, he had studied law, won the friendship of David Syme and George Higinbotham, and entered Parliament as a Liberal reformer. Wisdom and skill as an orator earned him a place in cabinet before he was twenty-four. His fine words were matched by able deeds. He made Victoria the leader in irrigation and factory legislation; undazzled by the great in London, he defied dictation to the colonies at the Colonial Conference. In the Convention debates he was without equal for his resolute patience and unselfish patriotism. Another powerful leader was Charles Cameron Kingston of Adelaide. A giant in size and strength, he liked to champion the weak as a lawyer, but as Premier he preferred to bully the opposition. His support for arbitration in industrial disputes and votes for women won him repute as a Democrat, but most of his reforms were designed to hurt his enemies more than to help the people. Unlike his bitterest foes, he did believe in federation and thus had a double reason for his vigorous support of the cause. Another able delegate was Sir John Forrest. He had lately turned from exploring to politics and, in spite of inexperience, steered his colony through its gold-rush difficulties. In five years of self-government, the west had separated church and state, made education free and secular and struggled to catch up with its neighbours. Forrest wanted Western Australia to benefit from federation; well aware of his colony's isolation and delayed progress, he insisted on the promise of a transcontinental railway and special tariff privileges. Another eminent federalist was Edmund Barton. Born and educated in Sydney, he became a lawyer before entering Parliament. In 1891 Parkes's mantle fell on his shoulders and he accepted the leadership of federalism in New South Wales. His powerful brain gave immense strength to the cause, but he disdained party politics and personal fame. When a less able man was chosen to be the Commonwealth's first Prime Minister, others had to press for Barton's appointment. Although he became the first leader of the federal government, he soon found a more congenial place on the High Court bench.

The Convention began in Adelaide, then moved to Melbourne and Sydney. Although it owed much to the constitution drafted by Griffith, many questions still had to be settled. Free trade within the continent solved the problem of border customs, but the subject of protective tariffs was postponed. A more difficult question was how to safeguard the rights of the less populous colonies. As one delegate said: 'In a federation diversity is freedom, uniformity is bondage; but state rights are the strongest bulwarks against despotism.' These fears were answered by giving each state an equal number of seats in the Senate, while equal electorates gave popular representation in the lower House. As a further safeguard the powers of the new Commonwealth Government were carefully enumerated, all else being left to the states. At last the constitution was ready for the people. The referendum in June 1898 attracted only half the electors, but large majorities accepted federation in Tasmania, Victoria and South Australia. In New South Wales, the wavering 'Yes–No' advice of its Premier, G. H. Reid, brought too few favourable votes to give the absolute majority required by that colony. The fate of federation trembled in the balance until the Premiers gathered at Melbourne and gave Reid more concessions, including the location of the federal capital in his colony. A newly elected government brought Queensland to share in a second referendum which gave decisive majorities in 1899. Next year Western Australians voted to join the federation soon after 'the Act to constitute the Commonwealth of Australia' had been placed on the Imperial Statute Book.

CHAPTER 8

FEDERATION: 1900–20

With bells ringing in a new year the Commonwealth of Australia was born on 1 January 1901. Sydney celebrated the event with processions, flags, triumphal arches and military displays. Everywhere optimistic speeches and waving banners hailed the achievement of nationhood: 'the crimson thread of kinship' was claimed to make 'one people, one destiny'. After elections in March and the opening of the Federal Parliament in May, it soon became clear that an additional government, not a new nation, had been created. It also became clear as the new Parliament gradually took up its duties that no sudden changes could be expected. The Commonwealth had gained the best political leaders and some of them dreamt of a united nation free from old-world inequality, but most of their followers thought of the past more than the future. Their awe of the Federal Constitution was matched by the people's reluctance to alter it when referenda gave them opportunity. The new government was hesitant and divided, uncertain of its rights to spend money. Many members seemed unwilling to look farther than their familiar colonial boundaries and regarded the Commonwealth as a mere managing agent for those joint functions that the states could not conveniently perform. Changes came very slowly as the government gained confidence and strength. Years passed before new financial arrangements, organized political parties and war transformed the Commonwealth from an agent into a controller of national policy. In 1920 this transformation was well advanced but still far from complete. With seven Parliaments the Australians were more fully governed, more heavily taxed and only slightly less devoted to regionalism than they had been in 1901.

The Commonwealth began in hard times; the northern half of the continent was in the grip of a record drought. Some inland places recorded no rain for seven years. When the drought broke in 1902 outback children were terrified to hear for the first time the rattle of rain on iron roofs, and it was claimed that thirsty young horses swam flooded creeks to drink at their accustomed water troughs. In the dry years Queensland lost two-thirds of its cattle and New South Wales lost half its sheep, while the continent's harvest in 1902 shrivelled to a quarter of the previous year. One farmer told of a harvest barely sufficient for next year's seed. Unable to borrow money, his household lived for months on home-ground grain. Rain came at last in heavy night showers; at daylight the teams were harnessed and ready, but the farmer turned back to the kitchen door to call to his wife: 'If the rain keeps up until lunch, we'll have that tin of raspberry jam.'

Although no other great castastrophe marred the uneventful progress of the Commonwealth's first decade, the big drought came as a climax after the hungry 'nineties to quicken many trends that had already become noticeable. The most important of these was the drift to the cities. Everywhere sheep-owners and farmers were heavily in debt, and hosts of disillusioned countrymen were leaving the land that seemed to mock their labour. The cities offered less discomfort but fewer opportunities. Too much oversea capital had been withdrawn and banks were extremely cautious. Money seemed almost as scarce as profitable employment. The building trade was stagnant and other important urban industries were falling into the hands of monopolists who kept prices high and wages low.

The depression lifted slowly as wool and wheat prices recovered and governments resumed their borrowing. By 1910 new records of prosperity were reached, but they owed very little to private investment from oversea. These changes of fortune kept the states busy with local affairs. The Federal Parliament took immediate control of customs, defence and postal communications, and trade between the states became absolutely free, but there was little change in pre-federation patterns. Most of the Commonwealth's revenue was given to the states and most of its early laws set the seal on existing state practices.

One of the first federal laws was the Immigration Restriction Act. Already the population (apart from Aboriginals) was mostly British stock and all the colonies excluded coloured immigrants Although a White Australia was the object, the Commonwealth Act dressed it more politely. On the advice of the Colonial Office it made no mention of racial distinctions and used instead an educational test. The undesirable newcomer could be excluded because of his health, morals or failure to write a few sentences dictated in a language that he was unlikely to know. These restrictions fulfilled their purpose; but apart from making and policing them, the Commonwealth took little part in immigration in spite of its constitutional power to do so. Until 1921 the states were left to attract their own newcomers.

These two decades brought an increase of 35 per cent in the population which passed four million in 1905 and five million in 1918. This rapid expansion was overwhelmingly due to natural increase. Oversea migration accounted for less than one-eighth of the gain. Although more people were desperately needed, the depression years had opened many eyes. Insecure wage-earners wanted no competition for their jobs, and other critics scorned the long-lived Wakefield scheme that had squandered the great national asset of Crown lands in order to lure inexperienced labourers. Other visionaries wanted to foster new urban industries that would justify appeals for skilled migrants and give the Commonwealth independence as well as population. But more disillusion and depression were needed before the lessons of the past were properly learnt. By 1910 all the states were bidding strongly in the United Kingdom for settlers and labourers. In the next four prosperous years more than 275,000 arrived, half of them with government assistance. Places in the colonial race were unchanged, but the gaps widened. By 1920 the two million people in New South Wales outnumbered the combined totals of Victoria, Western

PLATE XV

(a) South Australians about to depart for
'New Australia' in Paraguay, 1893

(b) The Federal Convention, Adelaide, 1897

PLATE XVI

(a) Imperial Bushmen's Corps about to depart
for South Africa, 1900

(b) First Australian Light Horse Brigade
in Palestine, January 1918

PLATE XVII

Copper mining in Queensland: the Mount Morgan mine, 1959

PLATE XVIII

Australia and Tasmania, while Victoria with one and a half million had twice the population of Queensland and three times more than South Australia.

Interstate migration continued at a slightly slower rate. After the great western gold discoveries there were few inducements for mass movements, though easier travel enabled the restless and ambitious to search for new opportunities and jobs. In spite of the heavy drift to the cities, the land was still a powerful attraction. Reformers had not given up hope of closer settlement by small farmers, and big pastoral holdings still caused envy and resentment. The Commonwealth's only contribution to land policy was made in 1910 with a graduated tax on big properties. When this was added to the states' land taxes, most of the remaining absentee owners hurried to withdraw their investments.

Most land reforms of the period were carried out in the states by 'Lib-Lab' governments in the face of strong opposition from conservative Legislative Councils. Queensland clung to its preference for leases instead of freeholds, and with a big revenue from rents saw no need of a land tax until 1915 when a Labor government came to office. Among the state's many reforms was a ballot system for re-allotting parts of the leased areas that became due for resumption each year. Too often they had gone to the sons of the original lessee; now equal opportunity was given to the landless. In New South Wales a hard fought battle for land reform empowered the government to buy large estates and re-sell them in moderate-sized sections on easy terms. In spite of scandals and evasion of the law, the plan was more successful, if more costly, than earlier attempts to unlock the land. The total number of holdings was increased, small settlers gained areas that gave them a better livelihood, and production multiplied. Although big sheep-breeding studs were exempted from subdivision, many large owners voluntarily reduced the size of their properties by the private sale of outlying paddocks. By 1920 half the big estates over 50,000 acres had been cut down and the number of holdings between 100 and 1000 acres increased by more than 10,000. In Victoria the same scheme was used, with an even larger increase in smallholdings. In South Australia and Tasmania there were fewer changes, but in Western Australia closer settlement laws increased the area under conditional purchase and tripled the number of moderate holdings. In addition to cheap land each state now corrected one serious mistake of the past by making substantial loans to small settlers for clearing, machinery, homes, wells, barbed wire and rabbit-proof fencing.

Conservatives grumbled bitterly about these changes, but the new forms of closer settlement had profound effects. The old selection systems had not developed a sturdy yeomanry. Few selectors loved their land; to most it was only a form of capital from which a little profit might be wrung with luck. Desperately poor and ill-equipped, they tried to tame new country with their bare hands, became disheartened and sank into shiftless ways. These old-fashioned 'cockie' farmers became the butt of city humour as conditions changed. Where a distant oversea market had taken only wheat and wool at highly competitive prices, motor transport and refrigeration now gave access to growing urban markets hungry for regular supplies of an increasing variety of foodstuffs. With this incentive and much technical advice from government Departments of Agriculture, mixed farming became more common and less risky.

The life on big sheep stations was as primitive as ever, although petrol engines slowly came into use for sawing wood, pumping water and supplying homesteads with electric light. These were too costly for most smallholders who relied on their families and used very little hired labour. Apart from shearers, few country workers were organized in trade unions, and their wages were seldom more than the earnings of an independent rabbit trapper. Although work was still heavy and poorly rewarded, the old rural isolation was banished by motor cars, telephones and better mail services. Roadmaking was still a novelty outside the cities, but dirt tracks could be used in dry weather even if tyres were often punctured by roots and stones. Easier transport helped lonely rural towns to blossom with cinemas, garages and more attractive shops. Big graziers still ordered their supplies from the cities, but less exclusive families came to depend on their nearest town for stores, repairs, sport, entertainment and schools. This slowly brought a new sense of community and, with it, life in the bush lost much of the need for romance to mask its discomforts.

The greatest rural expansion of the period was in wheatgrowing. One cause was the application of scientific methods. The careful experiments of a generation of wheat-breeders at last bore fruit. Among them, William Farrer, once a Cambridge mathematician, has gained the most fame. Near Queanbeyan in New South Wales he bred many new wheat varieties before the Department of Agriculture engaged him as an experimentalist in 1898. One of his best breeds was called Federation; it matured early, harvested well with machines and could be grown in drier, cheaper land. Other advances were made by the use of artificial manures. The soil in many wheat districts was deficient in phosphorus, but when superphosphate was first used at Roseworthy Agricultural College, many South Australian farmers believed it would have harmful effects. Slowly their suspicion vanished. By 1900 a quarter of the South Australian crop, and by 1920 over three-quarters, was artificially manured. The results were spectacular. The average yield of five bushels to the acre was more than doubled. With superphosphate, better seed and improved machinery, vast new areas came under the plough in each state. New South Wales raced ahead of Victoria as a wheatgrower in 1910. In Western Australia the meagre area cropped in 1901 was multiplied twenty times by the opening of a great new wheat belt. Although agriculture did not expand much in Queensland and Tasmania, the total results for the Commonwealth were amazing. Droughts often reduced the harvests, but by 1915 a good season brought a new record of 179 million bushels from 12 million acres.

Compared with wheat, the advance in woolgrowing was disappointing. In 1920 the output of wool was not much more than in 1901, although rising prices doubled its value. New South Wales was still the leading wool producer, while Queensland now challenged Victoria for second place. Nearly nine-tenths of the clip was still merino, but in some wetter areas growers were beginning to mate their merinos with English sheep to produce the crossbreds and comebacks that gave coarser wool and better meat. Beef also became more plentiful as the cattle herds doubled in northern Australia. As ice-works spread city families got better joints, and better milk and butter from dairies that now flourished in near-by coastal districts. With improved breeding, more country factories and motor transport, the export of refrigerated foods soared. These developments gave greater diversity to the whole livestock industry and helped its production to retain a high place as an earner of export income.

These two decades increased the Commonwealth male work force by more than half a million, but rural industries gained only one-tenth of them. Although more men were employed in agriculture by 1920, the number in pastoral pursuits was reduced. Gold-mining showed an even greater decrease. Its numbers fell each year as less alluvial gold was found. Big company mines still paid well, but needed deep shafts; some at Bendigo went down almost a mile. Many of the rich ores needed special treatment and much of the work was done by machinery. More than half the gold won in this period came from Western Australia, but everywhere the yield was falling. Other precious metals suffered the same fate; either mines became worked out or suffered from strikes and other industrial troubles. The great mining centres of Ballarat, Broken Hill and Kaigoorlie lost population. Only coal mines showed any substantial increase: by 1920 the annual output in New South Wales was more than ten million tons.

At federation the rural and urban populations were nearly equal, although there were big differences in some states. By 1920 the

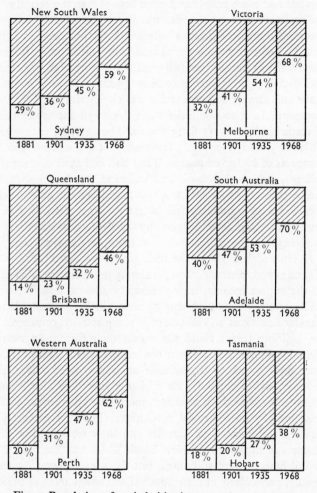

Fig. 3. Population of capital cities in proportion to total in each state, 1881–1968.

capitals had more people and more houses than the country. All the capitals had water supplies and electric trams and Melbourne was electrifying its suburban railways. Half the homes in Sydney and Melbourne were sewered and other cities were following slowly. Most housewives still used wood stoves but gas cooking and electric lighting were becoming common. Streets were better made and cleaner as horse traffic was slowly displaced by motor transport. In 1920 South Australia alone had one motor vehicle of some kind for every forty people. The capitals, each with its University and Teachers' Training College, offered the best prospects of higher education. They also had most of the private colleges, state high schools and technical training centres. The congregation of banks, business houses and factories gave the cities dominance in commerce and industry. More than ever before countrymen were dependent on city dwellers whose ambitions and needs began to shape the standards of living for the whole continent.

As cities stole the limelight, their growth increased the problems of state governments. Although primary products provided nearly all the export income, their seasonal variations and fluctuating prices greatly affected city employment. Banks and moneylenders remained cautious, and in spite of growing activity, commerce and the building trades could not regain their former importance. More local manufactures were obviously needed, both to provide work and to reduce dependence on imports. Few industries, however, could expand with labour alone; they also required costly improvements in transport, machinery and power. Federation brought no industrial revolution. The first twenty years doubled the number of factories and their workers, but three-quarters of them were in New South Wales and Victoria. Most establishments were still small, but the use of power expanded rapidly, particularly in New South Wales where most of the continent's metal-work and machinery was produced. In contrast, Victoria used more female labour and still made most of the boots and clothes. Small local markets did not encourage any great expansion of private enterprise, and governments were left to provide most of the big public utilities.

By 1920 the states' debts had doubled, though more loans were now raised locally than in London. Some loan money was spent on roads, a few country towns were supplied with water and great irrigation projects were commenced, but most loans went into railways as all the mainland states doubled their miles of rail. Queensland won first place in the railway race and the Commonwealth entered as a new contestant. It took over from South Australia the plans for a north–south railway, together with the two completed sections from Darwin to Pine Creek, and from Port Augusta to Oodnadatta. Port Augusta also became the eastern terminal of the transcontinental line that by 1917 enabled goods and passengers to travel by rail from Brisbane to Perth in less than a week despite five changes of gauge. Loan money also provided the cities with improved facilities. Some of these were taken over from private companies that failed to improve their services. Tramways were a notable example; by 1920 all the major lines in the capitals, except Brisbane, were brought under government or municipal control. Electric light and power continued to be supplied by private enterprise, but in Victoria were beginning to pass to public ownership.

The drift to the cities had greatly swollen the ranks of wage-earners and increased anxiety about employment. With railways, ports, roads, telephones, and most schools and savings banks under public control, government jobs offered the best security; but nationalization raised bitter political wrangling. Some people thought state enterprise was an abuse of privilege that threatened the old ideal of a fair field for all and no favours. Others believed that governments had a duty to provide public services. A few radicals wanted enough socialism to dispense with capitalists altogether. Although state Parliaments shunned theories and resisted sudden changes, the practical problems of urban employment and expansion hastened the organization of political parties.

Labor led the way. No other country had so large a proportion of trade unionists and this was supposed to be matched by a large faith in political action. Zealously Australian and isolationist Labor had other supporters too, but before it could win control of government it needed party unity. Its leaders decided to elect only those members who pledged themselves to the policies determined by regular party conferences; in Parliament these members must form a caucus to decide how to cast their joint votes. These tactics were scorned by old-fashioned Liberals; when they found that Labor discipline was forcing them to make too many concessions, they closed their ranks and organized their own parties. Although Liberals and Labor drifted apart, their old alliances had already gained shorter hours, workmen's compensation and wages' boards. With these reforms won, Labor had to broaden its fighting programme, and thus became more vehement against monopolies and big business combines that crushed competitors, exploited consumers and bullied working-men. When at last it won office, Labor was committed to a gradual expansion of state enterprise.

The first experiments aimed chiefly to save government departments from exploitation. State coal mines were opened in Victoria and Queensland, while New South Wales also had a host of state industries from brickworks to bakeries to provide government needs at low cost. With other state enterprises such as New South Wales's fishing trawlers and Queensland's butcher shops, they later served private consumers as well. Some of these projects made profits, others failed. Not one forced a competitor out of business, yet they were all ridiculed as government interference, and most were quickly closed when Labor lost office. In the Federal Parliament the Labor Party had varied success. As the constitution allowed the Commonwealth no power to nationalize industry, electors were asked in three referenda to give it this right. However carefully the question was phrased, the answer each time was 'no'. Undeterred, Labor gave the Commonwealth a shipping line, a small-arms factory at Lithgow and a woollen mill at Geelong. A more permanent triumph was the Commonwealth Bank created in 1911. Along with its savings bank it was wisely managed by Sir Denison Miller, a colonial-born financial expert with much banking experience in New South Wales. He opened business in Melbourne with one messenger boy to help him. As the Bank handled all the Commonwealth accounts it grew rapidly and won much public confidence before it had to finance the war effort. In raising over £250 million of war loans it saved the government large discounts and in many other ways proved its value. Private trading banks which disliked its privileged competition had another cause of complaint when Labor's Commonwealth bank-notes displaced their paper currencies.

In contrast to Labor's policy, Liberals saw the government more as a consumer than a producer; if public ownership became necessary at all, it must be independent of political control. They believed that government contracts gave legitimate encouragement to private enterprise. Thus in New South Wales a languishing smelting-works at Lithgow was saved from extinction by a large government order for steel rails. Other states used different methods to foster urban industry; unlike New South Wales they had protection, but their tariffs varied greatly. In 1901 when the control of customs passed to the Commonwealth, fierce debates between free-traders and protectionists made its first tariff a wishy-washy affair with few items and low duties. The list was lengthened in 1908 and duties became heavier, though a small preference was allowed for certain British imports. Further increases before and after the war gave a little more protection from oversea competition and from the dumping of goods unwanted elsewhere. To sidestep the tariff question one early federal government turned to bounties. The most important industries these affected were wool, iron and sugar. The makers of combed wool received small bounties for production that multiplied fifty-fold in eight years, put local woollen mills on their feet and provided a valuable part of the trade with Japan. The iron bounty helped the Lithgow smelting-works, but most benefit went to the Broken Hill Proprietary Company that stepped in to lay the true foundations of the Commonwealth's heavy industry. At first the company planned to smelt its rich Iron Knob ore at Port Pirie, but with expert American advice furnaces and mills were opened in 1915 at Newcastle near the best coal. To gather material from distant states, the company had its own railways, port installations and ships, and was soon supplying the continent's needs of iron and steel. The sugar bounty was a misnomer. An excise duty of £3 a ton was imposed on all growers with a rebate of £2 to those who employed only white workers. By this pressure, the repatriation of indentured islanders was completed by 1912. Although the first country in the world to grow cane entirely with white labour, Australia needed no sugar imports by 1920 and soon after became a big exporter.

The most remarkable policy of the Commonwealth's first decade was its 'New Protection'. In a narrow sense it applied only to bounties and excise rebates for protecting local industries. In a wider meaning it might be used to include a range of laws from White Australia to old-age pensions, each designed to give every Australian at least a minimum of economic security. In this wider meaning, the 'New Protection' laws were to become an important part of the national creed: birth into an unmixed race, sure access to education, guarantee of a fair and reasonable living and a shielded old age. One of its chief promoters was Alfred Deakin. In the confused jumble of early Commonwealth politics he forced attention to the great national purposes for which the country had federated; unless shared by all, the full benefits of peace, prosperity and progress would be ensured to none. As a whole-hearted Australian he dreamed of a young Commonwealth that might enrich the human spirit, and as a lawyer he tried to give his dreams a legal cloak. As a Liberal with great faith in equal opportunity he wanted no class legislation, whether it aimed at preserving privilege for the rich, or socialism and a welfare state for the poor. Deakin belonged to what he called the party of the centre. His middle-class eyes saw no escape from the clash of greed and need unless the Labor Party was civilized by reforms that protected wage-earners from exploitation. Opponents claimed that he was giving milk to a young tiger, and Labor's appetite later shocked Deakin himself.

The upheavals of the 'nineties had driven some states towards 'New Protection' before federation. The questions of race and free, secular education were already settled. To a youthful population, children seemed more worthy of care than the aged, but Victoria and New South Wales had old-age pensions and with other states provided many social services. 'Lib-Lab' reforms had also given each state some kind of industrial arbitration. Although the constitution left the states in charge of education and most bread and butter questions, the conditions of employment were indirectly affected when the Commonwealth took control of trade and other affairs. The most controversial of these was the power to make laws for 'the prevention and settlement of industrial disputes extending beyond the limits of any one state'. This question wrecked many governments before and after the federal court of conciliation and arbitration was created in 1904. The court's most notable president was Henry Bournes Higgins, immigrant son of an Irish Methodist minister. Thirty years in Victoria won him repute as a scholarly lawyer and a courageous reformer before he entered federal politics. He called arbitration a new province for law and order, and soon brought fame to his court.

An excise duty had been imposed on certain local manufactures, but a maker could be exempted from it if the working conditions in his factory were declared by the arbitration court to be fair and reasonable. In 1907 Higgins refused an exemption to the farm implement maker, H. V. McKay, on the grounds that his wage payments were too low to cover 'the normal needs of the average employee regarded as a human being living in a civilized community'. This important Harvester judgement deserves to be included in 'New Protection'. The Commonwealth public service and some states had already adopted the principle of a fixed minimum wage, but based it on the ruling rates that reputable employers were paying. Higgins's minimum wage of 7s. a day was no higher, but it was meant to be based on the rise and fall of living costs, beyond the reach of bargaining employers.

Although this reform did not stop industrial disputes, many trade unions formed federations and took their troubles to Higgins's court instead of going on strike. This made the states jealous for their own industrial controls, and overlapping authority sometimes had serious results. Queensland's government, for example, supported the private Brisbane Tramway Company in its refusal to recognize a federal union that some of its employees had joined. A stubborn dispute over the wearing of union badges led to a general strike. While Brisbane suffered, the state blamed the union and Higgins blamed the company; but an unyielding manager and coercive law drove the men back to work without federal benefits.

Commonwealth action also disturbed bigger states. New South Wales resented the long delay in choosing and building the federal capital of Canberra, while Melbourne grimly retained the temporary seat of government. New South Wales with its free-trade tradition also resented the payment of tariff duties, particularly on government imports. In defiance of Commonwealth customs officers, a big squad of state police once seized a large shipment of wire-netting bought by government for distribution among needy settlers. Less populated states had more serious problems.

At first the states did very well from their shares of the revenue collected by the Commonwealth in customs and excise duties. Free trade within the continent quickened interstate commerce and did not immediately disturb existing industries. These conditions changed when rising Commonwealth costs left less money for the states. In 1910 they lost their shares of customs revenue and received instead a much less valuable federal subsidy of 25s. per capita each year. This reduced subsidy bore most heavily on the smaller states whose public debts and taxes per head were already much higher than those of Victoria and New South Wales. More taxation was now needed and manufacturers could no longer compete with rivals in the wealthier states. In Brisbane and Adelaide factories were closed and urban employment shrank, while Tasmania and Western Australia had to be helped with special federal grants. Levels of prosperity were to become more uneven, though the differences were masked at first by growing Commonwealth responsibility. By 1914 Papua, Norfolk Island and the Northern Territory had been transferred to federal control, and federal old age and invalid pensions, quarantine services and maternity allowances relieved the states of other expense. The costs of federal government, however, were growing rapidly. One of the biggest items was defence.

At federation 'Imperial Bushmen' from each state were serving in the Boer War. When joined by Commonwealth contingents, these troops numbered 15,000. While they won distinction in South Africa, the federal government at home took over the states' naval and military forces and their shares in paying for the British fleet in Australian waters. In 1907 the Admiralty allowed the contribution to the Royal Navy to give place to a modern Australian squadron which after five years included one battle cruiser, three light cruisers, three destroyers and two submarines, as well as four old gunboats. Although their Australian crews were trained by British officers, a naval college for midshipmen was opened at Jervis Bay. After a visit from Lord Kitchener the militia was also reorganized. Compulsory military training for young men was introduced in 1910 and next year a military college was opened at Duntroon. Britain's declaration of war with Germany in August 1914 came as a startling shock. As part of the empire Australia was automatically at war and responded with patriotic fervour. Electioneering federal party leaders forgot their differences and promised to help the mother country with 'the last man and the last shilling'.

The navy was first in action. It sailed north with an expeditionary force to occupy German New Guinea and near-by islands, and thence to Samoa in search of an elusive German Pacific squadron. Thereafter it came under Royal Navy control. New ships were added each year, but not many engaged in actual fighting. Some were briefly in action off Gallipoli; the two submarines were lost, one in leading the British attempt to force the Dardanelles Straits; the *Pioneer*, a pre-federation relic, helped to destroy the *Königsberg* off East Africa, and the battle cruiser *Australia* narrowly missed a share in the battle of Jutland. The greatest triumph went to the *Sydney* for sinking the raiding cruiser *Emden* and its collier near Cocos Island. Apart from these actions the Navy's operations were mostly confined to uneventful convoys and patrols. By contrast the army moved in the thick of battle.

War found the Commonwealth with a small half-trained militia, committed by Defence Acts to home defence only, but volunteers from town and country were quick to enlist for oversea service in the newly formed Australian Imperial Force. Urban racecourses were transformed into training camps with officers from the permanent garrisons and Duntroon. Each day saw more khaki uniforms and more khaki hats with rising sun emblems decorating their upturned brims. Weeks before ships became available, 20,000 men, three-quarters of them colonial-born, were ready to sail. The first convoy swelled by transports from New Zealand left Albany in November, and others soon followed. In desert camps near Cairo the A.I.F. and New Zealand troops were joined together in one army corps under the command of General William Birdwood. Although an Englishman, he soon won the affections of the boisterous Anzacs.

While they trained for battle, strategists planned the capture of the Gallipoli Peninsula in order to divert Turkish attention from Russia and to open the Black Sea for Allied ships. The operation was a costly blunder. A long naval bombardment gave the Turks ample warning to strengthen their defences before the Allies

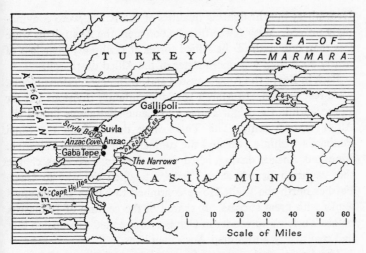

Map 5. The Gallipoli campaign, 1915.

attacked. The Anzacs had to seize Gaba Tepe at the narrow waist of the peninsula, but they were put ashore at the wrong beach. Instead of open country they faced steep broken ridges well manned by Turks with mountain batteries and machine guns. Nevertheless the gallant landing of 25 April 1915 gave the Commonwealth a day to remember with pride. The Anzacs left their transports in small boats and waded ashore dragging their equipment under withering enemy fire. In spite of heavy casualties they rushed the first ridges, and after a day of bitter fighting formed a line not far from the beach. Furious counter-attacks failed to dislodge them, but their own advance was foiled by strong Turkish resistance. In the next weary weeks small parties made heroic sorties to silence enemy guns and there was much individual valour. Losses were heavy and typhoid increased the toll. Other brave landings at Suvla Bay brought reinforcements and more costly battles. Mistakes, delays and wasted opportunities turned the campaign into a stalemate long before the Allies evacuated the peninsula in

December; but the fighting qualities of the A.I.F. were convincingly proved. With fewer than 80,000 men, the Australians were less than one-sixth of the Allied forces at Gallipoli; their loss of nearly 8000 men was one-quarter of the Allied death-roll.

Back in Egypt the Anzacs rested and, with new reinforcements, were reorganized. In March 1916 four infantry divisions left for France, while the Light Horse and Camel Battalions joined the Allies' eastern army. The Turks were driven from the Sinai Peninsula within a year and the campaign moved into Palestine. Mounted Anzacs distinguished themselves in a reckless charge that captured Beersheba and helped to open the way to Gaza. Farther north the Light Horse continued to harass the enemy's flanks with great success. It shared in the capture of Damascus before Turkey's surrender in October 1918 ended a campaign that had cost nearly a thousand Australian lives.

The Anzacs on the western front in July 1916 were concentrated near Amiens where an Allied offensive soon began. Part of the A.I.F. was thrown against the village of Pozières, where for a week they were bitterly tested by merciless shelling. According to the official war historian, 'a single hour of this battle caused more stress than the whole Gallipoli campaign'. They won the village and advanced beyond it to struggle for another month against savage counter-attacks, poison gas and flame-throwers. In these operations 12,000 Australians were killed and many more wounded before the onset of winter brought mud and cold, influenza and 'trench feet', to reduce their ranks still further. New recruits and men returning from hospital gave the A.I.F. a fighting strength of nearly 120,000 on the western front in spring of 1917. After the weather cleared, the Germans were slowly beaten back. The A.I.F. joined the attack on Bullecourt and won the goal with very heavy casualties. Further progress was barred by the Hindenburg Line. Months of tunnelling by Allied sappers destroyed some of its outer hill fortifications and cleared the way for the murderous third battle of Ypres. Although the A.I.F. won repute for hand to hand

Map 6. The war in the Middle-East, 1915-18.

fighting, its losses were very severe; by the end of 1917 another 20,000 had been killed. Next year a German advance aimed to split the British and French armies apart near Amiens. In April the fall of Villers Bretonneux brought the enemy close to this goal, but a ferocious counter-attack at night by two fresh Australian brigades recaptured the town, a fitting feat for the third anniversary of Anzac Day.

In May the A.I.F. gained a new leader in John Monash, an Australian engineer who was sometimes called the most scientific commander in the whole war. Like Birdwood he had immense faith in the tough A.I.F. and cared for his men well. At Gallipoli, the Somme and Ypres he had seen them mown down by machine guns and torn to pieces by wire entanglements. He came to believe that it was wrong to turn foot soldiers into martyrs however heroic; if properly covered by guns and tanks they could reach their goal and hold it without ruinous loss of life. In July he tested this plan in the battle of Hamel. In less than two hours the whole valley was taken with only 800 casualties including walking wounded. Four weeks later the plan was used by British generals in the great battle of Amiens. After an accurate and stunning barrage from 2000 guns came 450 tanks followed by the infantry. The battle raged for three days and some mistakes were made, but the German line was broken and enormous amounts of equipment were captured, while the prisoners taken by the Allies far outnumbered their own total casualties. The Monash plan was used again and again. In September it helped to smash the Hindenburg Line and hastened Germany's surrender. The end came with the signing of armistice on 11 November. The A.I.F. had shared in most of the major engagements of 1918, but its losses were only half the number of the previous year.

By the end of 1919 Monash had most of the A.I.F. back in Australia and demobilized. Of the 330,000 volunteers who had gone overseas, 60,000 had died and another 150,000 had been wounded. A grateful country fêted the returning men and promised

Map 7. Battlefields in northern France, 1916–18.

them land, homes, industrial training and employment; yet they found little difference in their homeland. Children had grown and friends were older. Houses and streets looked the same with a few more factories and telephone poles. Ports and railways were busier. Jobs were more plentiful and wages were higher, although money did not go so far. In the evenings drinks were harder to get except in Queensland and Western Australia; elsewhere liquor polls and regulations made public bars close at 6 p.m. The only marked changes were in politics; the Commonwealth had more power and rival parties were more bitterly opposed.

A federal election in September 1914 gave the Labor Party a decisive majority. Twelve months later William Morris Hughes became Prime Minister. Thirty years earlier this wiry Welshman had migrated to Queensland. In search of permanent work he battled his way at last to Sydney where he was drawn into Labor politics. A few stormy years in the state Parliament won him election as a federal member in 1901. Other Commonwealth leaders thought themselves better-brained, but none could match his sharp wit and biting tongue. He knew what his supporters wanted, and fought fiercely for their reforms even when curbed by cautious colleagues; but he never suffered defeat with any grace. Behind his daring impudence was a passionate will to win.

As Prime Minister Hughes had unusual opportunities. Immense war loans had to be raised in London and Australia. Wartime emergency added a Commonwealth income tax to those already imposed by the states. It was followed by a special tax on war profits. A War Precautions Act gave the Commonwealth very wide powers to make regulations for censorship, control of aliens and anything else connected with national safety. A Crimes Act guarded against all kinds of treason and, with a later Unlawful Associations Act, was used against strikes and other activities deemed harmful to the war effort. Laws against enemy contracts helped to break the German grip on Australian mining exports. State and Commonwealth regulations controlled prices to prevent exploitation of wartime shortages. Other regulations introduced wartime marketing schemes for wheat, sugar and wool.

Some of these wartime trade arrangements were made possible by Hughes's visit to Europe in 1916. In a heavy programme of civic functions, tours and public speeches he clamoured for a stronger, more united war effort. The war, he insisted, was not Britain's alone; the Dominions were in it too and deserved to be treated as partners, not as subject colonies. Another urgent need was more shipping for empire freights. When officials and owners insisted that ships could not be spared, Hughes proved them wrong by buying cargo vessels for the Commonwealth Line. Nevertheless British ministers and A.I.F. leaders did convince him that Australia must have conscription. Back in Melbourne in August he learnt that volunteer enlistment was falling in spite of a vigorous recruiting campaign.

Hughes discussed conscription with his colleagues and found them hopelessly divided. A long and troubled meeting of federal Labor members decided against conscription unless people voted in favour of it. This passed the question of a referendum to Parliament, and gave Hughes fresh hope. He called both Houses to a secret session and gave them 'facts of great moment' to prove that every available man was needed at the front. Next day after a gruelling debate Parliament voted in favour of a referendum. This decision brought Hughes expulsion from the New South Wales Political Labor League. More than Labor members, however, were divided on conscription. It disturbed many Irish who were mindful of recent troubles the subject had caused in Dublin. Many more were turned against it by the stern attack of the Coadjutor Archbishop of Melbourne, Dr Mannix, although other Roman Catholic leaders disagreed with him. Hughes's answers to Dr Mannix raised sectarian issues and other churches became divided. Although conscriptionists mostly appealed for patriotism, some charged their opponents with responsibility for the violent crime and sabotage that broke out at this time. Each day the issues became more confused and emotional. The referendum brought favourable majorities in three states, but they were outnumbered by a big negative vote in New South Wales, South Australia and Queensland. Two-fifths of the volunteers overseas were also against it. The conscription proposal was rejected by a majority of 72,000 out of two million voters. Two weeks later a meeting of the federal Labor caucus brought the dreaded split in the party. Twenty-three of the sixty-five members present walked out with Hughes. Soon the split spread to the states, shattering Labor's jealously guarded unity.

Hughes continued in office with Liberal support until an election in 1917 gave a sweeping victory to his new Nationalist Party. To Hughes this invited another conscription referendum; before it was held the country was torn by industrial disputes. The split in Labor had divided the trade unions and thrown militants together without moderate restraints. In New South Wales alone some 100,000 men were on strike for five weeks and new deep feuds were created against the 'loyalists' who stayed at work. Meanwhile recruiting figures rose and fell, but failed to reduce the numbers of unenlisted men thought fit for service. To save the army from withering away Hughes proposed to recruit 7000 men each month by compulsory ballot. This became the question for the second referendum.

The campaign revived bitter feelings everywhere. In Queensland the Labor Premier, T. J. Ryan, fought conscription tooth and nail. When the Commonwealth censor would not allow one of his pungent speeches to be reported in the press, Ryan repeated it in the state Parliament and had it printed in bold type in Hansard. On an order from the Prime Minister all copies of the offending volume were seized by the censor and a military guard. The rumpus died down after Hughes visited Brisbane. On his way back an anti-conscriptionist at Warwick hit his hat with a badly aimed egg. In the fight that followed the Prime Minister was pushed about and barked his knuckles. When he asked for the egg-thrower's arrest, the police sergeant declared himself to be under the sole authority of the Queensland Government. Elsewhere Dr Mannix and other churchmen were again on the war-path. To Hughes's disappointment conscription was rejected in the second referendum by a majority of 166,000; only two states gave favourable votes.

Six months later Hughes was in London at meetings of the War Cabinet, noisily pressing for full consultation with the Dominions. Soon he was at the Peace Conference defying any return of colonial territories to Germany; the captured Pacific Islands, he claimed, were essential to Australia's security. Because President Wilson wanted no annexations, the best that Hughes could win was a League of Nations mandate entrusting German New Guinea to Australian control. When islands further north were entrusted to Japan, the question of racial equality was raised. Hughes would have none of it; although Japan and Australia had been willing allies, nothing was to force the Commonwealth to change its immigration laws. His stubborn stand could not be shaken even by President Wilson and the question was dropped. At last the Treaty of Versailles was signed and the League of Nations Covenant adopted, with Australia a partner in both. War left behind, the Commonwealth moved into a new decade of peace, more strongly entrenched than ever in comforting isolation.

CHAPTER 9

DISILLUSION: 1920–40

The return of peace quickly brought a new optimism. The years of conflict were soon regarded as an unwelcome interlude that had halted progress. Everyone seemed eager for expansion, development and rising standards of living. War had brought the continent much closer to old-world problems, but although plans for universal peace could not be entirely ignored, marketing and migration seemed more pressing. Commonwealth and states increased their spending and extended controls in every direction. Fortune's favours were dearly bought with borrowed money, and prosperity appeared to spread its blessings widely throughout the 'twenties. Each year brought more co-operation between states and Commonwealth, and the people were drawn into closer unity as a nation with common goals. Then in 1929 economic depression arrived like a shattering blast from the outside world. Prosperity vanished as people and governments hastily scrambled for shelter. In the rush for self-preservation national ideals were forgotten. The financial position was soon adjusted by drastic retrenchment; but the rude shock of depression revived regionalism. Throughout the 'thirties the continent was troubled by uncertainty and suspicion. They were only banished when war brought new dangers that aroused a true spirit of nationalism.

In these two decades Commonwealth power increased greatly and the states lost much of their independence. There was also a great decline in the importance of Parliaments as more and more regulations were made by expanding government departments. A host of new boards and commissions was created; their semi-independence did not always please the Australian Labor Party whose members hoped for unification in one central government, and in 1921 pledged themselves to extend socialization. Except for two depression years, however, the Labor Party did not hold Commonwealth office, although it fared better in some of the states. During the 'twenties federal power was shared by the Nationalists and a new Country Party organized to give rural producers a stronger voice in government. This coalition complicated the making of national policies. As no single party often had an outright majority, Commonwealth politics were turned into a kind of upside-down auction where articles were left on the shelf if party competition seemed too keen, or sold with a great show if no one really wanted them. Elections were still vitally important and Parliaments still talked, but once party strengths were determined, the result of debates was always a foregone conclusion.

The 'twenties began with Hughes as Prime Minister leading the Nationalist Party, but his followers were restless. To some he seemed like a socialist and to others like an autocrat. In 1923 the Country Party refused to have him as a coalition leader and he was replaced by Stanley Melbourne Bruce. At forty Bruce was the Commonwealth's youngest non-Labor Prime Minister and one of the best mannered. He had three years of war service and was wounded at Gallipoli. He knew more about business than politics; though privately gracious, he resembled in public an aloof company director with a passion for efficiency. To him Australia was an undeveloped enterprise that could, under skilled management, enrich its shareholders. In many ways he was like Deakin, but less obviously humane. The slow routines of Parliament frustrated him nearly as much as the obstinacy of militant trade unions. On the other hand, his calm respect for British leaders at Imperial Conferences contrasted sharply with the stormy persistence of Hughes. Bruce made political blunders, but he also made Australia more credit-worthy, and long after he left office he continued to encourage investment from oversea. Bruce's political partner was Earle Christmas Grafton Page. This rural doctor rose quickly in the Country Party by prescribing decentralization as a cure for the continent's ills. In office he turned to other cures and advocated each one in turn with great gusto. The Country Party won a few special prizes and Page sometimes added warmth to Bruce's cold logic.

While boom times lasted the coalition flourished. In 1929 Bruce left politics; Page stayed on to share in another composite government created after Labor's unity was shattered by depression problems. The Nationalists, reformed as the United Australia Party, found a new leader in Joseph Aloysius Lyons who had left the Labor Party because he disagreed with its financial policy. Plain, homely and sincere, he had already won repute as Premier and Treasurer in Tasmania. Now as Australia's first non-Labor Roman Catholic Prime Minister he led his coalition government with ability for seven difficult years. But his outlook and manner remained insular. Where cartoonists had made fun of Bruce's too-English spats, they likened Lyons to a koala bear. This suggested a kind of isolationism that became increasingly dangerous as war clouds gathered, for Australians seemed far less interested in external affairs than in domestic questions.

In these two decades the population increased by 22 per cent but, like everything else, the growth was affected by depression. The rise from five to six million took only seven years; fourteen more passed before seven million was reached in 1939. Most of the gain came from natural increase, although there was an ominous decline in the birth-rate. In spite of the baby bonus, families were shrinking in size. The average of 5·5 children in 1881 had fallen to 2·2 in 1939, barely sufficient to replace the parents and maintain population numbers; this problem received little attention while migrants could be attracted.

These twenty years brought a great increase of visitors and Australian travellers oversea, and in the coming and going of migrants at their own expense. Among the unassisted immigrants many thousands came from Italy. At first most of them were males; their families came later. Like earlier German settlers, the Italians tended to band together either as labourers, fishermen or tenant farmers. Their frugal habits and readiness to toil long hours at low wages often brought them into conflict with local trade unions. Some were victims of savage riots at Western Australian gold mines and on Queensland canefields, and others suffered severely from prejudice during the depression. Even the Commonwealth Government once threatened to restrict the inflow of Italian immigrants who had no money. Some left the country, but others stayed to work hard for homes of their own, and many became naturalized as soon as they could.

Assisted passages were only given to immigrants from Britain. By an agreement in 1920, the Commonwealth took sole charge of migration and arranged to supply the states with the number and type of immigrants that they asked for. This enabled the Commonwealth to introduce passports, reduced competition between the states' agents-general in London and concentrated recruitment at Australia House. By another agreement Britain gave free passages in large numbers for the first time, as part of an ambitious plan made by Bruce and other empire leaders who dreamed of an Australia with one hundred million white people. The British and Commonwealth governments agreed to provide the states with special loans for approved settlement schemes that were to absorb hosts of immigrants each year. Some states were too cautious and others too bold, and not many of their schemes were approved before depression wrecked the plan and reversed the flow of migration.

Other enthusiasts aimed to encourage youthful immigrants. The Barwell Boys' Scheme was designed to replace the 6000 South Australians killed in the war. In Western Australia a South African Rhodes scholar named Kingsley Fairbridge struggled bravely for years to win support for his child migrants' farm school. After his death two more Fairbridge farms were opened in Victoria and New South Wales. The Dreadnought Fund and the Big Brother Movement also found places for British boys on Australian farms. With all these schemes government assistance was given to some

212,000 British newcomers in the 'twenties and to less than 7000 in the 'thirties.

One unusual project was Western Australia's Group Settlement Scheme. Aid was offered to poor British migrants who were placed in small groups to carve out dairy farms and orchards in the heavily timbered south-west. As a pioneering effort it was not very successful, but it brought the state a large proportion of oversea migrants and paved the way to closer settlement. In other states closer settlement mostly followed pre-war patterns. Big estates continued to be broken up either by private subdivision or by government purchase. In each state large areas were provided for the settlement of returned servicemen. This proved a very expensive venture. By the original wartime plan the Commonwealth was to lend each settler enough money to make a start. By 1924 more than 36,000 ex-soldiers were allotted farms and the plan had cost £35 million. Not many of the blocks were suitable for men with small capital; much of the land had to be cleared, and before it was in full production prices fell alarmingly. The soldier farmers were too heavily in debt to pay their way without great hardship. By 1940 more than half of them had sold or forfeited their blocks. Almost the only bright spots in this distressing experiment were in the irrigation areas. One of the most successful was at Red Cliffs near Mildura, where some 600 ex-servicemen transformed a drab wilderness of mallee scrub into flourishing orchards.

Each state had irrigation of some kind by 1940, both private and public. The largest works were on the River Murray and its tributaries. At its mouth long barrages stopped the inrush of the sea, and near its source the mighty Hume Reservoir held three times more water than Sydney Harbour. With more than twenty-five navigation locks and weirs the unpredictable flow of the great river was largely under control a century after Sturt's exploration. Although sheep stations still lined the Murray banks, its waters irrigated more than 250,000 acres of crops, nearly one-third of them grown by ex-soldiers. Old and new river towns also prospered, their ordinary trade and services supplemented by butter factories, canneries, packing sheds and wineries.

Queensland had a great dam on the Dawson River and Tasmania was harnessing some of its mountain streams and lakes for hydro-electricity, but Victoria was the leading state in irrigation. It shared the Murray water with New South Wales and had other schemes as well. The biggest was in the Goulburn Valley where miles of channels carried water from great reservoirs at Eildon and Waranga to large areas of farmland. Another network of channels supplied towns and holdings throughout the dry mallee areas and the Wimmera. By 1940 nearly one-quarter of the state was arti-ficially supplied with drinking water for homes and livestock. In New South Wales an immense dam at Burrinjuck stored the snow waters of the Murrumbidgee for summer use in the Griffith district 240 miles away. Rice-growing began here in 1924 with seed from California, and within five years was supplying the continent's needs. Another great dam at Wyangala on the River Lachlan, and water from the Murray, gave New South Wales several thriving new areas of closer settlement. Water for irrigation in South Australia was mostly supplied by pumping stations, and in dry seasons river levels were maintained by releases from the storage basin of Lake Victoria. On the lower river large areas of reclaimed swamp were turned into irrigated dairy farms.

The great achievements of irrigation and flood control produced a mighty national asset, but it was very costly in public and private investment. Millions were spent on the Murray works and millions more on the Goulburn Valley Scheme. As well as reservoirs and channels states had to provide roads, schools and a host of new services for isolated settlements that could not bear the cost them-selves. Irrigation also upset the habits of native birds that now feasted on crayfish in water channels instead of insect eggs on distant dry claypans. As a result vast pastoral areas were ravaged each year by invading myriads of grasshoppers. Meanwhile river settlers had other lessons to learn. Watering raised salt levels to lay waste promising orchards until deep drains were made. Frosts came without warning to ruin citrus crops, and unexpected summer rains sometimes spoilt drying fruit. Good seasons often brought over-production and weak markets. These difficulties were gradually overcome. By 1939 the great new irrigation areas were yielding a profitable return, much of it from dairies and livestock fattened on watered pastures. As in the other states fruit-growing had doubled. Tasmania led in apples, Queensland in pineapples, New South Wales in bananas and oranges, South Australia in wine grapes and Victoria in apricots, pears and peaches. The continent's fruit crop satisfied local needs and provided a steady income from exports. This great expansion was shared by sugar-growing. By 1939 the cane belt stretched for over a thousand miles from Clarence River to Cairns. More than 9000 cane farms and thirty-five sugar mills provided support for over 200,000 people, while production had multiplied five times in twenty years to leave a valuable surplus for export.

By contrast wheatgrowers made a poor showing. Although grain was worth 8s. 6d. a bushel in 1920, the accumulation of unshipped wartime stocks checked expansion. Ten years later, depression brought a new cultivation record of eighteen million acres of wheat and seven million acres of other cereals. For the first time more than 200 million bushels were harvested, but prices fell below 2s. 4d. and even then wheat exports were hard to sell. The annual crop area shrank until prices rose in 1936, but two years later they fell to the lowest recorded level of 2s. a bushel. In these uncertain years the most notable changes in farming were bulk handling and the increased use of tractors. New South Wales built its first government inland silo in 1920. Elevators filled it with wheat carted from the farms in open bags and railways carried the grain in bulk to the docks where it was poured into ships without heavy work by wharf labourers. Western Australia and Victoria ventured into bulk handling during the 'thirties. Meanwhile tractors multiplied, although nearly half the crop still depended on horses. Declining returns made debt-stricken farmers watch their costs carefully; while labour remained cheap and plentiful, many growers found hay for horses less expensive than fuel for tractors.

Woolgrowing followed much the same course as wheat. Sheep numbers rose steadily to pass one hundred million in 1925, and kept on rising. For the first time in sixty years, wool prices climbed above 20d. per lb. in 1924, bringing a short boom in which one Australian-bred merino ram sold for 5000 guineas. In spite of more care in breeding, wool prices fell below 8d. in 1931 when the clip first exceeded three million bales. After 1933 returns fluctuated around 13d. giving woolgrowers little promise of security; but although wool was being challenged by synthetic fibres in world markets, the value of pasture land rose rapidly wherever fat lambs could be reared. By 1940 more than ten million lambs were marketed each year as growers used more fertilizers and fodder plants for pasture improvement. This added to graziers' costs even though it made their returns more certain.

Gold-mining languished in the 'twenties, but hard times sent large numbers of unemployed to fossick for nuggets and reopen old workings. Rising prices in 1930 sent the gold yield soaring; by 1940 gold was selling locally for more than £10 an ounce. Rising prices also helped the silver, lead and zinc mines at Broken Hill, and another great silver-lead field opened at Mount Isa in west Queensland.

Although primary production still earned over nine-tenths of Australia's growing export income, the number of men in rural employment did not increase. Each state could boast new records in smallholdings, but closer settlement nowhere matched urban growth. By 1939 only one in every three Australians lived in rural isolation. Sydney and Melbourne each had more than a million people and another million lived in the other capitals. Unfortunately the increase in city and suburban dwellings did not keep pace with population growth. Thousands of old buildings were becoming sub-standard and slums were spreading, yet with one million more people the capitals gained less than a quarter of a million new houses. Nine-tenths of this expansion took place in the 'twenties when the Commonwealth spent heavily on war service homes. Some states also started housing schemes and moneylenders were eager to help home-builders, but the building trade came to a standstill in the depression and did not recover until 1936. The cities then had an acute shortage of houses for rent, a problem that could not be overcome by makeshift flats, shared homes or a swollen force of building tradesmen.

Other urban employment followed the same pattern. In the 'twenties the number of factories and hands rose rapidly. Twice as much machinery and power were used, and production doubled. But four-fifths of these industries were in New South Wales and Victoria. In the other states enterprise seemed to be strangled; only public establishments prospered. Apart from the heavy industries, most private factories were still short of capital, and contrived to keep open with the aid of subsidies and protective tariffs. This insecurity was exposed when depression brought stagnation. The employment and output records of 1928 were not reached again until 1936. By that time there were about one and a half million wage-earners; they outnumbered employers by less than three to one. In the towns this average was much higher; in the country districts most families could still claim independence, for only 14 per cent of the wage-earners were rural workers.

The growing cities needed a great extension of services, most of which made heavy demands on public funds. By 1940 most metropolitan houses were connected to water mains and sewers. The consumption of gas had doubled in twenty years, while electricity multiplied five times. In some states light and power were still provided by private companies, but increasing demand for improved services was making public ownership essential. Victoria took the lead in 1919 by creating a State Electricity Commission. Under the management of Sir John Monash the immense brown coal deposits at Yallourn were opened, a generating station and

PLATE XIX

(*a*) Perth from the air

(*b*) Melbourne from the River Yarra

PLATE XX

(*a*) Alfred Deakin

(*b*) Rt Hon. John Forrest

(*c*) Sir Charles Kingsford-Smith

(*d*) Sir Donald Bradman

Four famous Australians

PLATE XXI

(a) W. M. Hughes appealing for military recruits
in Sydney, 1939

(b) The Customs House, Darwin, after a Japanese air raid, 1942

PLATE XXII

Green Snipers' Pimple, Finisterre Range, New Guinea

town built, and power transmitted over 120 miles to Melbourne by 1924. In the next fifteen years power lines spread throughout the state to supply nearly half a million consumers in town and country.

Some services owed their expansion to the Commonwealth. By 1940 telephones quadrupled to connect over half a million subscribers. Broadcasting made even greater progress. The first radio stations built in 1912 near Sydney and Fremantle had proved their value during the war. In 1921 control of all public radio services was given to Amalgamated Wireless (Australasia) Limited, in which the Commonwealth became the major shareholder. When private wireless stations were allowed to operate five years later, some 60,000 listeners had been licensed. When new arrangements brought the Australian Broadcasting Commission into existence in 1932, nearly half a million homes had radio. By 1940 some thirty national stations and a hundred commercials entertained more than a million licensed listeners. Newspapers became more modern and, with broadcasting, brought the old world much closer, while local controversies such as Larwood's bodyline bowling in Test Matches agitated the whole continent and the cricket-playing world as well. Another priceless innovation was the pedal-driven transceiver designed in Adelaide in 1929. This 'pedal wireless' gave outback settlers communication with their neighbours and with the Flying Doctor Service inspired by Dr John Flynn of the Australian Inland Mission.

Civil aviation made good progress after an uncertain start. The first air services began between Geraldton and Derby, and between Adelaide and Sydney in 1921. Next year Brisbane and Sydney were linked, and Charleville with Cloncurry. Before long the mountain mining camps in New Guinea had regular services from the mainland. When depression played havoc with the early companies, only Queensland and Northern Territory Air Services (QANTAS) and Guinea Airways survived. By 1939 they had been joined by Australian National Airways and six other lines.

All had Commonwealth mail subsidies, and the continent had an air network of some 25,000 miles as well as several connections with the outside world.

Distance within Australia was also narrowed by motor vehicles. Their numbers multiplied rapidly in the 'twenties and more slowly in the 'thirties, to give an average of one car to every twelve people by 1940. This quick growth had many effects. Competition from motor transport brought railway building to a standstill, leaving the continent with some 28,000 miles of track that had cost more than £300 million, nearly one-third of Australia's borrowed money. Suburban passenger trains still prospered; Sydney followed Melbourne in electrifying its lines and added an underground city railway. The Commonwealth built the only important new country lines that ran from Oodnadatta to Alice Springs and from Pine Creek to Birdum. In spite of extra taxes on motor trucks, country railways were run at a loss in most states. In the cities horse-drawn traffic became rare as motor transport increased, and the accident rate rose rapidly. Cars and trucks also required immense government spending on roads and bridges. The cities had the best of them; although by 1940 the states claimed nearly half a million miles of country roads, three-quarters of them were not much more than surveyed tracks. One outstanding work was the Sydney Harbour bridge. It took nine years to build and, when opened in 1932, replaced countless passenger and vehicular ferryboats. With a span of 1650 feet, it carried tracks for trains and trams as well as six traffic lanes. Its cost of £9 million was steadily being repaid by passenger tolls. Most other bridges were free like the roads, and motorists helped to pay for them indirectly with state licence and registration fees and with Commonwealth taxes on petrol.

Motor transport also affected industry and trade. Many factories turned from building coaches to motor bodies. Assembly works and repair shops gave work to thousands of mechanics, and petrol distribution grew into such an important business that even the Federal Government became a major shareholder in the new

Commonwealth Oil Refineries Limited. Each year more money was invested in the motor industry. Car chassis and petrol, however, had to be brought from oversea and by 1939 represented more than one-tenth of Australia's total imports. They had therefore to be paid for with extra exports; this meant a search for new oversea markets which were found to be highly competitive. Primary production was increasing throughout the world, and in Australia seemed to have reached the limits of expansion, yet each year the growing population threatened to leave a smaller surplus for sale abroad. How then was trade to be balanced? If exports could not be increased, were Australians to run into more debt or go without the imports that improved their standards of living?

While prosperity lasted these problems did not seem difficult. The business-like Bruce tried to solve them by finding more markets and money. Most of his plans were spoilt by people who thought personal profits more important than national welfare. Wartime marketing schemes were replaced by voluntary wheat pools in most states and by the short-lived British-Australian Wool Realization Association. Price levels kept high, but once accumulated stocks were sold, woolgrowers returned jubilantly to their open auctions and wheatgrowers lost their enthusiasm for pools. Other producers were less optimistic. After 1924 an increasing number of government boards were created to find new oversea markets and to encourage production. They aimed to give growers fair and regular returns by charging a high price for produce sold locally, and using some of the money to pay a bounty on exports. Butter, sugar, dried fruit, wine and meat were assisted in this way, while some urban manufacturers were protected by higher customs tariffs. Although these schemes were designed either to increase exports or to decrease imports, they all increased local prices and thereby affected the level of wages.

In 1920 a Royal Commission appointed by Hughes found that the basic wage would have been £5. 16s. a week if the 'normal needs' principle of the Harvester Judgement had been properly applied. Although post-war inflation had reduced the value of the £ by two-fifths and living costs were rising everywhere, the actual basic wage was only £4. 2s. Next year Judge Powers of the Commonwealth Arbitration Court added 3s. to it on account of the boom in prices. Soon after automatic quarterly adjustments pegged the basic wage to the rise and fall of living costs as recorded by the Commonwealth Statistician. Many wage-earners, however, also received extra money as a 'margin for skill'. The adjustment of these margins and other special claims kept the industrial courts very busy. Delays could not always be avoided and some militant trade union leaders were quick to denounce the arbitration system. Many employers had similar doubts; some believed that unionists were dodging between Commonwealth and state courts looking for the highest benefits. A number of serious strikes brought the matter to a head. Bruce and Page tried to persuade the states to surrender all industrial arbitration to the Commonwealth; when this was rejected, they proposed that the Commonwealth should leave the entire subject to the states. This was turned down by the electors who threw out the Nationalist–Country Party coalition in 1929. Another important question raised by the Royal Commission in 1920 was the capacity of industry to pay a high basic wage; but high labour costs were not the only reason why some Australian manufacturers failed to compete with goods from oversea. The Tariff Board created in 1921 found that many protected industries used wasteful methods and poor equipment. In contrast, the youthful heavy industries paying the same high wages, produced the cheapest iron and steel in the world.

Most of the prosperity in the 'twenties was founded on government spending that increased public borrowing by more than £30 million each year. In 1923 Bruce invited the state Treasurers to join the Commonwealth in a voluntary Loan Council that aimed to prevent too many governments from borrowing all at once. Although New South Wales stood out at first, this Council was a useful step towards the Financial Agreement of 1929. By this important Act the Commonwealth took over the states' debts and contributed towards their repayment and interest charges. In return the states surrendered their rights to the Commonwealth's per capita payments. A Federal Loan Council of Commonwealth and state ministers was also formed to control all future borrowing. The Agreement was submitted by referendum to the people and approved by very large majorities in each state. Thus the states lost the long struggle to retain their financial independence. The Commonwealth no longer had to plead with state Premiers. They still had their income taxes and other revenues; but the Commonwealth through the Loan Council now had power over national borrowing as well as its old control of customs revenue.

The new order in public finance was long overdue and came at a convenient time. State debts amounted to more than £725 million and the Commonwealth owed another £380 million including war debts. About three-fifths of the total had been borrowed oversea. In 1929 prices for wool and wheat were falling fast and unemployment was rising. Next year exports brought £98 million and imports cost £131 million. This left an unfavourable trade balance of £33 million and another £34 million was due in interest charges on the oversea debts. To pay these sums the gold reserves in Australian banks had to be exported because no new loans could be raised in London. In 1931 imports dropped to £44 million and although exports fell to £78 million, accounts were nearly balanced after interest charges were paid. But gold stocks in Australia had become exhausted and the exchange rate with London rose quickly. It fluctuated for months until the Commonwealth Bank decided to make £125 Australian equal to £100 sterling. This rate helped to adjust oversea payments.

To outside eyes Australia seemed to be one of the first countries to recover from the world-wide depression, but within the continent the position was still deteriorating. The unemployment of unionists had averaged about 10 per cent in the 'twenties, but in 1932 it rose to 30 per cent. At the 1933 census a third of the 1,500,000 wage and salary earners were recorded as unemployed. Public works were stopped and many factories closed. In some states wages were taxed for unemployment relief. Family breadwinners, unable to find work, had to fall back on the small government dole, while others earned a few occasional shillings on relief works. Country roads swarmed with jobless swagmen, youngsters left school with no prospect of employment, thousands of marriages were postponed. Even the new 'talkie' picture shows were challenged by free community singing; but forced cheerfulness did not help governments to pay their way. Poorer states had not balanced their budgets for years, yet like the most prosperous still had to reduce their spending. In July 1930 the Commonwealth was visited by Sir Otto Niemeyer of the Bank of England. His message to a conference of state Premiers was that costs must come down even further. Six months later the Premiers planned to reduce their expenses by at least one-third. Although cost of living adjustments had already lowered the basic wage, the Commonwealth Arbitration Court reduced it further to £3. 4s. The Premiers had declared that all must share the burden; angry workmen found themselves carrying the heavy end of it. In Commonwealth and states the Premiers' Plan brought another split in the Labor Party, while in New South Wales there was further friction. The Labor Premier, John Thomas Lang, asserted that wages were more important than dividends, and refused therefore to pay interest to oversea lenders who, he believed, had conspired to wreck Australia's prosperity. He had other plans too that were no less threatening to property-owners. Although the Commonwealth met the payments that Lang repudiated, it also attempted to shut off his government funds. For some weeks Sydney was highly excited. The Treasury was barricaded and the state Savings Bank had to close its doors. Soap-box orators crowded the parks and streets, and fights were frequent. Young business-men formed a 'New Guard' and one of its venturesome knights with a sword hacked through the ribbon that Lang was about to cut at the Harbour Bridge opening ceremony; the Premier had him sent to a mental home for observation. Lang's followers were expelled from the official Labor Party and he himself was soon removed from office by the state Governor. For years the Lang group lingered on, a small noisy section in state and federal politics.

Under Lyons the Premiers' Plan was zealously carried out. Exports kept much higher than imports and enabled the Commonwealth to repay some of its oversea debt. In London Bruce did noble work in persuading bankers to convert their loans to lower interest rates. By 1939 only £20 million had to be sent abroad for interest payments and more than two-thirds of the public debt was owed to lenders inside Australia. Unemployment had fallen and the basic wage, raised by quarterly adjustments and by a 'prosperity loading', was now £4. 3s. Most of the recovery was due to the exchange rate that favoured Australian producers, but some of it came from new marketing arrangements.

An Imperial Conference in Canada aimed to increase trade between the Dominions and the United Kingdom. The Ottawa Agreement of 1932 gave some protection to Australian foodstuffs in Britain's markets, and in return Britain's manufacturers gained a greater preference in Australia. The plans were complicated and did not work very well. Britain took half Australia's exports and supplied 40 per cent of the imports. Although growers of perishable foodstuffs benefited, empire markets could not take all the wool, wheat and metals that still had to earn most of the Commonwealth's export income. In spite of the Ottawa plans, trade with foreign countries expanded. By 1935 Japan was Australia's second best customer, taking £17 million of wool and wheat exports and supplying only £4 million of imported goods. On the other hand, only £5 million of produce went to the United States whose tobacco, films, comics and cars cost Australia more than £13 million. Next year as part of a trade diversion policy, the Federal Parliament decided to reduce the imports from both these countries. They both retaliated, Japan by halving its wool purchases and the

United States by restricting the supply of car chassis. Fortunately this unnecessary quarrel did not last and new agreements soon restored trade. The diversion policy was only one of many signs that Australia could not prosper on empire trade alone. By 1938 the Commonwealth was again moving into depression. Once again falling world prices for wool and wheat proved the folly of too much dependence on primary produce.

However useful the Ottawa agreement, it had seriously hampered the growth of secondary industry, while the Premiers' retrenchment plan hindered improvements in education, hospitals and other social services, particularly in the less populated states. To relieve their pressing needs, a Commonwealth Grants Commission was created in 1933. It recommended generous payments each year to South Australia, Tasmania and Western Australia. In this way the poorer states were able to free themselves from stagnation and make a little progress. Other friction within the federation was less easily removed. Commonwealth marketing controls encroached on state rights and were often challenged. Interstate motor transport revived the problem of free trade within the continent. A proposal to give the Commonwealth control of air navigation was not approved when submitted to referendum. In some states there was talk of leaving the Commonwealth. Many Western Australians believed that they could have avoided depression but for the baneful effect of federation. At a poll in 1933 they voted by a large majority in favour of secession and petitioned Westminster to allow it. In New South Wales and Queensland jealousy of the capital cities led to demands for the creation of smaller new states. Everywhere town and country seemed at loggerheads and regional suspicions deepened. Even Federal Parliament's removal to its rural site at Canberra in 1927 did not end rivalry between Sydney and Melbourne.

In these two decades all Parliaments were so fully occupied with economic problems that little attention was given to political and social reforms. One valuable innovation was the Commonwealth

Scientific and Industrial Research Organization (C.S.I.R.O.). It shared in the successful control of prickly pear by cactoblastis caterpillars introduced from the Argentine. Other plant pests and animal diseases were later conquered by careful research and many new uses were found for primary products. The Organization's exacting work improved the standards of science throughout the Commonwealth. Social welfare was less well served. The pre-war pattern of 'New Protection' was undisturbed, but little more was added. Unemployment insurance was introduced in Queensland in 1923 and child endowment in New South Wales in 1927. In some states hospitals were given a share of the profits from public lotteries. Playgrounds and kindergartens became more common, while correspondence schools and broadcast lessons brought more opportunities for invalids and outback children. The Federal Parliament raised old age pensions, but its long-promised 'large, wise, contributory scheme of national insurance' remained an unfulfilled dream. Parliament chose instead to experiment with electoral reforms. The old method of first past the post had been replaced in 1918 by a system that took into account the second preferences of voters whenever no candidate had an outright majority. This innovation placated small groups like the Country Party and sometimes gave power to governments that represented only a minority of electors. Compulsory voting, first used in Queensland in 1915, was adopted by the Commonwealth in 1924 and later by all the states. Some states also widened the franchise for their Legislative Councils. Queensland went further; after years of bickering its nominated Council was abolished in 1922. Similar attempts in New South Wales failed; its nominee councillors were replaced in 1934 by members elected, not by the people, but by the state Parliament.

More momentous changes in the structure of the British Empire did not arouse much interest in Australia. However strong the traditional links with Britain, Australia was not greatly shaken by the discussions that led to the Statute of Westminster in 1931; ten years passed before Australia even endorsed it. In spite of Hughes's clamour for closer consultation, other Dominions had been left to press for a clearer definition of legal rights within the British Commonwealth. To many Australians, particularly supporters of the Labor Party, British ties suggested imperialist wars, while the League of Nations seemed to promise peace through collective action. The continent was regularly represented in the League Assembly, and after the Washington Treaties on disarmament the navy was greatly reduced and the battle cruiser *Australia* was solemnly sunk. But Bruce returned from an Imperial Conference in 1923 eager to co-operate with Britain in making Singapore a naval base that would defend the Pacific. He also began a costly defence programme that gave Australia by 1929 a small air force and a bigger navy than ever before.

Three years later depression wrecked this programme. Compulsory military training was abandoned, and navy and air force retrenched. Japan's growing strength was causing alarm, although her conquest of Manchuria was supposed to prove that no southern agression was intended. Fading hope in the League of Nations brought many excited arguments about the best defence strategy. Some favoured naval expansion and some a bigger army. Others wanted to concentrate on an air force to guard the narrow straits between the islands that screened the continent from northern threats. Many more doubted that any preparations for war were needed at all. As late as 1937 even the Prime Minister was sure that the British Navy would come to the rescue if any attacks were made on Australia. The menace of Hitler soon made it clear that Britain could spare little aid for any war in the Pacific. Australia must look to its own defence, although government leaders still talked of sending help to Britain if war broke out in Europe. The face of the continent rapidly changed. Years of depression had already exploded the myth of dependence on the wide open spaces; now defence preparation started something like an industrial revolution.

As war clouds gathered there was little difficulty in recruiting men for the armed services. In 1939 military training was made compulsory and before long industrial conscription followed. The country was desperately short of war materials. Money for defence was doubled, but some of it remained unspent because aeroplanes and other fighting equipment could not be spared by Britain, and were not easily obtained elsewhere. Because of exchange problems, imports and exports had to be controlled by licences. Railway workshops and private factories turned to defence production but machine tools were scarce. This meant more new factories and much training of new craftsmen. Mining was speeded up and large stocks of coal were stored in each capital for emergency use. Immense new steel works at Port Kembla made other quick expansion possible. Munition works and aircraft factories were built and preparations were made for holding large supplies, particularly of petrol and oil. Although Australia had never before built an aircraft engine, thousands were soon being made near Melbourne. Like many other industries, dockyards worked day and night. A new blast furnace and a five-berth shipyard came into being at Whyalla, while Sydney planned a mighty graving-dock capable of handling the largest ships. Everywhere new air-fields, training camps and industries called for more buildings, water, power and transport. Peace- and defence-production marched hand in hand. Destroyers were built in the same yard as cargo ships; machine guns and refrigerators often came from the same factory; Ford's motor works at Geelong assembled engines and made explosive mines. Strategic roads were improved and new highways were built; one important road link closed the six hundred mile gap between the railway termini of Alice Springs and Birdum, thus opening land communication between Darwin and the south. Many of these projects were shared by state governments which also prepared air-raid shelters and other protection for civilians.

Defence gave Australia its first large-scale national planning of economic activity. Production no longer depended on what consumers demanded; it was directed by governments for national needs. The work was gathering speed when Lyons died in April 1939. It moved faster when Robert Gordon Menzies became Prime Minister. Six years in Victorian politics and five in the Commonwealth had proved his unusual ability. Aloof as Bruce, Menzies was more openly impatient with those who did not follow his lawyer-like logic. Everyone had to be either for or against him; he allowed no middle choice, and in these days of crisis he was not popular. The Country Party withheld its full support and only voted with him to keep Labor out of power. Nevertheless Labor's strength was growing under John Curtin. He had no need like other politicians to protest that he was 'an average Australian'. His nationalism was born and bred, and backed by long years as a trade union organizer and a political journalist. Hard personal struggle made him an understanding leader even though he was unyielding on Party loyalty. Intelligent and shrewd, he united Labor and prepared it for wartime office.

After Lyons's death all parties supported the government in matters vital to defence. As Menzies said in his first broadcast as Prime Minister, it was everyone's business and everyone must get on with it. Four months later he announced on 3 September 1939 that Australia had followed Britain in declaring war on Germany.

CHAPTER 10

NATION: 1940–68

Defence was far from complete in September 1939, but the next two years gave valuable time for more preparation before total war spread to the Pacific. As in 1914, Australia's first duty was to protect its own coasts and the sea lanes that carried foodstuffs and supplies to Britain. This time no enemy islands or hostile squadron called for immediate attention, and for the first six months the war itself seemed at a standstill in Europe. By October two cruisers and five destroyers were serving with the Royal Navy, while at home reserves were called up for the R.A.N., merchant ships were armed and coasters were converted into mine-sweepers. A second A.I.F. was formed under a new commander, Thomas Albert Blamey, a farmer's son who had turned from school teaching to become a leading staff officer under Monash. In January 1940 his first brigade sailed from Sydney and others were preparing to follow for more training in Palestine. The R.A.A.F. had too many volunteers for its few aircraft, although the Empire Air Training Scheme was soon ready for thousands of recruits.

For most Australians business went on as usual until the German *blitzkrieg* roared through Belgium and Holland in May 1940. Next month France asked for an armistice and the British Expeditionary Force narrowly escaped from Dunkirk without its equipment and armour. August brought the Battle for Britain. With wave after wave of escorted bombers Hitler tried to smash British ports, airfields and industrial centres, but he was denied victory by the resolute pilots of Hurricanes and Spitfires. Some Australian airmen shared with distinction in this fearsome air fighting, and many more served later, not only with Fighter Command, but also in the flying boats that waged war on enemy submarines. By 1942 Australia had seventeen squadrons in Britain, some of them active in the heavy bombers that were beginning to spread nightly devastation in Germany. Before war ended the R.A.A.F. in Britain lost more than 5000 lives.

The fall of France brought Mussolini into the war in June 1940 and blew the lid off the Mediterranean powder keg. Germany's control of French ports and Italy's possession of Libya and Eritrea threatened British strength in the Middle East and its important oil supplies. Malta and Egypt thus became vital to Allied defence. An early attack on the headwaters of the Nile was defeated but British shipping between Suez and Gibraltar was badly beaten by dive-bombers. Although the long sea route around Cape Town had to be used, Malta and the northern ports of Egypt were held, forcing the enemy to use Tripoli and long land routes for the stores needed by its army in Libya. The North African desert war thus hinged largely on supply lines and the control of ports. The campaign began in September 1940 when 200,000 Italian troops crossed the Egyptian border. While they waited for reinforcements they were attacked by Allied forces which included one A.I.F. division. By February 1941 the Italians were driven back half-way to Tripoli. They lost much equipment and nearly half their army as prisoners, but their resistance was stiffening as Allied supply lines lengthened.

Australian cruisers and destroyers had scored notable successes against the Italian fleet before March 1941 when they helped to win the decisive battle of Cape Matapan that put British ships in control of the eastern Mediterranean. But a German invasion of Greece now threatened to bring enemy bombers within range of Suez and the oil ports of Syria and Palestine. Part of the Allied desert army was sent to Greece in April, only to be outnumbered on land and in the air by the Germans. Though the Allied withdrawal was skilfully planned, large numbers of men were hastily landed on Crete where they were soon overwhelmed by airborne German troops. In both places, Blamey's men had formed the rearguard and suffered heavy losses. Nearly six hundred were

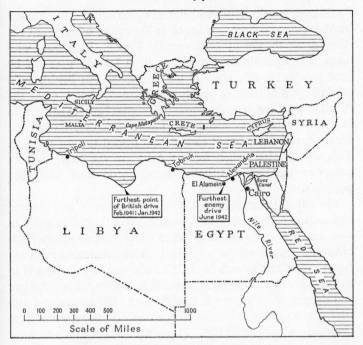

Map 8. The North African campaign, 1940–2.

killed and five thousand were taken prisoner. There were more casualties in June when an Allied force helped the Free French to regain Syria and Lebanon from pro-German control.

Meanwhile the Allied line in Libya had been attacked by strong German and Italian forces led by the Nazi General Erwin Rommel. His tanks and dive-bombers rolled back the Allies to the Egyptian border before he was checked by short supplies. Behind him the port of Tobruk was still held by a garrison of 31,000 including four A.I.F. brigades. Repeated attempts to relieve them by land failed, although British and Australian destroyers made risky runs on moonless nights to bring stores and carry off the wounded.

Each enemy attack was met with fierce counter-attacks. The Tobruk 'rats' remained defiant from April to December when at last the Allies drove the enemy back towards Tripoli. Reinforced with tanks and planes Rommel turned again in January 1942 and by June was within fifty miles of the Nile delta, but British naval action kept him short of supplies, particularly petrol, while the Allied strength was steadily growing. The great battle of El Alamein in October 1942 was mainly an infantry victory, though the timely arrival of anti-tank ammunition helped to turn the tide. This was the last action for the A.I.F. in the North African campaign that cost Australia nearly 3000 lives and 1900 prisoners.

The fall of France, Dunkirk and Italy's entrance into the war had caused great shocks in Australia. Men flocked to enlist in such numbers that recruiting had to be checked so that defence industries would not be weakened. More shocks came when Japan moved into French Indo-China and seemed eager to add to its empire. Australian troops were sent to Malaya, Timor, Ambon and Rabaul, and Darwin was strengthened. Defence expenditure tripled as munition industries speeded up. Harbour booms were prepared and minefields laid. Planes were added to the air force and corvettes to the navy. The R.A.N. had 68 ships and 20,000 men, many of them patrolling the sea routes to Singapore.

Labor had just taken office under John Curtin when disaster struck in November 1941. The cruiser *Sydney* was lost with its entire crew off the west Australian coast, victim of a disguised German raider that was also sunk in the engagement. A few days later, on 7 December, Japanese planes bombed Pearl Harbor while seaborne forces attacked a dozen places in South-east Asia. The United States was now drawn fully into the war, but the Allies seemed powerless before Japan's lightning assault. Hongkong, Borneo, Manila, Rabaul and Ambon were lost in quick succession. With no proper air cover, Australians joined stubbornly in the defence of Malaya, but when Singapore fell on 15 February 1942 over 15,000 of them were taken prisoner. Four days later Darwin was bombed by Japanese planes from aircraft-carriers and from Ambon. In this first enemy raid on the Australian mainland 238 people were killed, eight ships sunk and much damage done to port, town and airfield. Dutch Timor was next attacked with more Australian losses, and more air raids on Broome, Wyndham and Darwin soon followed. Two A.I.F. divisions hastily withdrawn from the Middle East were too late to reinforce Singapore. British and American leaders wanted them for Burma's defence, but Curtin and his advisers insisted that Australia's need was greater. Before their convoy was ordered home 3000 of these seasoned troops were landed at Batavia to be taken prisoner when Java surrendered in March.

Within three months the Japanese had gained complete control on land and sea within a vast semi-circle reaching from Burma to Kamchatka. Their navy ranged far into the Indian and Pacific Oceans. By April 1942 Australia was cut off on north and west, and in danger of being isolated on the east. Its navy was battered and its land forces outnumbered in spite of reinforcement by American troops. It was pitifully weak in the air; although Beaufort bombers were beginning to be made, most of its aircraft were light training planes and few northern airfields were completed. In this grave peril, command of the South-west Pacific area was given to the American General Douglas MacArthur, hero of the last gallant stand in the Philippines.

Japanese submarines played havoc with coastal shipping, Sydney and Newcastle were shelled and two underwater midgets actually entered Sydney Harbour. To complete Australia's isolation from America Japan needed airfields in the Solomon Islands and Papua. A powerful convoy was sent on these missions, while the Allies mustered a fleet to reinforce Port Moresby in New Guinea. The two forces approached each other and although they did not meet, their planes began the Battle of the Coral Sea on 7 May. Both sides suffered big losses and the Japanese turned back, their first reverse in the

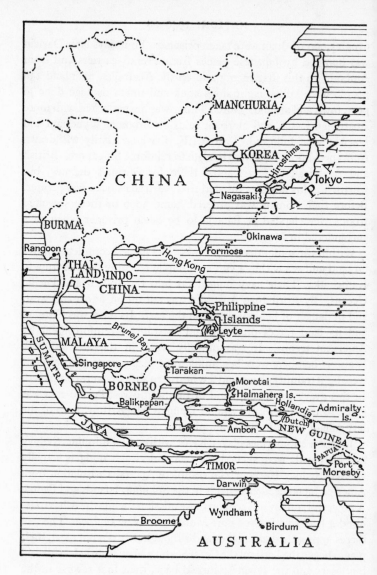

Map 9. The war in the Pacific, 1941–5.

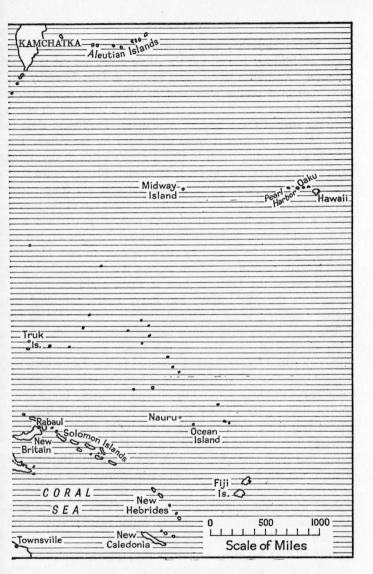

Map 9. The war in the Pacific, 1941–5.

war. Next month they were repulsed again in another naval air battle off Midway Island, but the Allies could not yet take the offensive. Australian troops were rushed to Port Moresby and even untrained militia were sent to Milne Bay, while larger Japanese forces were gathered at Buna for a land and air attack over the rugged Owen Stanley Mountains. They were close to Port Moresby in August when challenged by the Allies. The airstrip at Milne Bay was held after a week's battle in drenching rain, Japan's first failure on land. Meanwhile Blamey's men were winning on the Kokoda trail. With valuable aid from native porters, the A.I.F. steadily drove the Japanese out of the mountains, a long gruelling fight through malarial jungle and over 10,000-feet heights. Supplies were dropped from the air, but the wounded had to be carried by stretcher back to Port Moresby until Kokoda airstrip was taken. Beyond it many trails had to be cleared before the Japanese base at Buna could be attacked. Meanwhile the Allied Navy had heavy losses, including the cruiser *Canberra*, when American marines were landed in the Solomons to struggle for months against enemy airfields.

By the end of 1942 the tide was slowly beginning to turn. Although Allied leaders were determined to beat Hitler first, the United States Navy was hammering at Japan's outer defences and even Tokyo had been bombed by Flying Fortresses. In the south Pacific, shipping lanes were beginning to be cleared and American planes and tanks were reaching Australia in greater numbers. Strategy was changing too. For the attack on Japan the United States had good springboards in Alaska and Pearl Harbor, but Darwin was still being bombed and, like Sydney, was too distant to serve as a southern base. MacArthur now aimed to capture Rabaul which was only 2800 miles from Tokyo. His plan gave new importance to the enemy airfields within range of Rabaul and decided Australia's fighting role throughout 1943.

Buna had already been taken from the Japanese though enemy pockets still had to be cleared from near-by jungle. To Blamey's

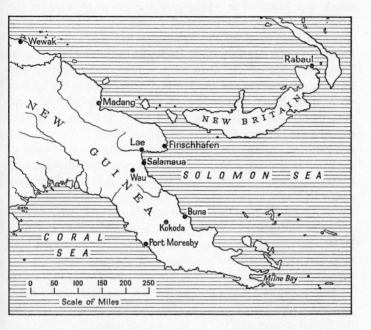

Map 10. The New Guinea campaign, 1942–4.

growing annoyance this slow and dangerous guerrilla warfare was left to the Australians, and sometimes took them far inland. The R.A.A.F. gave valuable support, although crews often complained of too much 'biscuit' bombing and transport duty; but Australians took a prominent part in the capture of enemy coastal bases and shared in the sea and air landings at Salamaua and Lae. After Finschhafen fell, part of the Allied force attacked New Britain; but long before Rabaul was taken, MacArthur changed to a new strategy. Instead of driving the enemy from one base after another, he decided to hurl his strength at the key points that guarded Japanese supply lines. More American forces arrived and an attack was launched at Madang, which led to invasion of the Admiralty Islands and provided a base three hundred miles closer to Tokyo. Soon the Americans had taken Wewak and jumped even farther forward to Hollandia in Dutch New Guinea. These big leaps left the Australians with more mopping-up and less support from sea and air. The R.A.A.F. shared in the landing on Morotai Island in the Halmaheras in September 1944, and next month Australian ships joined the Allied task force that crippled the Japanese fleet off Leyte Island in the Philippines. In this battle an enemy plane crashed and exploded on the bridge of the flagship *Australia*. Many officers and men were killed; among the seriously wounded was John Augustine Collins who six months earlier had been appointed Commodore, the first graduate of the Royal Australian Naval College to command the R.A.N.

Enemy strongholds still abounded in the islands but the main Pacific war moved away from Australia as MacArthur planned his promised return to the Philippines. An Australian army corps trained for months to share in it, but was sent instead to Borneo. In May 1945 the A.I.F. captured Tarakan and soon after Brunei Bay and Labuan. Although war had come to an end in Europe, the Japanese were still full of fight and casualties were heavy on both sides. In July more Australians seized Balikpapan and its big oil refinery, while the Americans pressed further north. Next month atomic bombs were used against Hiroshima and Nagasaki and on 15 August Japan surrendered.

In the islands the A.I.F. now had the task of guarding the many Japanese who gave themselves up. A more moving task fell to those who shared in liberating prisoners of war. For these the war years had been nightmares of sickness, hardship and short rations. Of the 9000 Australian prisoners in Italy and Germany, about 250 died, some 700 escaped and the rest were repatriated in 1945. Greater losses were suffered under Japanese hands. Some Australians were sent to camps in Manchuria and Formosa, but most were at Changi on Singapore Island. After May 1942 thousands were taken to work with natives and other Allied prisoners on the Siam–Burma railway, a dreadful ordeal from which one-fifth of them did not return. Others were sent to Borneo where poor food and ruthless treatment also levied a heavy toll. Of the 22,000 Australian prisoners taken by the Japanese only a handful escaped; nearly 8000 died and many of the men repatriated were too weak to walk.

Altogether more than 750,000 Australians joined the armed services; 64 per cent of them were in the army and 28 per cent in the air force, and about one-tenth were women; as in the first World War, Western Australia had the highest proportion of enlistments among the states. The death-roll numbered more than 29,400, two-thirds of them lost in the Pacific war. This was much lower than in 1914–18 in spite of more deadly weapons. Fatalities from wounds were greatly lessened by more efficient medical services. Much use was made of blood transfusions and of penicillin. Although war in the tropics brought serious health problems, the menace of sickness was reduced by sulpha drugs and new insecticides. The sources of quinine came under Japanese control, but atebrin proved more effective against malaria. Nutrition experts gave troops better diets, and more suitable uniforms were provided; but nothing reduced the horrors of war in its wasteful destruction.

To many Australians it seemed important that war criminals should be punished, but interest waned as the trials dragged on. Some thought that the Axis powers should be permanently crushed by reparations and harsh treaties. Many more also wanted Australia, however small its population, to have some say in the United Nations that offered fresh hopes of an enduring peace and a world free from the fear and want that caused wars. Labor leaders, and particularly Herbert Vere Evatt, insisted that the peace talks should not be dominated, as wartime policies had been, by the great powers. Evatt was an impetuous, forceful intellectual whose faith in the Labor movement made him step down from the High Court Bench to enter federal politics, but his ideals were not always understood by his enemies or his supporters. One difficult question was whether Australia should act independently or in co-operation with the British Commonwealth. Evatt believed it could do both, for he was not frightened of antagonizing men in power. When Britain had its hands full in Europe in 1944, he helped to make a pact between Australia and New Zealand that claimed for both countries a large share in the future affairs of the South-west Pacific. Next year at San Francisco he worked hard to improve the United Nations charter. Although his attack failed to remove the Great Powers' right of veto, he won Australia a name as a fearless, if rough and ready, champion of the smaller nations. When an Allied army disarmed Japan and began its occupation, Australia was given command of the British Commonwealth Occupation Force (B.C.O.F.) and from 1948 provided most of its strength.

War cost Australia nearly ten times more than in 1914–18. At its peak in 1943 defence expenditure amounted to almost half of the government spending. About two-thirds of the staggering cost was paid by taxes and the rest by loans raised this time wholly within Australia. In addition the Commonwealth received munitions, equipment and petrol from the United States under a lend-lease plan made before America entered the war because of exchange difficulties between dollar and sterling countries. In return Australia provided the United States forces with food and facilities. When the lend-lease account was settled after the war Australia owed about £8 million, most of which was later devoted by America to Senator Fulbright's scheme for travelling scholarships.

During war the power of the Federal Government was greatly increased by a multitude of security regulations and new laws. Many state responsibilities were taken over by the Commonwealth. The most important was income tax which had varied widely in different states. The maximum tax rate on personal earnings was 15s. in the £ in Queensland and only 8s. 6d. in Victoria. In 1942 income tax was made uniform, with the Commonwealth as the sole collector. Each state reluctantly agreed to abandon the field and received instead a yearly grant based partly on population. To pay war costs the Commonwealth tripled income taxes, increased others and imposed new ones; but where the states had previously raised more than three-quarters of the income taxes, they now received less than a quarter of the total under uniform taxation. Thus they became almost wholly dependent on the Commonwealth, and in turn it had to give them more assistance. In wartime this additional federal aid was needed for state roads and duplication of state railway tracks to cope with the transport of troops and munitions. Other special help was given to such projects as the pipeline that carried water from the River Murray more than 200 miles to Whyalla. Although the Premiers met each year to discuss their state needs, defence requirements came first.

The war effort brought many limits on individual freedom. Enlistment remained voluntary for service oversea, but single men were called up for the militia and part of it was sent, for the first time, outside Australian territory. Civilians were directed in their work and encouraged to put their savings into war bonds. Private investment was checked, building came to a standstill, house and land sales almost stopped, rents were pegged, and share selling was restricted in the stock exchanges. Manpower regulations limited civilians in their choice of occupation, and more than 200,000 women were drawn from their homes to become wage-earners in shops and factories. Civilian travel by interstate trains and planes was restricted by priorities that favoured servicemen. Civilian standards of living were severely cut in order to maintain supplies for Britain and for Allied forces in the Pacific. Rationing began with petrol in 1940 and private cars were soon limited to sixteen miles each week. After Darwin was bombed, identity cards and coupon books were issued; clothing, butter, tea, sugar and meat were rationed. These measures made civilian life less rigorous than in Britain but more so than in the U.S.A. The armed services and a thousand public and private defence factories drew labour away from the farms, and drought brought further austerity. Phosphate supplies were shut off when Japan seized Nauru and Ocean Island, and crops went short of fertilizers; but more tractors and machinery helped the farmers, and many labour problems were solved by a land army of women until men could be released from war work. Although yields of wheat and butter fell far below pre-war levels, meat production remained high and canned supplies increased.

The transition from war to peace was slow, but not haphazard. Reconstruction had been carefully planned by Labor leaders who believed that the nation's forces should now be mobilized for a vigorous peace-effort. To Joseph Benedict Chifley national planning was as important for winning the peace as it had been for winning the war. Experience had taught him to hate the sequence of reckless booms and disastrous slumps that had bedevilled Australia's progress. At twenty-four he had been the youngest engine-driver in the New South Wales railways, but for taking part in the 1917 strike he was reinstated only as a cleaner. Undaunted he set himself to study banking and public finance and he entered federal politics as the depression began in 1929. In the next years he nearly lost his voice as he urged the Labor Movement to unite and fight for a better deal for more people. This great object he liked to call 'the light on the hill'. It led him back to Canberra where as Treasurer he managed Australia's war economy. At Curtin's death on the eve of victory, Chifley became Prime Minister. He saw the light glow brighter as his peace aims began to provide jobs and rising standards of living for all, but his plans were difficult to turn into laws. Federal Parliament was still limited by its constitution, and neither states nor electors were always willing to allow the Commonwealth to extend its powers. Some of Chifley's plans went awry, but in success and disappointment he remained calm, watching his policy of full employment begin a new epoch in Australian history.

By the end of 1946 more than nine-tenths of the fighting forces were back in civil life. Many returned to their old jobs, and the rest were not left at a loose end. Gratuities, paid in instalments, gave them money to spend; loans from government helped many to start in business and trade, and work was found for others. This time soldiers were settled on the land with more care. Commonwealth and states co-operated to select and train applicants. Most blocks were equipped with water, homes, fences and sheds, and some were cleared for crops by powerful bulldozers. These preparations took time, but gave ex-soldiers profitable work and experience as well as better prospects of comfort and success before they were allotted their own holdings. Although only 3500 soldiers were settled by 1950, their numbers rose to 16,000 in the next decade. In the cities the Commonwealth Reconstruction Training Scheme helped thousands more ex-servicemen and women to complete university courses and to learn vocational skills. All received free instruction, and living allowances were given to full-time students. Help to build and buy homes was also available for servicemen, and those with war injuries received pensions and free medical treatment.

Restrictions on wheat growing were lifted in 1945 and more than 100 million bushels were exported in the next two years. Although oversea prices rose, the Commonwealth with the states' consent still bought each harvest at fixed rates and controlled the cost to local consumers. Production passed old records in 1948 and oversea sales soared above 21s. a bushel, but next year an International Wheat Agreement gave Australia an export quota of 80 million bushels a year and fixed the price at about 16s. The area under wheat declined and many farmers turned to wool-growing which had advanced rapidly once the accumulation of wartime stocks was sold. Sheep numbers rose each year and wool prices leaped from 15½d. per lb. in 1946 to 63d. in 1949.

The great advance in rural production was not all due to better prices. The states planned many new irrigation projects and great extensions of existing schemes, while the Commonwealth planned further increases, and hydro-electricity as well, by diverting the waters of the Snowy River through mountain tunnels into the Murray and Murrumbidgee. The C.S.I.R.O. and smaller expert groups helped to solve many other farming problems. With careful plant study, tobacco-growing quadrupled in Queensland and doubled in Victoria and Western Australia. Wool yields were increased and improved by better pastures; soon the rabbit pest was to be checked by myxomatosis and new poisons. Attention was given to the quality as well as the quantity of wheat when soil study revealed important mineral deficiencies in many districts. Some wholly unproductive areas were treated with trace metals and became amazingly fertile. The activities of the C.S.I.R.O. were almost without limit. In pre-war days it had paved the way for new paper-making industries by improving production of wood pulp from eucalypt trees. Now it advanced other primary industries and even experimented with rain-making.

While science increased the employment of rural resources, high prices for primary produce gave Australia an export income that was six times higher in 1949 than before the war. To Chifley this swollen income was an invitation to make the Commonwealth more independent of oversea borrowing. By restricting imports he gave Australia a very favourable balance of trade that helped to pay oversea loans as they fell due and to build up a big reserve fund in London lest export values should fall. To make Australians pay for their country's development he kept taxes high. With few imports to buy, people were encouraged to save, and much of their money found its way into Commonwealth Security Loans. Governments were thus able to undertake the public works that soon led to rapid industrial growth.

Although the war had proved that Australia could make anything, the tests of peace production were more varied. People were not content with austerity; they wanted things that not only worked well but also looked smart. Individual needs, however, had to wait. Although defence production ended sharply, there was little unemployment. New jobs abounded, though many raw materials were scarce and power supplies were inadequate. Post-war coal production rose to sixteen million tons by 1950, but strikes and shipping shortages often left cities without gas and electricity. This brought more fuel oil and diesel engines into use and more dependence on local coal supplies. The yield from Queensland mines doubled and even South Australia opened its remote brown coal deposits. One after another the states followed Victoria's example and took full public control of electricity supply. Immense new power stations were built and more had soon to be added to meet the growing demands.

At first most of the new post-war factories were small, but by 1950 every secondary industry was bursting at the seams. Many were making goods that used to come from abroad. Notable expansion took place in the manufacture of textiles and clothing, chemicals and paints, electrical apparatus and rubber goods. The largest increase was in metal-work and engineering which also employed the most labour. Farmers were demanding new and more varied equipment to replace their worn machinery and their sons and workmen who now preferred city jobs. Housewives wanted refrigerators and many other electrical appliances, and factories required more machines to make them. Everywhere production depended on transport, and, with restricted imports, new vehicles were scarce. Railways needed modern engines and carriages, and their main lines needed relaying to a standard gauge. Trolley cars and motor buses began to replace trams in each capital city except Melbourne. Motor trucks had become a necessity for rural producers and city firms, while even wage-earners no longer thought of cars as a luxury. Before long a dozen major companies from Britain and the United States had large assembly plants in Australia, and locally made motor vehicles followed. The pioneers, General Motors–Holden Limited, began producing in 1948; by 1969 they had made two million cars.

Each state was eager for development and regional rivalry revived, though with less of its earlier bitterness. All needed money to expand their public services, but Chifley wanted to disperse industries. This seemed to favour the poorer states who now claimed that they got what they asked for more often than their richer neighbours at the Loan Council and Premiers' Conferences. One desperate common need was housing. The war years and a record marriage-rate had aggravated the shortage. Although this was a state problem, Chifley agreed to help. Many materials were in short supply and most private building was restricted, but by 1949 large federal grants and heavy state spending had brought more than 100,000 new houses, while another 60,000 war service homes were provided. These new records were not sufficient for the nation's natural increase. The shortage of houses became more acute when the Commonwealth began an immense immigration programme.

A post-war agreement with the United Kingdom gave free passages to ex-servicemen and assisted passages to other British residents. Migrants were also brought from other European countries and many more were sent by the International Refugee Organization. A greater number came with no assistance at all, though many did not stay. Altogether by 1949 the permanent newcomers added 200,000 to the population and carried it past the eight million mark. Some assisted migrants went to private homes; most were temporarily housed in hastily built hostels and disused military camps. Before European refugees could choose their own work, they had to stay for two years in jobs found for them by the Commonwealth Government. Thousands were sent to such projects as the Snowy River Diversion and many others were employed on urban roads and waterworks. Before long these new Australians were doing a large part of the nation's heavy manual labour; old Australians turned to the mechanical equipment that was rapidly reducing the strain of work throughout the continent. Where men had toiled for decades with bare hands and

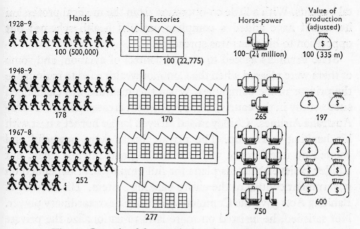

Fig. 4. Growth of factory industries, 1928/9–1967/8.

crude tools, post-war workers had power-driven machines for every job however great or small. They had better wages and working hours too. In 1946 the Commonwealth Arbitration Court increased the basic wage, and next year awarded a 40-hour week spread over five working days.

By 1949 less than 1 per cent of the labour force was out of work and over 40 per cent of the population was gainfully employed. The number of employers and those who worked for themselves had not risen since 1939, but wage-earners increased to more than two and a half million; only 6 per cent of them were rural workers. Many new services were added to 'New Protection'. Menzies had given the Commonwealth a limited child endowment in 1941 and Curtin followed with widows' pensions, funeral payments for the aged, unemployment and sickness benefits and increased maternity allowances. To pay the rising costs, Chifley introduced a special social service tax on incomes. This was deducted together with general income tax from wages each pay-day on a pay-as-you-earn plan. By agreement with the states Chifley also introduced hospital benefits. With a little co-operation from the medical profession he would have added a complete national health scheme; but opposition to his plans was spreading.

State Premiers agreed to central control of aviation, and some of them were pleased when the Commonwealth tried to nationalize the private airline companies. When this measure was challenged successfully in the courts, the Government created its own Trans-Australia Airlines. Chifley raised an even larger hornet's nest with his banking legislation. The private banks were powerful and wanted no interference with the lending and interest rates; but Chifley believed that his plans for full employment depended on government control of the entire banking system. His first set of Banking Acts gave the Commonwealth Bank extraordinary power. Not satisfied, he insisted on more laws to nationalize the private banks. When these were declared to go beyond the powers of the Federal Constitution, Chifley used the expanded Commonwealth Bank as a check on its rivals' business. Australia's credit had never been higher oversea, but by 1949 prices were rising everywhere and inflation was threatening.

Chifley's toughest problems came from the ranks of labour. On waterfronts and coalfields trade unions insisted on strikes over every trivial complaint. Although the Commonwealth Government gave them special tribunals they refused to be placated. Many unionists seemed not to care who led them. Their apathy played into the hands of militants who by trickery with voting papers had themselves elected as union officials. Some were Communists who thought 'class war' was much more important than full employment. Their control of waterside workers, coal miners and ironworkers became more serious as the worldwide spread of communism developed into cold war. To Chifley the control of unions was their own affair. Again and again he appealed to unionists to throw out their false leaders in fair and open fight, but the Communists hit back. In the winter of 1949 the entire nation was disrupted by a severe coal strike. Chifley

PLATE XXIII

A modern 'Mullenizer'—a five-ton steel ball dragged by two heavy tractors—clearing Soldier Settlement plots in the Heytesbury Forest, Victoria

PLATE XXIV

(a) A condemned terrace, Adelaide

(b) One of the houses that replaced it

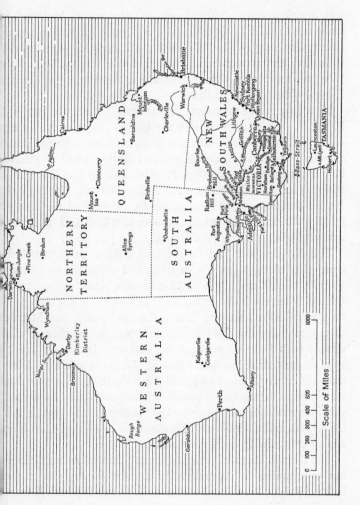

Map II. Australia, 1863–1968

213

took drastic action against the miners' union and its leaders. The strike soon ended but it added to the popular grievances against Labor. Too many of Chifley's plans, particularly his banking laws seemed to aim at socialism. Federal elections at the end of the year gave a sweeping victory to Menzies, now leading a reformed Liberal–Country Party alliance.

Next July the Commonwealth was again at war. Its men with B.C.O.F. were the first to join the United States in the United Nations' fight against Communist invaders in South Korea. More recruits were sent and the Australians distinguished themselves in bitter rearguard actions at Pakchon and on the Chongchon River. The R.A.N. and R.A.A.F. also did well, although the United States provided most of the forces and had the heaviest losses. Australian casualties numbered 281 killed and 1250 wounded when the armistice was signed in July 1953.

The Korean War had far-reaching effects. It hastened the treaty that brought peace with Japan and ended the occupation For mutual defence in the Pacific, Australia, New Zealand and the United States made the Anzus Pact; in London it was thought to be a withdrawal from the British Commonwealth but Menzies soon proved that this was not intended. R.A.A.F. squadrons were already with British forces fighting terrorists in Malaya and by 1954 an Australian battalion followed. In 1950 the United Kingdom and other nations had joined Australia in the Colombo Plan which aimed to help the countries of South-east Asia whose newly won independence was threatened by poverty and low standards of living. Australia's main contribution was in money, machinery and special training for Asian students.

The Korean War sharpened Menzies's determination to stamp out communism in Australia. As militant leaders still caused industrial disputes, a new law armed the Commonwealth Arbitration Court with power to use secret ballots in trade union elections and proposals to strike. To dissolve the Communist Party another Act was passed, but it was challenged and found unconstitutional.

Undaunted, Menzies asked electors to give the Commonwealth the necessary powers. At first a favourable vote seemed certain, but a vigorous campaign by Labor convinced many people that any critic of government might be denounced and punished as a Communist. In the referendum nearly five million voted and the proposal was rejected by an overall margin of 52,000 with 'no' majorities in New South Wales, Victoria and South Australia. But the Communist question still caused trouble. A few vigorous Roman Catholic laymen and other enthusiasts had encouraged unionists to form Industrial Groups in 1945 to fight communism within the Labor Movement. They gained strength from the reports of new Australians who had suffered under Communist rule in Europe. Many militant union officials were soon replaced by anti-Communist Groupers, whose tactics and criticism of the Labor Party were often as disturbing as those of the Communists. Evatt, who had become leader after Chifley's death, tried to keep the Labor Party united in its traditional policies, but the Groupers in the eastern states were implacable. Open revolt came in 1954 when Evatt recklessly attacked the Royal Commission on Espionage which examined the documents taken by the Russian diplomat Vladimir Petrov from his embassy in Canberra. The anti-communists broke away and soon formed the Democratic Labor Party. Although its supporters were too few to win elections, their votes were sufficient to keep the official Labor Party out of office in the Commonwealth and in some states. Long after the Communist threat had subsided, the Liberal–Country Party alliance was left to govern without much danger from its divided opponents.

The Korean War hastened Australia towards inflation. After Menzies's victory in 1949, Chifley's checks on enterprise were swept away by a flood of private spending while demands for labour pushed up wages and prices soared. In 1950 imports rose sharply to £600 million and 153,000 immigrants arrived. Oversea private investment reached new records and the Commonwealth Government borrowed abroad for the first time in twenty years.

Over 76,000 new homes were built, and Commonwealth subsidies encouraged the states to order thousands of prefabricated houses from Europe. Inflation was well under way before American stockpiling under threat of war shattered all records on oversea markets. In 1950-1 the Australian wool clip reached the un-dreamed-of total of £651 million, over ten times higher than pre-war levels. Prices fluctuated during the season to give an average of 12s. per lb. A Commonwealth plan to reserve some of this windfall for future use was rejected by woolgrowers and little could be done quickly to limit the spending spree that followed. By the end of 1951 imports had risen to £850 million, another 85,000 houses were finished and another 110,000 immigrants arrived, but retail prices and living costs had nearly doubled.

To limit inflation the Commonwealth added an extra 10 per cent to income taxes and dismissed thousands of civil servants. They quickly found work because the government also started a large and costly defence programme. But ships still crowded the ports with goods from oversea and Australia soon had an unfavourable balance of trade. Reserve funds in London dwindled alarmingly as wool prices fell below 7s. Drought played havoc with pastures, oversea investment dropped sharply and more than 100,000 wage-earners lost their jobs. This recession proved that some controls were necessary if Australia's prosperity was not to rise and fall with every change in the prices of pastoral produce. By drastic import restrictions Menzies protected oversea reserves, and unemployment was soon reduced. The huge surplus of oversea goods was quickly absorbed after the government eased taxes and encouraged banks to lend more freely. The building trade revived and industry recovered as eager spenders took advantage of the hire purchase offered by equally eager moneylenders. Homes became so full of radiograms and labour-saving appliances that each housewife almost required an engineer's certificate.

In 1950 the Commonwealth Arbitration Court had increased the basic wage and awarded females three-quarters of the male

ates. By the end of 1952 quarterly adjustments made the basic
wage almost three times higher than it was in 1939. Living costs
continued to rise, and employers clamoured for lower wages and
longer hours. The Arbitration Court rejected these claims but
decided to replace the automatic quarterly adjustments by regular
reviews of conditions in particular industries. Award rates and
the basic wage became almost dead letters; many employees in
private industry had much higher earnings. Wage disputes and
strikes became rare, and their revival in the mid-1960s was mainly
by government employees.

By 1953 the lead in national progress seemed to have passed to
private enterprise, leaving governments with little more than the
provision of public services and social security. Federal Parliament
had already increased child endowment and introduced free milk
for schoolchildren and life-saving drugs for the sick. Now it
added a voluntary Benefits Scheme by which contributors were
repaid part of the cost of medical treatment for themselves and
their families. Much larger sums went into defence, and into vast
public works that provided producers with power and water. The
state Parliaments had other heavy costs as births and immigration
swelled the population to nine million in 1954 and twelve million
in 1968. Hospitals and roads, ports and sewerage all cried for
expansion while the demand for housing was insatiable and
youngsters threatened to swamp the schools from kindergartens to
universities. Traffic jammed the roads and workers had to spend
long hours in reaching factories, shops and offices. New buildings
changed the skyline of cities and sprawling suburbs while radio,
television and newspapers helped to transform old attitudes of
isolation.

In 1954 Australia had joined other nations in a collective
defence treaty. Under the name of S.E.A.T.O. it was designed to
give South-east Asia protection from armed attack and freedom
from 'those subtle forms of aggression which undermine self-
government and subvert men's minds'. When Soekarno launched

his policy of confrontation to crush the newly-created union of Malaysia, Australian forces were committed to repel the Indonesians. The battalion stationed in Malaya was responsible first for mopping-up operations after Indonesian landings in the Malay states and in 1964 was sent to Borneo to cut off Indonesian attempts to invade Sarawak. These hostilities gradually ceased in 1965. By that time American troops had been engaged for more than three years against Communist forces in South Vietnam. Under pressure from President Kennedy, the Menzies Government sent a token contingent of forty men to widen America's diplomatic base for the conduct of the war. These moves were generally approved in Australia where it was widely agreed that aggression in South-east Asia should be checked. In 1964 the government decided, because of the Indonesian confrontation, to reintroduce national service. The decision aroused some opposition but enabled the increase of the army from four battalions to seven in 1965 and nine in 1967. When the South Vietnamese Government and army collapsed and the Viet Cong threatened Saigon, President Johnson decided in mid-1965 to fight the war with American forces: by 1967 they had over 500,000 troops in Vietnam. The Menzies Government, beholden to the United States for guaranteeing Australian forces during the Indonesian confrontation, decided with reluctance to commit a battalion to Vietnam in 1965. This move, and the further commitment of national servicemen, made opposition more vocal but an election failed to dislodge the government. The first Australian battalion was assigned to the area around Bien Hoa air base and in May 1966 the government committed more troops. The first Australian Task Force was made responsible for Phuoc Tuy province with freedom to conduct the war according to Australian methods evolved in Malaya. This province dominated the land link between the port of Vung Tau and Saigon and had long been held by the Viet Cong. The Australian force was increased to three battalions in 1967. Involvement in Vietnam had cost Australia 254 dead and 1144 wounded by 21 January 1969.

Four days before Sir Robert Menzies resigned as Prime Minister on 17 February 1966, his government introduced decimal currency based on dollars (worth 10s.) and cents (1.2d.) as legal tender. On 1 August 1967 it became the only legal currency in Australia. The political stability he had helped to create, together with Australia's potential, had attracted an increasing flood of oversea investment. By 1967 over $2500 million had arrived, half of it from the United Kingdom. Hundreds of British and American firms also came to make Australian associates or subsidiaries, most of them in Sydney and Melbourne. Apart from a short recession in 1960–1, industrial expansion appeared to have no limit.

The old problems of oversea markets and fluctuating prices shrank in significance beside the immense urban and industrial development, yet the expansion of rural industries was scarcely less spectacular. The limit of twenty million acres, accepted for nearly fifty years for Australian agriculture, was doubled in the 1960s. The wheat harvest rose from 164 million bushels to nearly 500 million and overflowed storage capacities in spite of large gifts to India and sales to mainland China. Crops of barley, rice, sugar cane and cotton doubled while tobacco and peanuts tripled and new sources of vegetable oil sufficed the nation's needs. The gross value of agricultural produce in 1968 reached a new record of $888 million. This was slightly more than half the wool cheque from a new record of 177 million sheep. Supplies of beef, mutton and dairy produce also increased while timber products helped to swell the export of rural produce to $2300 million. Japan had become the largest buyer of Australian exports, taking nearly a fifth of the total of $3000 million and slightly less than the combined share of Britain and the U.S.A.

What probably caused most excitement in the 1960s was the invasion of Australia's wide empty spaces by men and machines in search of minerals. In the 1950s coal production had crept up slowly to 16 million tons a year; in the next decade it doubled as many mines were mechanized and exports rose to 10 million tons.

Gold remained constant at about one million fine ounces a year and tin increased steadily from two thousand tons to five in 1966 while copper rose sharply from 30,000 tons to 120,000 in the 1950s and retained that level in the 1960s. The radio-active deposits at Rum Jungle in the Northern Territory were over-shadowed by mines at Mount Isa, where a large expansion pro-gramme added copper, lead and zinc to its output. The search for petroleum, mainly in New Guinea, had been long and unsuccessful but rich oversea oil companies began large-scale operations in 1950. On the mainland a dozen companies were at work in different states when a small flow of oil was struck in 1953 at Rough Range in Western Australia. The wild excitement on Perth's stock exchange outshone the golden days of Kalgoorlie. Everywhere oil shares brought fabulous prices. The boom soon passed but drilling went on in likely places, with generous subsidies after 1958 from the Federal Government. By 1967 more than 1300 wells were sunk and Australia had three commercial oilfields, Moonie and Alton connected to Brisbane by pipeline, and Barrow Island, Western Australia; between them they produced about 8 per cent of the nation's needs and oil refineries were established in each mainland capital. Other spectacular drilling produced natural gas, some from off-shore wells in Bass Strait. By 1968 plans were well advanced to pipe the gas to domestic consumers in Brisbane, Adelaide and Melbourne.

In the mid-1960s the stock exchanges in capital cities again went wild with new discoveries of nickel and copper, but the greatest expansion in minerals was in northern Australia. For many years the deposits at Iron Knob in South Australia had been the nation's main supply of iron ore, with production limited to about three million tons by an export embargo. Broken Hill Proprietary Company had a vast complex of smelters and steel works at Newcastle, Port Kembla and Whyalla. In the 1950s it opened more works near Perth for its rich iron ore from Yampi Sound. It had long been known that the Pilbara Division in the north-west corner of

Western Australia abounded in high-grade ore 'enough to supply the whole world', but the area remained empty except for scattered sheep stations and nomadic Aboriginals. In 1960 the export embargo was lifted. Geological surveyors were soon at work, using helicopters and modern equipment to speed their progress. Goldsworthy Mining Proprietary Limited, with some backing from an American firm, was first in the field. With a hastily-constructed railway to Port Headland, the firm won iron ore export contracts for over $200 million to be fulfilled at the rate of five million tons a year. Other large deposits were opened with more railways, and the tidal harbour at Port Headland was quickly transformed to load huge ore carriers. The tempo of exploration rapidly increased as other companies decided to exploit their mining leases. In 1962 Rio Tinto, mainly a British firm, merged with Australia's Consolidated Zinc; they were soon joined by Kaiser Steel of America to form Hamersley Iron. Their chief mine, Mount Tom Price, named after a Kaiser vice-president, was 180 miles from the coast but was estimated to yield 500 million tons of 60 per cent ore, with reserves of 4000 million tons of lower grade. With incredible speed gigantic machinery was at work, opening the mine, laying a railway, constructing the new port of Dampier and building two towns with modern air-conditioned houses and a desalination plant for water. In December 1964 Hamersley won a Japanese contract for 65 million tons of ore, the first of it to be ready for loading by July 1966. The programme was disrupted by a cyclone that swept away part of the railway and wrecked a train of 200 loaded ore cars. But the railway was finished a few days ahead of schedule and the first ship for Japan, the 52,000 ton *Huon Maru*, was loaded to capacity in seventeen hours in August. By 1968 the production of mines near the Northern Territory railway was being exported from Darwin, while other new deposits at Koolyanobbing, 300 miles east of Perth, and Port Latta in Tasmania helped to swell Australia's annual output of iron ore to more than twelve million tons.

Other spectacular developments were in bauxite and the aluminium industry. Great deposits of the mineral were opened at Weipa, not far from where Wilhelm Jansz made the first recorded landing in Australia, and at Gove in Arnhem Land; both were on Aboriginal reserves and raised questions of royalty rights. The mines were developed by Australian and American capital and required new towns and harbours. For smelting the alumina, refineries were opened at Bell Bay in Tasmania, Gladstone in Queensland and Newcastle, while the ore from other deposits in Western Australia went to Perth.

Prosperity and closer links with the rest of the world banished the evils of regional rivalry. The varied extensions to 'New Protection' had not created a welfare state, but they did reinforce the minimum foundations of security on which anyone might build with freedom and certainty. This security, together with full employment and patriotism bred by war, helped to bring old and new Australians together in a common purpose, conscious at last of their unity as a nation. Some critics still prophesied depression; others were alarmed by creeping inflation which brought unexpected hardship to many families. Blind to these dangers, most people chose to believe that national prosperity had come to stay. Visitors praised the Commonwealth for its splendid possibilities, but for complacent Australians the promise seemed already fulfilled. The golden age for work and leisure appeared to have dawned.

CHAPTER II

DESTINY

The Australian story is something like a fun-fair. The same things happen again and again. Ferris wheels go round and round, hurdy-gurdies grind out the same tunes, swings and see-saws move up and down. Everyone appears to have something to spend. Worries are left behind and troubles are forgotten. People press from one sideshow to another eager to sample everything. The biggest crowds throng round the lucky dips where anyone may draw a winning ticket. From outside the scene appears featureless and dull. The shouts and laughter are too carefree and light-hearted. Apart from the showmen no one seems more important than any-one else. What is the purpose of it all? How can a fun-fair give a young nation an inspiring history?

The pioneer writers of Australian history were not bothered by these questions; they gave the story very simple patterns. The early Governors and their officers appeared as men of varying worth who made good use of their lucky dips in land and convict labour. The explorers followed, almost superhuman in endurance and resolution. On their heels came the squatters with more lucky dips in land and wool. Then came gold, the winning ticket that brought population and self-government. Democracy and more free dips in land followed. The colonies flourished and soon had to federate, a lucky device that left history-making to the Common-wealth. Later historians looking more closely added more human touches and more lucky dips. Immigrants appear, tempted by free passages to take a chance on starting life anew. Governments, jealous of each other's progress, try their luck in reckless borrow-ing. City merchants and trade unions bid for bigger shares of prosperity. Beyond the public eye crowds move restlessly always eager to get rich quick. Lotteries and race-courses take a prominent place, but opportunities abound everywhere. Nobody wants to believe there are more shavings than prizes in the lucky dips.

This homely story omits more than it tells; it cannot be applied to every decade or all the people. Compared with old-world glories it seems to give the young continent scarcely any history worthy of the name. Here was no cradle of civilization. No enemies invaded these shores to quicken fervent nationalism. No colonizing crusade ever left this land to conquer and rule other countries. No local battles or revolutions disturbed this peaceful isolation. Only the beginnings appear unusual and the early years seem to account for every peculiarity. For good or ill the national character is supposed to have sprung from these humble origins. Too many attempts, however, have been made to interpret Australian history wholly through its beginnings. Now that Australia has come of age it needs a more complete survey, even if growing pains are hard to describe and harder to explain.

Some find an answer in geography. Isolation, climate and distance are sometimes seen as subtle forces that are shaping the Australians as the Aboriginal natives were moulded before them. The struggle for existence appears to be driving men into tribes with physical well-being as their sole concern. Even the fun-fair seems like a grotesque corroboree. This dismal view is unfair to the Aboriginal, and as a prophecy it has little appeal. Most geographers prefer to see a great triumph in the taming of a strange country by white settlers who came to terms with a wilderness and forced it to meet their needs. Sheep and cattle graze where kangaroos once roamed. Pine forests and rich pastures flourish where only scrub grew before. Fields of corn and irrigated orchards defy the ravages of drought. No wolves wait at these doors with threats of famine; instead each year brings new resources to swell the abundance. This triumph has been shared by many Australians whose descendants now live in cities and still resemble transplanted Europeans. Their clothes and houses and even their tight-lipped speech are little different from those of Britain. Each year the distinctive colonial marks become less noticeable. Most new arrivals, if they see anything strange at all, find it easy to make themselves at home. Only isolation persists as newspapers head-line local affairs more prominently than oversea news.

Other writers find economic explanations of Australian history. Some see the success of private enterprise, some the exploitation of labour, some the ravages of imperialism. Ample evidence can be found for each of these views. In the colonies' long fight with poverty everyone rode on the merry-go-round and the lucky dips were very important. The story always had two sides: one of success, the other of frustration. From the beginning speculators were eager for quick profits and had little care who paid the public cost so long as they lined their pockets. But most early investment went into land, and in spite of occasional booms its value rose very slowly. Many owners found themselves tied to Australia by their acres. Unwilling to work their land, they left it idle or leased it on terms that did not encourage careful improvement. Too often their land delayed colonial development by forcing genuine settlers further afield. Too often land hunger left immigrants with no use for their special skills and forced them to turn to manual labour. Heavy work and poor reward killed their enterprise and lowered their outlook to earthy levels. In town and country there was little advance in the art of living; instead everyone talked of standards of living, while wages and costs became national obsessions.

Some historians try to colour this story with Marxist theories. Here and there they are successful. The landless did struggle with squatters, trade unions have fought with employers and the little goldfield rising at Eureka provided a moral for many occasions. But anything like sustained oppression is hard to find. More obvious than any prolonged class war in Australia is the blurring of class distinctions. The miserly are everywhere scorned, however great their wealth. Local traditions defy the extremes of grandeur and poverty. Although this is supposed to cast the whole nation in a mediocre mould, a very wide range remains for each man to do what he likes. The equality that Australians boast is a freedom from gross inequality. In popular terms, if you 'have a go' it must be a 'fair go'.

Australia's quiet story is perhaps best explained by combining geographic and economic influences with the British tie. Botany Bay was chosen as a place of reform at a time when Britain faced revolutions in America, France and its own industries. British prisoners were working out their salvation in New South Wales when victory over Napoleon gave Britain command of the seas and altered the face of empire. The old search for naval stores, trade and strategic coastal bases was still important, but attention slowly turned to the vast hinterlands of Canada, South Africa and Australia. From haphazard beginnings the settlement of empty continents became more systematic as cheap land opened new prospects for British money and migrants. Australia's share of them was small and irregular but new settlements multiplied. Some survived early hardships to become Crown colonies, but British investment and British demand for raw material shaped their progress. Their long struggle for self-government was thoroughly British too, for the political freedoms won by the colonists were those they had wanted before they emigrated. Gold brought other freedoms but the colonists remained dependent on British markets, shipping and protection. The British tie was taken for granted. The few who questioned it were thought disloyal by the many who remembered their patriotism only on special occasions. Political reforms still had their origins in England although the colonies sometimes won them first. Only when federation brought 'New Protection' was there any clear Australian policy and even then it was partly British. To this day some British training is considered essential for Australian scholars and leaders, while each visiting Englishman is assumed to have more knowledge than local experts. Britain still supplies Australia with money and migrants, and the British tie still saves many Australians from thinking for themselves about international affairs.

Australia owed much to this link with Britain, but one of its ill-effects was a curious sense of inferiority. Measured by European standards everything colonial seemed to bear a stigma. For long decades local art, music and literature were dominated by the British tie. Old-world traditions were not seriously challenged until the 'nineties brought an upsurge of Australianism; but the new culture soon became timid and uncertain. Some writers and artists remained aggressively national, flaunting Australia's tears and triumphs with a wild abandon that delighted the irreverent. Others seemed scared of British reviewers and failed to please anyone. The creative fires that still burned were well-nigh quenched by war and depression. Although the Australian Broadcasting Commission gave welcome aid to local talent and Australian galleries encouraged local art, little Australian writing was thought worth publishing without the promise of sales in England. British readers were taught to see Australia as a land where convicts were brutally flogged, where bushrangers and dingoes thrived, where life was in peril from snakes and sharks. As late as 1935 a learned English visitor could announce that 'the rewards of literature in Australia were not good enough to make it attract the best minds'. Some writers jeered at his patronizing pessimism; others scorned their compatriots as uncultured and unappreciative. A more balanced approach, truer to the Australian spirit, came when local demand slowly expanded after the second World War. Although oversea publishers flocked in, and imported cinema, records and glossy magazines captured youthful imagination, Australian film producers and musicians faced another struggle for recognition.

The sense of inferiority also intruded at first into Australian sport. Racing, cricket and athletics were brought by early newcomers to flourish as widely in the antipodes as anywhere in the world. No peculiar local sport emerged until the gold rush when Victoria ventured into football according to Australian rules. The game spread through the southern states and became immensely popular, but found no international devotees. The gold rush also brought a closer organization of cricket clubs and the beginnings of intercolonial matches, but local standards were considered low. The first test match against an English eleven in 1877 told a different story and later triumphs added greatly to Australia's confidence. By 1900 Australian players were competing in international tennis and before long were winning prized world trophies. But old-world problems of amateur and professional status disturbed tennis supporters and hopelessly divided the patrons of Rugby football in New South Wales and Queensland. The Rugby 'Union' separated itself from the professional 'League' and thereby weakened its own chances in international games. The other football code of 'Soccer' was thought too English and had few followers outside the coal towns until newcoming Europeans formed their own clubs. In the twentieth century Australia was one of the few countries to take part in each of the Olympic Games, yet there was much hilarity and harsh criticism when Melbourne was chosen as the site for the Games in 1956. The result was a victory for local organizers as well as for the Australian runners and swimmers who won gold medals.

Whilst prominent sportsmen helped to put Australia on the map, other great men were sought by local biographers. The marks of personal prowess were abundant, but the ablest Australians seemed to prefer to remain anonymous. Although six thousand names will appear in the *Australian Dictionary of Biography* not many of the outlines fill more than a page. As elsewhere the men who blazed their trails most clearly are often less worthy of remembrance than those whose lives were too full for diaries. Revealing studies of great Australians are scarce; too many biographies have been written by admirers and overfilled with praise. Men like Polding, Robertson, Mitchell and Hanson remain almost forgotten while endless books are published about British Governors like Macquarie and explorers like Sturt.

In great part the Australians were themselves to blame for their apparent inferiority, although much of it was a pose. With profound affectations of their own, they have always been ready to decry pretence in others. Their unpolished manners seem to match their aggressive denial of any talent outside their own sportsmen. Their hospitality is generous and sincere, but their casual habits and crude language often invite criticism that brings them more smiles than frowns and never changes their ways. They always assert that Australia is the best place in the world to live in and that Australians have clear distinctive marks. They never willingly describe themselves as an old-fashioned oversea British society without a recognized élite. However unpalatable this judgement, it has strong historical support.

Remote and outlandish, the continent never gained the cream of British gentility. The convicts and assisted immigrants were unpromising material for nation-building; the poor relations and dependants of absentee investors were not much better. Exile in a strange land left many cowed and beaten, but some accepted the tough challenge of the bush in company with the venturesome young colonial-born. Before long two Australias seemed to emerge: the towns and coastal districts struggling to apply their old-world ideals, and the outback primitive and vigorous. From early years the 'typical Australian' was thought to be the nomadic bushman. In different decades he was shepherd, stockman, shearer and drover, but always an independent wage-earner with no permanent place of his own. Stifled by farm life and urban traditions and fearful of endearing family ties, his outback world was almost wholly masculine, rough and full of improvisation. After each spell of punishing work he spent his earnings in wild sprees with reckless improvidence. His lawless ways were supposed to infect some gold-diggers, and if he did not become a bushranger himself, his sympathies were never with the police. His great redeeming virtue was mateship; he stuck to his cobbers through thick and thin even when they were in the wrong.

The tense Australianism of the 'nineties elevated this legendary figure into a literary hero. To A. B. Paterson, son of a dispossessed squatter, writing from a city office, the bushmen with their horses and simple skills were the backbone of Australia. To Henry Lawson, wandering son of an unsuccessful selector, outback mateship was the secret of trade union solidarity that could free Australia from need and greed. But the old bush life was already passing when the *Bulletin* printed their robust verses. The 'wild colonial boys' were gone; the bushmen's last great spree ended with the drought of 1902 and mateship had its last fling with the A.I.F.

The ghosts from a romantic past filled some Australians with national pride and some with unhappy longing. The glories of the great outback lingered on, but it could scarcely support its own legend. The 'typical Australians', lean, tanned and tall, were never numerous and they became fewer as farmers drove them inland. They lasted longer in Queensland and northern Australia, but even there, pastoral expansion was checked by deserts. In this shrinking outback 'hard cases' may still be found, odd relics of a breed too restless and too primitive to fit into any pattern of civilized life. The roving bushman lives on in fiction losing his peculiarly Australian marks as he becomes confused with the legendary American frontiersman.

The bushman belonged to Australia's first century. Before 1880 many of them were drifting into the towns they affected to despise. What made the outback important to Australia was not its independent people but its wool and cheap land. However free the pastoral patriarchs and their casual labourers, their wool went to British factories and kept Australia dependent on British markets. As the chief source of export income, wool had much to do with the rise and fall of prosperity. Carried on the sheep's back, the colonies relied on imported supplies and neglected local manufactures. Sheep numbers soared but wool-growing kept the continent primitive and sparsely populated. Cheap land also had some of these ill-effects. It dispersed settlement and delayed industrial growth by drawing men and money from the towns.

Unlike wool, it did attract immigrants, and thus helped to make a second Australia in the temperate coastal belt.

The coastal settlers worked and sometimes drank as hard as the bushmen, but families kept them grimly practical and allowed no scorn of agriculture. They learned much from the bushmen, but the need for more skills soon made them more self-reliant and more ingenious than their teachers. Their home-made implements and rough dwellings were displaced by better homes and more efficient tools long before bushmen thought of improved techniques. The farming settlers fed their families and carted their heavy wheat into the towns to make the colonies independent of imported grain a century before Australians had locally made woollen goods.

Unlike the nomadic bushmen, many of the coastal families were *bona fide* settlers. They wanted places of their own, land by legal possession, land they could work and nurture with their own tears and sweat. They had other ideals that came from Britain too. They wanted to pay their way as many of them had paid their own passages. They took pride in austerity and frugal living. They hated waste and made do with old things in their homes. They were intrigued by short cuts to fortune but saved zealously for rainy days. Above all they expected all men to better themselves.

Where bushmen felt an urge to escape from urban civilization, farming settlers welcomed it and kept close to the towns that were their only market. The kind of independence they wanted sprang from ownership of land. Their property might be small and often change hands, but ownership gave them respect for the law. It also gave them a permanent stake in the country and warranted a voice in local affairs. Although they distrusted the distant government that allowed influential speculators and absentee investors to snatch the choicest land, they had no wish to cut the ties of empire. Their fight for self-government meant a fair field for all and no favours. Their victory armed them against the squatters who claimed special rights to grass and water.

The self-dependent farmers valued stability more than expansion, but after the gold rush settlement was spread farther afield by cheap land. In many districts selectors wavered between livestock and crops until railways solved their transport problems and confirmed their faith in farming. Southern colonies found export markets for their wheat, and lost some of their dependence on wool, but cheap land carried agriculture too far inland. Like the pastoralists, farmers seemed to have reached the limit of expansion in the 'eighties, although superphosphate and irrigation were soon to give them a new lease of life. New farm land beckoned in New South Wales and Western Australia, but by 1880 hosts of disappointed countrymen were turning to the cities to work for wages.

They found the city centres ringed by working-class suburbs with narrow streets, cramped tenements and tiny backyards. In these old-world conditions cockneys and poor Irish thrived with ideals of mateship and carefree living not unlike those of bushmen. These urban characters were glorified by C. J. Dennis in *The Sentimental Bloke*, but neither Dennis nor his larrikin hero Bill could resist the self-dependent faith that each family should have a place of its own; both found peace by marrying and by settling down on their own plots of land. Although many countrymen had to live in these inner suburbs, they saved hard for separate houses with space for a lawn at the front and fruit trees and vegetables at the back. Quarter-acre blocks seemed to be the desired pattern but years passed before it became common. Although the building trade was well established long before 1880, the countrymen's demand for new houses made it more vigorous and helped to give urban prosperity some independence of fluctuations in the wool market. The cities began to sprawl and speculators made fortunes while self-dependent families spent half their lives paying for their homes.

Self-dependence took other forms in the cities. It sometimes denied schooling to children and sometimes made struggling families help their sons to places reserved for the rich in Universities and learned professions. It gave immense fervour to regional pride, but resisted public works. It gave some individuals dignity and made others selfish. It gave an urge to work that helped to postpone clashes between trade unions and employers, and often provided 'free labour' that broke the strikes when they came. Always its sober influence robbed the fun-fair of much glamour.

When cheap land came to an end, immigrants were invited to Australia as a paradise for working-men. Newcomers found the self-dependent faith bewildering and out-of-date. They were more in sympathy with the Labor parties that were gaining support among the miners and shearers of the outback and among the workers of the ports and inner suburbs. Self-dependent families, even among the wage-earners, remained conservative. Their distaste for government interference and social security slowly vanished as reformers proved that these blessings still left room for men to help themselves. Federation and 'New Protection' gradually blended self-reliance with the idea of national independence. Both gained new vitality and purpose when war and depression shattered the illusion of isolation. The Japanese threat showed that Australia was part of a wider world and lagging far behind it. Outmoded notions of self-dependence and the dominance of wool had too long delayed development. Peace brought challenging plans to make good the wasted years. Confidence replaced caution as full employment, heavy immigration and free spending rallied Australia's energies. Old savings, carefully tucked away, were invested in vigorous new enterprises. New industries and oversea money poured in to make dramatic changes. In half a generation Australia shot forward towards maturity leaving no place for fear or want in the national creed. The *bona fide* settlers had sought a fair field where all might better themselves; that part of their dream found fulfilment in their children's children.

Burra, 92
Burrinjuck dam, 177
bushrangers, 68–70, 78, 111–12, 226, 228

Cairns, 40, 178
Cambridge Gulf, 38, 40
camels, 40, 140
Campbell, Robert, 58
Canada, 1, 32, 47, 120, 131, 187, 225
Canberra, 160, 188, 207, 217
Cape Leeuwin, 5, 12
Cape Northumberland, 12
Cape of Good Hope, 5, 7, 11, 18, 194
Cape York, 5
cattle, *see* industry
Chaffey brothers, 131
Charleville, 181
Chartists, 47, 99, 119
Chifley, J. B., 206–7, 209, 211–12, 214–15, 217–18
Chinese, 77, 90, 98, 106, 120–1, 134
Chisholm, Caroline, 90
churches, 50, 58–9, 70, 82, 96, 100, 124–5, 144, 169
Clarence River, 14, 178
clearing land, 27, 50, 55, 85, 113–14, 150, 176, 207
Cloncurry, 181, 218
closer settlement, 19, 35, 63, 73, 75–8, 129, 138, 149–50, 176–9
coal
  New South Wales, 14, 29, 47, 50, 92, 123, 133, 137, 152, 191, 209, 215
  Queensland, 156, 210
  South Australia, 210
  Victoria, 156, 180
Cobar, 132
Cobb and Co., 112, 144
Cockatoo Island, 21
Cockburn Sound, 71–2
Collins, David, 31

Collins, J. A., 202
Colombo Plan, 216
Colonial Land and Emigration Commission, 89, 98, 115, 117
Colonial Office
  appeals to, 66, 70, 72, 79
  Colonists' criticism of, 63, 65, 72, 82, 87–91, 105, 142
  control, 63, 65, 76, 84, 86, 90, 99–101, 103–4, 106, 113, 115, 140, 148
  displeasure, 13, 57, 62, 70, 73, 141–2
Commonwealth Oil Refineries Limited, 183, 218
Commonwealth Scientific and Industrial Research Organization, 189, 208–9
Commonwealth Shipping Line, 22, 156–7, 169
Communists, 215–17
conscription, 169–71, 191
Constitutions
  Colonial, 92, 100–1, 103–6, 119, 125, 139
  Federal, 143, 145–6, 156, 159, 162, 207, 214
convicts
  assigned servants, 47–52, 55–8, 60, 67, 69, 84
  conditional pardons, 50–1, 58, 62, 65, 90–1
  cost to Britain, 44, 53–4, 63, 84–5
  labour, 27–8, 30–1, 47, 50, 57, 61, 63, 70, 79, 107
  numbers, 45–7, 90
  penal settlements, 26–8, 49–50, 54, 69, 81
  probation, 84–5
  secondary punishments, 47–50, 55–6, 69, 226
  transportation, 10–12, 45–9, 61, 81, 84, 90–1, 104
  transports, 12, 15, 27, 46, 48
Cook, James, 8–9

INDEX

Aboriginals, 1, 5–6, 8, 10, 28, 35–6, 70, 72, 78–9, 221–2, 224
Adelaide
  government, 76, 83–4, 96, 100, 103, 120, 144
  population, 76
  port, 15, 95, 137, 140
  settlement, 3, 35, 74–5, 85, 93
  trade and industry, 75–6, 83–5, 92–3, 161, 220
  transport, 39–40, 116, 128, 181
agricultural machinery, 85, 113–14, 130–1, 178–9, 206–7, 209
Albany, 18, 140, 162
Albury, 114
aluminium, 222
Anzac, 162–4, 166
Anzus Pact, 214
arbitration and conciliation, 136, 138, 144, 159–60, 184, 186, 211–14, 216–17
Arnhem Land, 6, 222
Arthur, George, 69–70, 78–9
assisted passages, 15, 73–7, 80, 87, 90–1, 97, 117–18, 127–8, 134, 148, 175, 210
Australian Imperial Forces
  First, 162–4, 166, 169, 230
  Second, 193–7, 200–2, 207
Australian Natives Association, 141, 143
aviation, 23–4, 41, 181–2, 188, 191, 205, 212, 221
  see also R.A.A.F.

Ballarat, 94, 96, 99, 121, 131, 152
Banks
  British, 18, 65, 80, 128, 186–7
  Colonial, 62, 67, 70, 80, 109, 119, 124, 138, 147, 154, 212

Commonwealth, 157, 185
  Savings, 155, 157, 186
Banks, Sir Joseph, 8, 11
Barcoo Creek, 38
Barton, Sir Edmund, 144–5
basic wage, 160, 183–4, 186–7, 211, 216–17
Bass, George, 11, 13
Batavia, 5–7, 10, 27, 197
Bathurst, 30, 93–5, 98, 139
Batman, John, 78
Bendigo, 94, 112, 152
Bent, Ellis, 61
Berry, Graham, 124
Bigge, J. T., 63–4, 68
Birdum, 182, 191
Birdwood, William, 162, 166
Black, T. C., 23
Blamey, T. A., 193–4, 200
Blaxland, Gregory, 30; John, 58
Bligh, William, 59–60
Blue Mountains, 29–30, 94, 115
Botany Bay, 8, 10, 11, 26, 29, 45, 226
Bourke, 114
Bourke, Sir Richard, 78–9, 81
Bowen, John, 31
Brisbane
  government, 122, 160, 170
  settlement, 2, 16, 104
  trade and industry, 116, 134, 161, 220
  transport, 23, 128, 155, 181
Brisbane, Sir Thomas, 32
British Commonwealth Occupation Force, 204, 214
Broken Hill, 42, 132, 136, 152, 187
Broken Hill Proprietary Company, 132, 158, 220
Broome, 197

Bruce, S. M., 173–5, 183–4, 187, 190, 192
Burke and Wills, 38–9
Burra, 92
Burrinjuck dam, 177
bushrangers, 68–70, 78, 111–12, 227, 229

Cairns, 40, 178
Cambridge Gulf, 38–40
camels, 40, 140
Campbell, Robert, 48
Canada, 1, 32, 47, 120, 131, 187, 226
Canberra, 160, 188, 206, 215
Cape Leeuwin, 5, 12
Cape Northumberland, 12
Cape of Good Hope, 5, 7, 11, 18, 194
Cape York, 5
cattle, see industry
Chaffey brothers, 131
Charleville, 181
Chartists, 47, 99, 119
Chifley, J. B., 206, 208, 210–15
Chinese, 77, 90, 98, 106, 120–1, 134
Chisholm, Caroline, 90
churches, 50, 58–9, 70, 82, 96, 100, 124–5, 144, 169, 215
Clarence River, 14, 178
clearing land, 27, 50, 55, 85, 113–14, 150, 176, 207
Cloncurry, 181
closer settlement, 19, 35, 63, 73, 75–8, 129, 138, 149–50, 176–9
coal, 212, 219
    New South Wales, 14, 29, 47, 50, 92, 123, 133, 137, 152, 191, 209
    Queensland, 156, 209
    South Australia, 209
    Victoria, 156, 180
Cobar, 132
Cobb and Co., 112, 144

Cockatoo Island, 21,
Cockburn Sound, 71–2
Collins, David, 31
Collins, J. A., 202
Colombo Plan, 214
Colonial Land and Emigration Commission, 89, 98, 115, 117
Colonial Office
    appeals to, 66, 70, 72, 79
    colonists' criticisms of, 63, 65, 72, 82, 87–91, 105, 142
    control, 63, 65, 76, 84, 86, 90, 99–101, 103–4, 106, 113, 115, 140, 148
    displeasure, 13, 57, 62, 70, 73, 141–2
Commonwealth Scientific and Industrial Research Organization, 189, 208
Commonwealth Shipping Line, 22, 156–7, 169
Communists, 212–15, 218
conscription, 169–71, 191
Constitutions
    Colonial, 92, 100–1, 103–6, 119, 125, 139
    Federal, 143, 145–6, 156, 159, 162, 206, 212
convicts
    assigned servants, 47–52, 55–8, 60, 67, 69, 84
    conditional pardons, 50–1, 58, 62, 65, 90–1
    cost to Britain, 44, 53–4, 63, 84–5
    labour, 27–8, 30–1, 47, 50, 57, 61, 63, 70, 79, 107
    numbers, 45–7, 90
    penal settlements, 26–8, 49–50, 54, 69, 81
    probation, 84–5
    secondary punishments, 47–50, 55–6, 69, 227
    transportation, 10–12, 45–9, 61, 81, 84, 90–1, 104
    transports, 12, 15, 27, 46, 48

Cook, James, 8–9
Cooktown, 10
Coolgardie, 139
Cooper's Creek, 38–9
copper, 16, 92–3, 98, 112, 132–3, 220
Corio Bay, 32
Crown land
  free selection, 108–12, 130
  grants, 28–31, 34, 44, 50–60, 63,
    65, 67–73, 77–8, 107, 118, 140,
    223
  sales, 35, 67, 73–7, 79–81, 83–4,
    87–8, 92–3, 103–4, 129, 150,
    230–2
  squatting, 32, 34–7, 77–81, 86–8,
    107–11, 129, 149, 231
Cunningham, Allan, 32
currency, 52–9, 62, 66–7, 72, 75–6,
  157, 219
Curtin, John, 192, 196–7, 206, 211
Cygnet Bay, 6

dairying, 19, 22, 108, 130, 137, 152,
  176–7, 183, 205–6, 219
Dampier, 221
Dampier, William, 6
Darling Downs, 32
Darling Ranges, 72
Darling River, 32, 34, 37–8, 42,
  114
Darwin, 2, 23, 40, 116, 155, 191,
  196–7, 200, 205, 221
Davey, Thomas, 68
David, Sir Edgeworth, 43
Dawson River, 177
Deakin, Alfred, 144, 158–9, 173
defence, 20–1, 51, 106, 142–3, 147,
  161–2, 190–6, 200–6, 214
Dennis, C. J., 232
Derby, 181
Derwent River, 31
Dirk Hartog's Island, 5, 7
drought, 30, 67, 96, 99, 110, 146–7,
  206, 216
Duntroon, 161–2

East India Company, 7, 11, 13,
  14
Ebden, C. H., 80
Echunga, 95
education
  free, secular and compulsory,
    124–5, 144, 158–9
  schools, 62, 70, 82, 155, 177, 189,
    217
  universities, 81, 154, 157, 217,
    232–3
Egypt, 18, 164, 194–6
Eildon Reservoir, 177
elections
  Colonial, 86–7, 100, 107, 125
  Commonwealth, 146, 168, 170,
    184, 214–15, 218
electorates, 86, 92, 100–1, 104,
  145
electricity, 133, 150, 154–5, 177,
  180–2, 191, 208–9, 217
Emancipists, 28–9, 50–1, 54, 57–61,
  63, 65–6, 68, 99
Eureka, 99, 100, 136, 225
Evatt, H. V., 203, 215
Exclusives, 58–66, 68
Expansionists, 44, 54, 56, 63–4
exploration
  Antarctic, 10, 43
  land, 1, 29–35, 37–40, 42, 64, 72,
    74, 80, 84, 104, 110, 114
  sea, 1, 4–7, 10–12, 70
exports
  agricultural, 16, 18–19, 22, 86,
    114–15, 139, 158, 178, 187,
    207–8, 219
  income from, 130, 133, 138, 179,
    183, 185, 208, 219
  mineral, 16, 18, 92, 94, 97–8, 133,
    168, 219–22
  pastoral, 14–15, 18–19, 22, 30,
    65, 73, 80, 129–30, 152, 187,
    207, 216, 219
  whale products, 12–15
Eyre, E. J., 35

Fairbridge, Kingsley, 175
Farrer, William, 151
Fawkner, J. P., 79
federal grants, 157–8, 161, 180, 183, 188, 205, 207, 210, 216, 220
federation, 20–1, 42, 91–2, 120, 127, 140–5, 154, 159–61, 188, 226, 233
Fiji, 6, 23, 122, 143
Fingal, 95
Fisher, J. H., 74–5
FitzRoy, Sir Charles, 98, 100
Flinders, Matthew, 11–13
Flinders Island, 36
Flinders River, 39
flour mills, 73, 113–14
Forrest, Alexander, 40
Forrest, Sir John, 40, 144
France (French)
  expeditions, 7, 10–12, 30–1, 35
  threats, 18, 35, 70, 142
  war in, 164, 166, 193–6
franchise, 86, 92, 99–100, 103–4, 137, 144
free trade, 120, 123, 137, 143, 145, 157, 160, 188
Fremantle, 140
Fremantle, Charles, 71
fruitgrowing, 19, 22, 130–1, 139, 176–8, 183, 232

Gallipoli, 162–4, 166, 173
Garden Island, 71
Gascoyne River, 38
Gawler, George, 75–6, 83–4
Geelong, 34, 80, 95, 157, 191
Geraldton, 181
Germany (German)
  settlers, 76, 130, 174
  threats, 21, 141, 171
  trade, 18, 168
  war, 162, 164, 166, 193–6, 202
Gibson Desert, 40
Giles, Ernest, 40

Gipps, Sir George, 87–8, 98
Gippsland, 80
gold, 3–6, 104–5
  discoveries, 92–7, 111, 121, 149, 223
  fields, 16, 93–9, 107–8, 114–15, 120–2, 125–6, 132–4, 139–40, 144, 152, 175, 181
  licences, 99–100
  miners, 93–100, 103, 114, 133–4, 141, 229
  yields, 94, 97, 132, 152, 179, 220
Goolwa, 115
Goulburn River, 177
Goyder, G. W., 110
Grant, James, 12
Greenway, F. H., 61
Gregory, A. C., 38
Grey, George, 84
Griffith, 177
Griffith, Sir Samuel, 143, 145

Hamilton, 115
Hannan, Patrick, 139
Hanson, Sir R. D., 120, 124, 228
Hargraves, E. H., 93–4, 139
Harrison, James, 19
Hawkesbury River, 28, 59
Henty family, 34, 78
Higgins, H. B., 159–60
Higinbotham, George, 120, 124, 144
Hindmarsh, John, 74–5
Hinkler, Bert, 23
Hobart
  government, 79, 103
  port, 13–14, 16
  settlement, 2, 31, 68
  trade and industry, 14, 35, 69–70, 72–3, 75–6, 85, 116
horses, 30, 34, 40, 96, 112–14, 139, 154, 179, 182
Horsham, 115
Hotham, Sir Charles, 99

housing, 27–8, 37, 119, 133–5, 179, 205, 210, 216, 221, 231–2
war service homes, 180, 207, 210
Hughes, W. M., 168–71, 173, 183, 190
Hume and Hovell, 32
Hume Reservoir, 176
Hunter, John, 56–7
Hunter River, 14, 17, 29

imports, 52–60, 62, 160, 183
American, 13, 22, 167
British, 18, 20–2, 27, 37, 96, 157, 187
Japanese, 22, 187
restriction, 122, 157, 187, 191, 208, 216
value of, 80, 84, 98, 134, 185, 187, 215, 219
Indonesia, 218
industry
agricultural, 16, 19–20, 26–9, 42, 50, 53–6, 59, 61–2, 69–73, 85–6, 106–16, 130–3, 139–40, 150–2, 175–9, 206–8, 230–2
building, 119, 133–4, 138–9, 147, 154, 179–80, 205, 210, 216, 221, 232
manufacturing, 21–4, 42, 49, 121–3, 130–1, 133–4, 139, 147–8, 154, 157–8, 161, 180, 182–3, 186, 188, 190–1, 196, 205–6, 208–11, 216, 219–22, 233
pastoral, 17, 19, 22, 26, 29–32, 34–42, 58–9, 63, 65, 69–70, 72–3, 76–81, 85–8, 104–12, 128–30, 136–9, 147, 149–52, 179, 207–8, 216, 219, 230
intercolonial rivalry
economic competition, 41–2, 73, 81–2, 105–7, 127–8, 133, 139–40, 160–1, 172, 175, 210
government conflict, 68–9, 81, 123, 145–6, 188, 205

regional pride, 38, 76, 91, 115–17, 143
Ireland (Irish), 32, 46–7, 58–90, 99, 113, 115, 120, 159, 169, 232
iron, 21, 92, 157–8, 184, 191, 220–1
irrigation, 41, 131, 144, 155, 176–8, 207–8, 210, 217, 232
Isolationists, 44, 63–4, 68, 106, 156, 174, 190
Italy, 174–5, 194–6, 202

Jansz, Wilhelm, 5, 222
Japan, 21–3, 158, 171, 187, 190, 196–7, 200–4, 206, 214, 219, 221, 233
Java, 40, 116, 197
Jervis Bay, 161
Johnston, George, 60, 63

Kalgoorlie, 139–41, 152, 220
Kanakas, 121–2, 158
Kangaroo Island, 35, 74, 76
Kapunda, 92
Kennedy, Edmund, 38
Kimberley goldfield, 139
King, P. G., 28, 57–9, 68
King George Sound, 11–12, 31, 35
Kingston, C. G., 144

Lachlan River, 32, 177
Lake Alexandrina, 34
Lake Amadeus, 40
Lake Eyre, 26, 38–9
Lake George, 32
Lake Victoria, 177
Lane, William, 137
Lang, J. T., 186–7
La Trobe, C. J., 81
Launceston, 2, 31, 68, 70, 79, 81
Lawson, Henry, 141, 230
League of Nations, 171, 190
Legislative Councils and Assemblies, see Parliament
Leichhardt, Ludwig, 38, 40
Light, William, 74–5

Lithgow, 157–8
Liverpool Plains, 32
Loan Council, 184–5, 210
Lockyer, Edmund, 31
Lodden River, 94
Lonsdale, William, 79
Lord Simeon, 51,
Lyons, J. A., 174, 187, 190, 192

MacArthur, Douglas, 197, 200–2
Macarthur, John, 29, 31, 58–60, 63, 68
McKay, H. V., 131, 159
McKinlay, John, 39
McMillan, Angus, 80
Macquarie, Lachlan, 30, 60–7, 228
Macquarie Harbour, 31, 69
Macquarie River, 32
Macqueen, Potter, 67, 71
mails, 18, 52, 83, 89, 116, 147, 150, 182
Malaya, 196, 214, 218
Mallee District, 131, 176–7
Mannix, Dr, 169–71
markets
    local, 17, 19, 93, 96, 98, 111, 122, 150, 154, 216
    marketing problems, 18–22, 40–1, 109, 172, 178, 187–8, 232
    marketing schemes, 169, 183, 187, 207
    oversea, 3, 19, 41, 128, 150, 187, 207, 219, 221, 226, 230
Marsden, Samuel, 57, 61
Mary River, 40
Mawson, Sir Douglas, 43
Melbourne, 228
    government, 79, 81–2, 87, 92, 121, 145, 154, 160, 182, 188
    population, 79–80, 133, 179
    port, 15, 18, 95, 140
    settlement, 2, 34, 79–81
    trade and industry, 80, 85, 91, 93–4, 96, 117, 133–4, 138, 157, 181, 191, 219–20

transport, 23, 42, 112, 116, 128, 209
Menzies, Sir Robert, 192, 211, 214–16, 218–19
migration
    Asian, 77, 90, 98, 106, 120, 122, 141, 143, 148, 158
    British, 16, 21, 35, 44, 46, 65, 68, 70–7, 83–5, 96–8, 117–18, 140, 148, 175–6, 210, 215, 217
    European, 24, 76, 174, 210, 217
    intercolonial, 76, 78–80, 95, 121, 127, 139–40, 149
    laws, 106, 148, 171; and see assisted passages
    opposition to, 119, 121, 134, 175–6
Mildura, 131, 176
Miller, Sir Denison, 157
Mitchell, John Henry, 228
Mitchell, Sir T. L., 34, 38
Monaro Tableland, 32
Monash, Sir John, 166, 180, 193
Moonta, 132
Moreton Bay, see Queensland
Morgan, 116
Mort, T. S., 17, 19
motor transport, 21–2, 41–2, 150, 152, 154, 182–3, 187–8, 205, 209, 217
Mount Alexander, 94, 96
Mount Isa, 170, 220
Mount Lyell, 132
Mount Morgan, 132
Mullen, Charles, 113
Murchison River, 38
Murray River, 33–4, 41–2, 80, 114, 116, 131, 133, 176–7, 205, 208
Murrumbidgee River, 32, 34, 177, 208
Myall Creek, 36

Newcastle, 14, 29, 31, 47, 92, 136, 158, 197, 220, 222

New Guinea, 4–7, 20, 141–3, 161–2, 171, 181, 197, 201–2, 220

New Holland, 7–8, 12, 65, 71

'New Protection', 158–9, 189, 211, 222, 226, 233

New South Wales
agriculture, 28, 54–5, 59, 63, 86, 112, 129, 139, 151, 177–8, 232
exploration, 10–12, 30, 32, 34, 37–8, 80
federation, 120, 142–5, 159–61, 184
government, 35, 44, 48–69, 77, 81, 86, 98, 101, 106–9, 119, 125, 128–9, 137, 186, 189
mining, 93–4, 97, 114, 121, 123, 132–3, 139
partition, 70, 92, 104, 188
trade and industry, 11, 13–14, 42, 49, 51–9, 62, 67, 123, 133, 152, 154, 156–7, 180, 220
transport, 36, 112, 115–16, 128, 139
woolgrowing, 29, 35–6, 41, 59, 63, 65, 90, 106–7, 129, 147, 152

New South Wales Corps, 51–2, 55–60

New Zealand, 6, 13–14, 97, 120, 143, 162, 204, 214

Norfolk Island, 13, 27, 31, 47, 49, 57, 61

Northern Territory, 40–1, 110–11, 161, 181, 220–2

oil, 182–3, 191, 196, 202, 204–5, 209, 220

Oodnadatta, 155, 182

Ophir, 93–4

O'Reilly, Dowell, 141

Ottawa Agreements, 187–8

Oxley, John, 31–2

Page, Sir E. C. G., 173–4, 184

Parer, Ray, 23

Parkes, Sir Henry, 119–20, 122, 125, 142, 144

Parliament, 89, 100–1, 103–4, 106–7, 115, 119, 124, 135, 138, 140, 143, 146, 149, 155–6, 188, 217
Federal, 146–7, 149, 156, 169, 187–9, 206, 217
Imperial, 13, 16, 18, 45–6, 65–6, 71–2, 74, 84, 87, 89, 91, 103–4, 106, 142–5, 188–9
New South Wales, 66, 78, 86, 88, 92, 98, 101, 108, 120, 144, 189
Queensland, 122, 129, 170, 189
South Australia, 87, 92, 100, 103, 110
Tasmania, 69, 87, 92, 103
Victoria, 92, 99, 103, 108, 120–1, 123, 144, 168, 172–3
Western Australia, 72

Parramatta, 27, 29, 49, 55

passports, 22, 175

payment of members, 123–4

Peel, Thomas, 71–2

Perth, 2, 15, 25, 40, 71–2, 91, 116, 139–40, 155, 220

Phillip, Arthur, 11, 26–8, 48, 51–2, 54–6

Pine Creek, 155, 162

Pinjarra, 36, 72–3

Polding, J. B., 228

police, 47, 51, 62, 69, 79, 95–6, 98–9, 112, 136, 160, 171, 229

political parties, 89, 107, 146, 155, 161, 168, 173
Country, 173–4, 189, 192
Democratic Labor, 215
Labor, 22, 123, 137, 143, 149, 156–9, 168–70, 172–4, 186–7, 190, 192, 196, 203, 206, 214–15
'Lib-Lab', 137–8, 149, 156, 159
Liberal–Country, 214–15

Liberals, 107–8, 115, 117, 136–7, 144, 156–8, 170
  Nationalists, 170, 173–4
  United Australia, 174
population, 1, 46, 70, 152, 175
  numbers, 36, 65, 106, 127, 148–9, 174, 210, 217
Port Arthur, 69
Port Augusta, 155
Port Elliot, 115–16
Port Essington, 31, 37, 40
Port Headland, 221
Port Jackson, 12–13, 26–7
Port Kembla, 191, 220
Portland Bay, 34, 78
Port Lincoln, 34
Port Macquarie, 31
Port Moresby, 142, 197, 200
Port Phillip District, see Victoria
Port Pirie, 132, 158
public debts
  Colonial, 117–18, 128, 138–40, 155, 161, 182, 185
  Commonwealth, 185, 187, 208, 215
  financial agreement, 184–5
  war, 157, 204–5
public servants, 51, 54–61, 69, 75, 79, 89, 106, 124, 216

Queanbeyan, 151
Queensland
  federation, 143–5, 160, 170–1
  government, 20, 104, 117–18, 120–2, 125, 128, 149, 188–9, 204
  mining, 97, 114, 120–1, 132–3, 156, 220, 222
  pastoral industry, 41, 91, 110, 129–30, 136, 152
  separation, 104
  settlement, 31
  sugar growing, 121–2, 131, 139, 175, 178
  trade, 42, 130, 178

rabbits, 19, 42, 46, 129, 113, 137, 150, 208
radio, 24, 41, 181, 189, 216–17, 227
railways
  Commonwealth, 144, 155, 182, 191, 221
  gauges, 115, 205, 209
  State, 16–17, 20, 40–2, 112, 115–17, 130, 132–3, 139, 155, 205–6
  suburban, 154, 182
rainfall, 25–7, 37, 41, 80, 85, 95, 130, 147, 208
Red Cliffs, 176
Redfern, William, 61
referenda, 145–6, 156, 169–71, 185, 188, 215
refrigeration, 19, 40–1, 130, 139
Reibey, Mary, 51
Reid, G. H., 145
Renmark, 131
Ridley, John, 85, 113, 131
ring-barking, 19, 111, 121
Risdon Cove, 31
Riverina, 133
Robertson, Sir John, 108–9, 228
Robinson, G. A., 70
Royal Australian Air Force, 190, 193–7, 200–3, 214
Royal Australian Navy, 21, 161–2, 190, 193–7, 200–3, 214
Royal Navy, 20–1, 122, 142, 161–2, 190, 193–6
Ryan, T. J., 170

Scott, C. W. A., 23, 41
Shark Bay, 7
Shearer, John, 114
shearers, 36, 42, 95, 111, 128, 134, 136, 150, 229, 233
sheep, see industry
ships
  building, 11–14, 16–17, 23, 73, 191

explorers, 4–8, 11–12, 30
owners, 16, 68, 77, 88, 118; *and
see* R.N., R.A.N.
sailing, 11, 15–16, 18, 26–7, 51–
2, 54–5, 58, 71, 74, 89, 93–4, 117
steam, 1, 17–19, 22, 41, 95, 133,
136, 169, 191, 193
whaling, 12–14, 35
silver-lead, 92, 132–3, 136, 179
Singapore, 18, 190, 196–7, 202
Smith, Sir C. Kingsford, 23
Smith, Sir Ross, 23
Snowy River diversion, 208, 210
socialization, 155–8, 173, 206, 211–
12
social services, 158–9, 161, 188–9,
211–12, 217
soldier settlement, 176, 207
Sorell, William, 68–9
South Africa, 1, 5–6, 29, 161, 175,
226
South Australia
agriculture, 84–5, 93, 106, 112–
14, 130–1, 139, 151, 177
exploration, 34, 37, 39–40
factories, 130
federation, 91–2, 142–5, 161, 188
government, 20, 35, 75–6, 83–4,
87, 96, 100–1, 103, 110, 112–
13, 120–1, 124–5, 137, 150
mining, 92, 95, 98, 106, 132–3,
220
pastoral industry, 36, 76, 110
settlement, 74–6
trade, 41–2, 75, 83–4, 93, 114,
134, 185
South-east Asia, 1, 3–4, 18, 20, 38,
113, 196–7, 214, 217–18
Spencer Gulf, 12, 32
Stirling, Sir James, 70–3
strikes and lockouts, 135–8, 160,
170, 184, 206, 209, 212–14,
217, 233
Stuart, J. M., 39–40
Sturt, Charles, 32, 34, 37, 176, 228

sugar, 121, 131, 139, 143, 157–8,
169, 175, 178, 183, 205, 219
superphosphate, 20, 42, 141, 206,
232
surveys, 11, 30–1, 35, 38–9, 67,
71–2, 74–80, 108–10
Swan River, 14, 35, 70–1, 73, 78
Sydney
government, 31, 47, 61, 68, 77–
82, 87–8, 92–3, 142–6, 154,
168
harbour, 15–16, 18, 20–2, 27, 91,
137, 187, 197
settlement, 1, 26–7
trade and industry, 14, 17, 19,
28–9, 35, 55–7, 62–3, 67–9,
75–6, 88, 94, 134, 136, 191,
219
transport, 115, 128, 181–2
Syme, David, 123, 144

tariffs, 22, 122–4, 131, 137, 144–5,
157–60, 180, 183–5, 187
Tasmania
exploration, 6, 8, 11
government, 35–6, 65, 68–70,
78–9, 91–2, 95, 103, 128, 145,
150, 161, 174, 188
settlement, 31
trade and industry, 14, 34, 69,
76, 79–80, 84–5, 112, 130,
132, 151, 177–8, 221–2
Tasman Peninsula, 36, 69–70
taxes
income, 138, 161, 168, 186, 204–
5, 211, 216
land, 88, 138, 149
telegraphs, 40, 116–17, 143, 147,
155
Throsby, Charles, 32
Timor, 1, 7, 40, 196–7
Torrens, R. R., 113
trade unions, 42, 134–7, 150, 156,
160, 170, 173, 175, 184, 212–
15, 223, 225, 233

Treasury bills, 53, 56, 60, 62–3, 69
Twofold Bay, 14

Ulm, C. T. P., 23
United Nations, 203–4, 208, 214
United States
  investment, 209, 219, 221
  Pacific defence, 196–7, 200–2, 204–5, 214, 217–18
  ships, 13, 16, 18
  trade, 21–2, 187–8, 219
uranium, 220

Vancouver, George, 12
Van Diemen's Land, *see* Tasmania
Victoria
  agriculture, 85, 95, 109, 112, 131, 151–2, 177–8, 208
  factories, 19, 123, 131, 133–4, 144, 154–5, 180, 219
  federation, 142–5
  government, 20, 38, 79–82, 92, 98–9, 103–4, 106–9, 117–18, 120–5, 142, 150, 177, 180
  mining, 94–100, 132–3, 139, 152, 156
  settlement, 31, 34, 78–81
  trade, 42, 80, 94, 97–9, 116, 130, 133–4
  transport, 23, 42, 112, 115–17, 128, 133
Victoria River, 38, 40
Vietnam, 218

Wakefield, E. G., 73–4, 76–7, 112, 120, 148

Wangaratta, 115
war, 20–1, 142, 161
  First World, 21, 157, 161–72, 178, 183, 203–4
  Second World, 23, 43, 190–207
  Korean, 214–15
Waranga, 177
Warrego River, 38
Warwick, 170
water supply
  city, 23, 81, 117, 133, 154–5, 180
  rural, 37, 41, 111, 128, 140, 150, 177, 205, 208, 217, 221
Wentworth, W. C., 30, 66, 101
Western Australia
  explorers, 38, 94
  government, 35, 71–2, 128, 139–40, 144–5, 161, 188
  settlement, 70–3
  trade and industry, 41, 72–3, 91, 112, 139–40, 175–6, 220–2
  transport, 115, 140, 221
Westernport, 11, 31
whaling, 12–16, 34, 73–6
wheat, *see* industry; exports
White Australia, 90, 98, 106, 121–2, 134, 141, 143, 148, 158, 171
Whyalla, 191, 205, 220
wool, *see* industry; exports
Wyangala dam, 177
Wyndham, 40, 197

Yallourn, 180
Yampi Sound, 220
Yarra River, 79